CONTENTS

ACKNOWLEDGMENTS

Who can do this sort of thing alone? Not I. Thanks are due to many.

For permission to include passages from my article, "*Heartbreak Soup*: The Interdependence of Theme and Form" (*Inks* 4:2, May 1997), the Ohio State University Press. For shepherding that article in the first place, *Inks* editor Lucy Shelton Caswell.

For the use of copyrighted material, the many artists and other rightsholders represented herein.

Special thanks to the following, without whom my vague aspirations and tentative arguments could not have become a book:

For guiding my first draft, my advisors at the University of Connecticut: Tom Roberts, Jean Marsden, and Tom Recchio. For information and images: Robert Beerbohm, Cécile Danehy, Gary Groth, John Morrow, Mark Nevins, Nhu-Hoa Nguyen, Nick Nguyen, Eric Reynolds, Michael Rhode, Patrick Rosenkranz, Randall Scott, R. Sikoryak, Tim Stroup, Brian Tucker, and the Comics Scholars' Discussion List (comix-scholars@clas.ufl.edu). For the correspondence, Gilbert Hernandez. For patience and counsel, Seetha Srinivasan and Walter Biggins. For design, Pete Halverson.

For mentorship and friendship, Joseph (Rusty) Witek. For help of all sorts and friendship in all weathers, my fellow traveler Gene Kannenberg, Jr.

For inspiration and conversation, my brother Scott. For unstinting moral and material support, my parents Ella and Jerry and my parents-in-law Ann and Bob.

For the spark, Jack Kirby.

Finally, and above all, to my own dear family: Michele, Coleman, and Nicholas. *Norp!*

INTRODUCTION

ALTERNATIVE COMICS AS AN EMERGING LITERATURE

This book is about comics. Specifically, it is about the growth, over the past thirty-odd years, of the American-style comic book and its loosely named offshoot, the graphic novel. In the English-reading world, the graphic novel in particular has become comics' passport to recognition as a form of literature. Through this book I aim to cast light on both the necessary preconditions for and certain key examples of this newly recognized literature, while unashamedly holding up as a backdrop the form's populist, industrial, and frankly mercenary origins. In all, this book offers an entry—or rather several points of entry, including the socio-historical and the aesthetic—into that most fertile and bewildering sector of comic book culture, *alternative comics*.

Alternative comics trace their origins to the underground "comix" movement of the 1960s and 1970s, which, jolted to life by the larger social upheavals of the era, departed from the familiar, anodyne conventions of the commercial comics mainstream and provided the initial impetus, the spark of possibility, for a new model of comics creation. The countercultural comix movement—scurrilous, wild and liberating, innovative, radical, and yet in some ways narrowly circumscribed—gave rise to the idea of comics as an acutely personal means of artistic exploration and self-expression. The aesthetic and economic example of the underground (as related in this book's scene-setting first chapter) spurred the development of what eventually became a highly specialized commercial venue for comics: the comic book specialty shop, as it blossomed in the seventies and eighties. Within this specialized environment, the collision of "underground" distribution with mainstream comic book publishing resulted in the growth of a hermetic yet economically advantageous market, one that catered to mainstream comic book fans but sustained, at its margins, the fevered sense of artistic possibility ignited by comix.

"Alternative" comics, responding to that spirit, sprang up within the specialty market during the 1970s, and more vitally and self-consciously from the early 1980s onward, with the advent of iconoclastic magazines such as *Raw* (1980–91) and *Weirdo* (1981–93), both rooted in underground comix, and *Love & Rockets* (1981–), deeply indebted to both underground *and* mainstream comics. These publications participated in a burgeoning movement of so-called independent comics, but stood out even within that context because of the animating influence of the undergrounds, which inspired them to flout the traditional comic book's overwhelming emphasis on comforting formula fiction. Even as the growing sophistication of mainstream genre comics led to revisions of familiar formulas—leading, for instance, to a boom in darkly revisionist superheroes in the late eighties—alternative comics skirted those shopworn genres. They were the boot up the backside of comic books, pushing and kicking against the calcified limitations of the medium.

Though driven by the example of underground comix, many alternative comics cultivated a more considered approach to the art form, less dependent on the outrageous gouging of taboos (though that continued too, of course) and more open to the possibility of extended and ambitious narratives. Alternative comic creators of various pedigrees—from venerable comic book pioneer Will Eisner (1917–2005), to underground veteran Art Spiegelman, to underground latecomer Harvey Pekar, to such newcomers as Gilbert and Jaime Hernandez—raised the intoxicating possibility that comics might be viewed not only as a crackling, vital repository of supercharged Pop Art but also, and crucially, as a literary form.

From this reenvisioning of comics has sprung a vital if underappreciated literary movement—and it is to this movement that the following book is devoted. Crucial to this new movement were the rejection of mainstream formulas; the exploration of (to comics) new genres, as well as the revival, at times ironic recasting, of genres long neglected; a diversification of graphic style; a budding internationalism, as cartoonists learned from other cultures and other traditions; and, especially, the exploration of searchingly personal and at times boldly political themes. What's more, alternative comics invited a new formalism, that is, an intensive reexamining of the formal tensions inherent in comics (which are the focus of chapter 2).

Indeed among the best of alternative comics are many that have expanded the formal possibilities of comic art: out of a struggle with the conventions of serial publication, they have created breathtaking experiments in narrative structure and density. One such experiment, Gilbert Hernandez's recently collected Central American epic *Heartbreak Soup*, is the subject of chapter 3. Unfolding on a vast social and temporal canvas, *Heartbreak Soup* tested the limits of comics form in order to broaden the artistic horizons and question the political responsibilities of comic books.

Alternative comics, in addition, have enlarged the comic book's thematic repertoire by urging the exploration of genres heretofore neglected in comics, such as autobiography, reportage, and historical fiction. Autobiography, especially, has been central to alternative comics—whether in picaresque shaggy-dog stories or in disarmingly, sometimes harrowingly, frank uprootings of the psyche—and this has raised knotty questions about truth and fictiveness, realism and fantasy, and the relationship between author and audience. These topics are essayed in chapters 4 and 5, which turn on the question of artistic self-representation, arguing that self-reflexive and mock-autobiographical devices paradoxically serve to reinforce autobiography's claims to truth. Chapter 5 further argues that self-reflexive autobiographical comics, far from devolving into navel-gazing passivity, can become, indeed have become, a means for radical cultural argument.

In sum, this book shows how alternative comics have breached the limits of the traditional comic book on every level, including packaging, publication, narrative form and thematic content. In the process they have spawned the vital yet often misunderstood genre of the "graphic novel," whose origins are addressed in chapter 1 (and whose constraints are addressed, finally, in chapter 6). This genre, again, has become a passport to new recognition; indeed the graphic novel has been repeatedly invoked as a radically "new" form, even the harbinger of a new visual literacy. Such claims, of course, mislead: graphic novels are neither "post-literary" nor without precedent. They are comics, thus examples of a venerable tradition. Yet the graphic novel genre is of recent coinage, and its commercial upsurge even more recent; moreover, its recognition has invigorated the critical discourse about comics. At last comics are being recognized as a literary and artistic form deserving of sustained attention.

The recent influx of artistically ambitious graphic novels has led to salutary changes in the critical environment—a trend borne out in rigorous academic study as well as greater attention from reviewers. For telling academic evidence of this trend, consider, for example, two articles in the *Chronicle of Higher Education* that appeared, bookend-like, to bracket my final round of work on this volume: The first, by cartoonist and art instructor James Sturm, appeared in the April 25, 2002, issue and urged art schools and art departments to take up the teaching of comics as a discipline. The second, by historian Paul Buhle, appeared in the May 16, 2003, issue and noted, albeit in an underresearched way, the recent growth of comics study as an academic field. (Unfortunately, Buhle failed to mention the rise of academic conferences and publications devoted to comics study, the interdisciplinary nature of the field, or its mushrooming diversity—full acknowledgment of which would have drawn a drastically different picture of the field.)

This recent growth in comics study is reflected in, and has been much affected by, the increasing self-awareness of practitioners, which has resulted in such seminal works of autocriticism as Will Eisner's textbook *Comics & Sequential Art* (1985) and Scott McCloud's much-debated theoretical comic *Understanding Comics* (1993). Both of these books, but especially McCloud, have had a strong impact on artistic practice and academic research (see, for example, Witek, *Inks*, and Beaty, "Critical Focus"—and *this* book, frankly, for McCloud's work sparked my own, or at least rerouted it). These watershed studies have changed the way the field talks about itself and have given rise to a new, or newly self-conscious, breed of comics formalism, as well as a wave of sequential art

curricula and pedagogically minded cartoonists. For example, the National Association of Comics Art Educators, founded by James Sturm in 2002, advocates the development of comics programs in educational institutions; it represents a summing up of recent gains and a hopeful next step after Eisner and McCloud. (Much to the enrichment of the field, NACAE has encouraged the exchange of teaching materials between studio art and non-studio instructors, for example, teachers of literature and media studies.)

In short, comics are clearly in the process of being repositioned within our culture. This is not because all comics are changing (such is never the case) but because *some* comics have stimulated profound changes in the ways the form is received and understood. At the forefront of this development are alternative comics. In particular, Art Spiegelman's two-volume family memoir *Maus*, recipient of a special Pulitzer in 1992, constituted a signal moment in the emergence of book-length comics from obscurity—a major intervention in the history of the form and its attendant criticism. Spiegelman's achievement, unprecedented in English-language comics, served to ratify comic art as a literary form; the reception of *Maus* suddenly made serious comics culturally *legible*, recognizable, in a way they had not been before. Yet Spiegelman's success only crystallized a larger trend of which he had been a part: the development of a new breed of cartoonists and comics writers, for whom comics were first and above all an acutely personal means of literary expression. This revolution in reception and practice, solidified by *Maus*, is what is meant by *alternative comics*—and it has publicly redefined the potential of the art form.

THE DEVILS OF STATUS AND DISTINCTION

Some will nonetheless scoff at the labeling of comics as "literature"—and among the scoffers will be some practitioners. Alternative comics, coming as they do out of a marginalized subculture, uneasily straddle two different attitudes about comic art: one, that the form is at its best an underground art, teasing and outraging bourgeois society from a gutter-level position of economic hopelessness and (paradoxically) unchecked artistic freedom; two, that the form needs and deserves cultural legitimatization as a means of artistic expression. (That would include academic legitimization.) Alternative comics waver between these two positions—between the punk and the curator, so to speak.

Both of these attitudes have their attendant dangers. The former, at its worst, reeks of willed naiveté or reverse snobbery. The latter, at *its* worst, reeks of status anxiety and an over-earnest bidding for gentrification. Either position may be blinding, but together these contrary attitudes form the inescapable setting for any discussion of comic books as literature—so in what follows we will not be able to ignore them entirely. The contemporary comic book field, especially in its alternative wing, embodies a curious mix of values, a blend of countercultural iconoclasm, rapacious consumerism, and learned connoisseurship. It is a highly specialized if thinly populated consumer culture, one that holds tightly to a romanticized position of marginality and yet courts wider recognition. Its best authors have to navigate this swamp of conflicting values (both without and within). Scholars must do the same.

Suffice to say that this book cannot resolve the lowbrow/highbrow conflict, nor does it seek to. Respectability, of course, can be stifling—some cartoonists think so—but marginality can likewise be suffocating. Ambivalence on this score is hard to avoid, for, ever since the earliest published attacks on comic books (that would be 1940), critical discussions of the medium have always been implicitly tied to beliefs about class. This tendency finally became explicit in 1955 with Leslie Fiedler's bravura essay, "The Middle Against Both Ends," in part an ironic defense of the medium: Fiedler famously claimed that comic books, as a lowbrow form, attracted the same sort of middlebrow scorn as did avant-garde or highbrow art; that both kinds of attack were grounded in the middlebrow's "fear of difference" (428). In so saying, of course, he was joining a midcentury discussion of taste framed by such critics as Clement Greenberg and Dwight MacDonald, known for their Olympian disdain of the middlebrow. He was, more specifically,

attacking a peculiar consensus of leftist reformers and rightist censors who had in common but one thing: a hatred and dread of the lowbrow comic book. Fiedler's defense of comic books proved prescient, in that it effectively prophesied the odd meeting of lowbrow form and highbrow attitude that was to occur in the underground comix of the 1960s, and especially in the alternative comics of the 1980s and after. Though the subculture of alternative comics is lowbrow and shabby in origin, it tends to be highbrow both in its material obsessions and in its self-conscious rejection of bourgeois norms.

Because critical discussions of comic art in America remain stubbornly connected to such ideas about class, both the prosecution and the defense have always leaned heavily on the notion of comics as an under-art or paraliterature, one that (to invoke Art Spiegelman's oft-quoted phrase) flies below critical radar. Fiedler understood the inevitability of this in 1955, and the problem persists. For this reason, those who seek to study comics as a literary form often find themselves pulled between two impulses, neither of which yields a wholly satisfactory outcome.

On the one hand, status anxiety may drive scholars to import traditional literary standards to comics without respect for the comics' unique origins and nature. As an example (one I can cite with impunity), my own earliest writings on the subject favored nuts 'n' bolts formalism, almost New Critical in character, as a self-conscious corrective to sweeping content analysis. I wanted formal rigor to displace sociological maxims about "popular culture"; I wanted readers to appreciate the complexities of the art form. To get to that promised land, though, I felt obliged to bypass some of the more distracting elements of the comic book landscape, including its industrial origins and its fervid emphasis on certain market genres (cue some remark about superheroes here). Such an approach allows one to appreciate the layered complexities and ironies of the most challenging comics but falsifies the comics reading experience in two ways: one, it soft-pedals the essential role of popular genre comics in establishing both a public taste and the scholar's own passion for the form; and two, it does not allow one to recognize the seminal achievements of popular comics creators from the past. (It ought to be as easy for critics to appreciate the work of a commercial cartoonist like Carl Barks or Jack Kirby as it is for them to admire the work of a filmmaker like Griffith or Ford.) Thus status anxiety can doubly handicap the critic's work.

On the other hand, scholars may argue from an iconoclast's position, and point out, with a nod of the head toward Pierre Bourdieu, that taste differentials are based not on inherent qualities in art so much as on the exercise of political power by privileged classes. By this argument, it makes no sense, and indeed would be bitterly ironic, to erect a comics "canon," an authoritative consensus that would reproduce, within the comics field, the same operations of exclusion and domination that have for so long been brought to bear against the field as a whole. This iconoclast argument questions the needfulness of making hierarchical distinctions among comics (indeed, why even single out *alternative* comics as such?), and argues for a more open, less canon-obsessed view of the field. Such a position is tempting, as it allows one to keep all of the field in focus, sans status anxiety, and to discuss the ceaseless interchange between popular genre works and more critically favored ones. That interchange is crucial: doubtless our sense of literary history would be richer had past scholars not lost sight of it, that is, had they not neglected the popular traditions which stoked the development of what would later become canonical literary works (*Northanger Abbey*, anyone?). Why should we repeat the same critical exclusions, the same mistakes, with comics?

Yet the iconoclast position, grounded though it is in a necessary Marxist critique of taste, cannot explain the bracing experience of reading and rereading excellent work in the comics form—work that not only engages us emotionally and intellectually with its vision of life but also tutors us in the possibilities of the form and makes us hunger to read more good work in that form. Simply put, a critical stance that posits no meaningful distinctions among comics cannot do justice to the art form. Nor can it explain its recent rejuvenation. That is why the following study, while acknowledging the history of the comic book as a lowbrow or no-brow medium (and referencing comics of all kinds), finds its center of gravity in alternative comics. Though many are wretched, and the subculture from which they spring is admittedly an ideological rat's nest, alternative comics have also been the seedbed of much that is vital and transforming in the comics field. I think readers of contemporary literature should be specially introduced to them.

THE VIRTUES OF UNFIXABILITY

Both socially and aesthetically, comics are likely to remain an unresolved, unstable, and challenging form. This is what makes them interesting. Indeed, for the general reader, the collateral benefits of comics study may be found in this very instability: if comic art is some kind of bastard, to recruit a popular metaphor, then maybe bastardy is just the thing—our culture has it in for aesthetic purity anyway. In our age of new and hybrid media, interartistic collaboration is king. Popular culture and high art alike are saturated with text/image combinations; we are encircled by imagetexts (a phrase I lift from W. J. T. Mitchell). What better form than comics to tune up our sensibilities and alert us to the possibilities of such texts? Among the popular traditions, none mix text and image more persistently, or diversely, than comics; they make an ideal laboratory for the sustained study of text/image relations. In my own teaching I have learned that bringing comics into contact with other hybrid forms (for example, picture books, illustrated novels, artist's books, concrete poems) enriches my and my students' understanding of text/image relations in general.

Comics are challenging (and highly teachable) because they offer a form of reading that resists coherence, a form at once seductively visual and radically fragmented. Comic art is a mixed form, and reading comics a tension-filled experience (as I posit in chapter 2). Recent criticism both within and without the academy has recognized that comics solicit the reader's participation in a unique way; through their very plurality of means, they advert to that incompleteness or indeterminancy, which, as Wolfgang Iser has argued, urges readers to take up the constitutive act of interpretation (*The Act of Reading* 166–70). The fractured surface of the comics page, with its patchwork of different images, shapes, and symbols, presents the reader with a surfeit of interpretive options, creating an experience that is always decentered, unstable, and unfixable. As Robert P. Fletcher observes, this fragmentation urges readers to take a critical role, for comic art "calls attention to its fictionality by displaying its narrative seams" (381). The reader's responsibility for negotiating meaning can never be forgotten, for the breakdown of comics into discrete visual quanta continually foregrounds the reader's involvement. The very discontinuity of the page urges readers to do the work of inference, to negotiate over and over the passage from submissive reading to active interpreting. In the words of McCloud's *Understanding Comics*, "Every act committed to paper by the comics artist is aided and abetted by a silent accomplice. An equal partner in crime known as *the reader*" (68, his emphasis).

The comics form is infinitely plastic: there is no single recipe for reconciling the various elements of the comics page. Granted, readers are guided by expectations born of habit, and artists by "rules" born of long usage, but the makeup of the page need not follow any set pattern. In the reading of a page there is always the possibility that different protocols may be invoked, different elements stressed. Perhaps that is why, within the larger field of word/image study, comics are a wandering variable, and can be approached from so many perspectives. The restless, polysemiotic character of the form allows for the continual rewriting of its grammar; each succeeding page need not function in precisely the same manner as its predecessor. The relationship between the various elements of comics (images, words, symbols) resists easy formulation. The critical reading of comics therefore involves a tug-of-war between conflicting impulses: on the one hand, the nigh-on irresistible urge to codify the workings of the form; on the other, a continual delight in the form's ability to frustrate any airtight analytical scheme.

The inherent plurality of comic art makes it apt for critical study, as it promises to shed light on verbal-visual dynamics in many different kinds of hybrid texts. Indeed comics have the potential to illuminate the entire field of word/image relationships. If, as W. J. T. Mitchell argues in *Picture Theory* (5), all media are "mixed," and all representations "heterogeneous," then comics may serve as a way of honing our critical sensibilities to approach the material and visual dimensions even of more traditional texts. Through the exploration of comics we can work on assembling a much-needed vocabulary for the study of hybrid texts old and new, a vocabulary that will help us better understand the visual elements of literature as well as the possibilities of interartistic collaboration. Comic art, after all, represents a vast experimenting with word/image combinations, a thus far neglected inheritance that may make it possible for us to reapproach whole bodies of marginalized work from the past (as well as the burgeoning possibilities of an increasingly on-line future).

WHAT (NOT) TO EXPECT

While establishing a cultural milieu for alternative comics, this study views comic art primarily as a literary form. This is not the only productive way comics can be viewed, but it is an important and thus far neglected way. Granted, comics are an unusual kind of literature and should not be carelessly subsumed into prevailing models (a caveat raised in chapter 6). What's more, comics study encourages eclecticism, for comics urge the dissolution of professional boundaries and the mingling of theories and methods drawn from various fields. In this sense they are antidisciplinary. Yet embarking on comics study requires, no less than other fields, a provisional commitment to some discipline, some particular way of seeing. (Otherwise, how can one get started?) In what follows, then, I have stressed the literary, while happily stretching out toward other fields and modes of inquiry. At the core of this book is an interest in comics as a narrative form, in the broadest sense: fiction, recollection, reportage, exposition. These are not the only things to look for in comics—narrative drive is not the only, nor always the best, criterion for evaluating a comic—but I continue to be drawn to comics that tell stories.

I am, however, not drawn to arguments based on presumptions about the "essence," proper scope, or limitations of comic art. (Such arguments are routinely flouted by alternative comics.) And, emphatically, I am not interested in problems of definition or origin, issues that have consumed much energy among comics scholars. Regarding the "origin" of modern comics, suffice to say that several competing narratives of comics history, some clearly shaped by cultural nationalism, are now in place (readers are urged to consult Diereck and Lefèvre, as well as the essential David Kunzle). Regarding definition, I consider the question a detour—the outlines of the field are by now agreed upon, despite continued wrangling over fine points. What definitions I propose in this book are either purely local, meaning tactical, or else based on histories of practice rather than abstract formal criteria (as in chapter 1's discussion of the comic book). Though chapter 2 offers a toolbox of notions for the aesthetic analysis of comics, it does not presume to be definitive; rather, it consists of an unfinished series of questions about what comics can do and how they can do it. In short, I do not propose a new, overarching definition of comic art—though I hope I have treated certain familiar questions more comprehensively than readers have seen before.

Finally, this study is but a progress report from one who is working as fast as he can to keep abreast of a rapidly accelerating field. Comic art is now wide open for reassessment, as many of the limiting assumptions behind previous scholarship have at last been overturned (no longer do we assume that comics are American in origin, that they are just over one hundred years old, or that they are reducible to a handful of popular genres). In fact this is an exhilarating moment for comics study, for, aesthetically, critically, and economically, things have changed and *are* changing so fast that it is hard to keep up. I take this as an encouraging sign. When I began drafting this book, prospects for the continued popular growth of comics were unpromising: the U.S. comic book market was in retreat, and the "graphic novel" had yet to make a strong mark on the mainstream publishing industry. Since then, the landscape has changed: the graphic novel has carved out a healthy niche in the book trade, so that even this skeptic has finally dropped the habit of bracketing the term in quotation marks (when in Rome . . .). In a space of just a few years, market trends and patterns of reception have undergone terrific shifts, and alternative comics in particular—through acclaimed work by such creators as Spiegelman, Harvey Pekar, Gilbert Hernandez, Jaime Hernandez, Lynda Barry, Chester Brown, Dan Clowes, Joe Sacco, and Chris Ware—have leapt into the spotlight.

At the moment, comic art in North America happily suffers from a fever of promise, commercially and artistically, so much so that a larger critical audience is at last waking up to its possibilities. Readers are therefore urged to use what follows as a springboard for their own explorations.

ALTERNATIVE COMICS

CHAPTER ONE

COMIX, COMIC SHOPS, AND THE RISE OF ALTERNATIVE COMICS, POST 1968

Comics have most often come in small packages: broadsheets, panels, strips, pamphlets. Yet recent emphasis on the graphic novel suggests that the form's further artistic growth, or at least recognition, depends on the vitality of longer stories that exceed these small packages. Critical attention has turned to longer works that cannot fit within the narrow straits of the strip and other miniature formats. Notwithstanding the many brilliant uses of the newspaper strip as a ritualistic genre—one thinks of George Herriman, Charles Schulz, and a pantheon of others—the current renascence and critical reassessment of comics stems mainly from book-length works. Many of these works, not coincidentally, are alternative comics, determined to push back the thematic horizons of the form—and to avoid the colorful yet diversionary byways of familiar market genres such as the superhero.

Critical study of these alternative comics and graphic novels begs certain historical questions: What conditions have allowed for the creation of such extended, formula-defying comics? What cultural and commercial circumstances have enabled the growth of alternative comics and the recognition of comics as a distinct literature? If, as Lee Erickson argues in *The Economy of Literary Form*, the evolution of a genre reveals an "economy of readers' demands and authors' productions" (3), then what "economy" accounts for the innovations seen in recent comics? The following chapter tries to answer these questions by placing the development of alternative comics—as literary form and as reading culture—within the history of American comics publishing, and in particular the history of that most puzzling of artifacts, the "comic book."

I offer here a new take on the comic book and its reading culture. While some recent studies describe the world of contemporary comic book readers in detail, most notably Matthew Pustz's participant-observer study *Comic Book Culture* (1999), none satisfactorily explains how this culture, in particular its "alternative" subculture, has reshaped comics as a literary form. This is because none has acknowledged the current field's contested origins in 1960s-era counterculture or the way those origins still inform and enliven the field. None has succeeded in explaining why this seemingly narrow and specialized field continues to generate such explosive work or why the field should be of interest to the general reader. By reexamining the history of the comic book as commodity *and* as literary form, and specifically by demonstrating the importance of countercultural or "underground" comic books within that history, I hope to answer these questions. Thus we will establish a cultural and economic milieu for alternative comics (and for the remainder of this study).

FORMAT VERSUS ART FORM

Let us begin by taking a step back, so that we can gain a sense of overview, or topsight:

The history of comic art has been bound up in the histories of certain *packages* or publishing formats. In the United States, the most dominant of these packages have been the newspaper comics page and the "comic book." The former consists of a miscellany of features and genres, most bound by the rigid constraints of the daily strip or the Sunday; it appears within the larger miscellany of the newspaper, and comics produced for it are seen as secondary features at best. The so-called comic book, on the other hand, is a small, self-contained magazine or pamphlet (roughly half-tabloid in size). In the early days of the industry, this magazine incorporated a miscellany of features, both narrative and non-narrative; more recently, though, it has come to concentrate on a single character or group of characters and, more often than not, a single story (typically between eighteen and twenty-four pages in length). Since the late

1980s, a third way of packaging comics has gained ground in American print culture: the "graphic novel," which in industry parlance means any book-length comics narrative or compendium of such narratives (excepting volumes reprinting newspaper strips, which comprise a long-lived yet critically invisible genre of their own). Each of these three packages, the newspaper page, the comic book, and the graphic novel, has its own horizons in terms of content, audience, and cultural cachet.

As Samuel R. Delany has observed of "comics" in general, these formats are *social objects* (in the sense established by sociologist Lucien Goldmann), and as such are defined more by common usage than by a priori formal criteria (Delany 239). As social objects, they come to us encrusted with connotations—or rather *we* come to them with associations and habits of thought inculcated through repeated use. If we are to see comic art more clearly, we have to distinguish between these connotatively charged objects and the art form itself. To this end, it helps to distinguish broadly between *short-form* comics and *long-form* comics. Each of these categories, the short form and the long form, may come in a variety of packages, though each has traditionally been associated with one medium, or package, in particular.

The *short form*, through the medium of daily and weekly newspapers, remains the type of comic most familiar to general readers in the United States. Under "short form" we may also group panels and strips in magazines, as well as a smattering of short features within comic books. Yet the kernel of the short form remains the newspaper strip, which, despite the recent plunge in newspaper reading, remains an entrenched part of American culture. Strips are small, formally rigid and ephemeral, though the more popular ones are routinely gathered into best-selling books. While they have recovered a degree of formal playfulness in recent years, thanks to the interventions of popular artists such as Bill Watterson (*Calvin & Hobbes*), strips remain an editorially conservative medium, bound by inflexible formatting constraints. Artists and historians have written lovingly of the full pages that strip cartoonists once enjoyed, and have lamented the gradual crowding of the medium into its present cramped conditions, but the fact is that the age of the large-format newspaper strip passed decades ago. Though some artists have adapted well to the smaller format, strips continue to be cramped by unyielding editorial policies. The ability of such strips to insinuate themselves into daily routine has been at once their greatest asset and greatest obstacle to continued growth: to remake a newspaper comics page is to disrupt the habits of many readers. This fact apparently looms so large in the minds of editors that the newspaper page tends to remain within its predictable bounds, with little change, year after year. Thus comics in the short form are, by and large, severely hobbled in terms of graphic and thematic potential.

Comics in the *long form*, though in some ways freer, are hemmed in by other factors. Most spring from the comic book industry, which in essence depends on the hobby of comic book collecting rather than appeals to a mass audience. From this enclave of specialized consumer ritual, some long-form comics have emerged to make claims on critical attention as "graphic novels" (a convenient if often inaccurate label). But the serialized graphic novel, as practiced both by publishers within the so-called mainstream of the hobby and by those on its alternative fringe, has until recently made little impact on the book trade. The most notable critical success among graphic novels, Art Spiegelman's Pulitzer-winning *Maus*, appeared not in serial comic books per se, but in Spiegelman and Françoise Mouly's oversized art 'zine *Raw* (the seminal journal for the comics avant-garde, 1980– 91). Though *Raw* depended to an extent on the support of comic book fans, its unusual origins, format, and attitude pushed it to the margins of the hobby (see Spiegelman and Mouly, Interview, *Read*, and Interview with Cavalieri et al.). *Maus*, then, unlike most volumes christened "graphic novels," did not have immediate roots in the periodical comic book. Long-form narratives that *have* been born out of the traditional monthly comic book have fared notably less well over the long term—at least until very recently. (Of late, graphic novels have become a growth area for bookstores, a phenomenon spurred in part by the new popularity of translated *manga*, that is, Japanese comics.)

In the years after *Maus*, an initial fit of commercial enthusiasm for the graphic novel gave way to at best flickering interest, as it became clear that Spiegelman's project was sui generis and did not necessarily herald an explosion of comparable books. Only recently (especially since 2000) have graphic novels of similar density and ambition begun to reach bookstores more regularly. Despite this, the term "graphic novel" has become common parlance—a curious thing, as few of the volumes so christened aspire to be anything like novels in terms of structure, breadth, or coherence. Indeed a graphic novel can be almost anything: a novel, a collection of interrelated or thematically similar stories, a memoir, a travelogue or journal, a history, a series of vignettes or lyrical observations, an episode from a longer work—you name it. Perhaps this very plasticity helps explain the currency of the term. What might have seemed at first to denote a distinct genre has instead become an all-purpose tag for a vague new class of social object (one that, unlike the "comic book," need not be grounded in the exact specifications of a given physical format).

Format *is* important. As Pascal Lefèvre has remarked, format "influences the total concept of [a] comic, not only the style, but also the content"; furthermore, different formats "stimulate different manners of consuming" ("Published" 98). What we think about comic art is circumscribed by what we think about, and the ways we consume, the dominant formats of strip, comic book, and graphic novel. In fact, the cultural connotations of format, if accepted uncritically, can obscure or mystify the development of the art form itself. Terms like "comic book" and "graphic novel" are, strictly speaking, inaccurate; worse yet, they may encourage expectations, positive or negative, that are not borne out by the material itself. The phrase "graphic novel," for instance, seems to imply a breadth and cohesion to which few graphic novels aspire, let alone achieve. The label, taken for granted within the narrow straits of the comic book hobby, threatens confusion as the graphic novel bids for acceptance within the wider field of literature and criticism. (Ironically, the novel—once a disreputable, bastard thing, radical in its formal instability—is here being invoked as the very byword of literary merit and respectability.) Conversely, the term "comic book," fraught with pejorative connotations, seems to undersell the extraordinary work that has been done, and is currently being done, in the long form. Yet to reject such terms completely is to run afoul of common usage and to risk obscuring the subject behind neologisms that are clumsy, counterintuitive, and ahistorical. (I have therefore grudgingly retained these familiar phrases but try to use them in specific and historically contextualized ways—hence my positing of *short-form* and *long-form* as larger, more inclusive categories.)

Though this study makes occasional reference to newspaper strips, its center of gravity is comics in the long form, specifically extended stories and novels—as opposed to the anecdotal, repetitive, or episodic structures of the short form. Since the field of alternative comics (notwithstanding alternative newspaper cartoonists such as Lynda Barry, Matt Groening, or Carol Lay) tends to be associated with sporadic comic books and graphic novels, we will concentrate on the genres of the self-contained story, the novel, and the memoir, rather than the open-ended daily or even monthly serial. This is to say that, for the duration of this study, we will privilege the kinds of comics for which the phrase "graphic novel" was originally coined. At the same time, though, readers should stay mindful of the restrictions and possibilities inherent in serial comic book publication—issues that have complicated the aesthetic growth of the art form, and that will necessarily turn up, again and again, in the chapters ahead. Indeed one cannot begin to discuss alternative comics, nor the recent recognition of comics as a literature, without first dealing with what the "comic book" is, how it has been distributed, exhibited, and received, and how the entrenchment of the comic book hobby has affected the aesthetic horizons of the form.

UNDERGROUND COMIX AND WHAT THEY DID TO THE COMIC BOOK

If the history of comics is necessarily a history of objects, then in the United States the comic book (in the narrowest sense) has been the most influential of those objects in terms of shaping critical opinion. In fact the comic book has so monopolized the critical conception of comic art that it must be dealt with at length. Periodical in origin, typically populist in nature, and often characterized by the most mercenary of aims, the comic book is well-established as the dominant identity of anglophone comics in the long form, and has also been the target of some of the most sustained and intense critical savaging of any cultural product in American history. Vilified, often misread, ill-understood, the comic book in its heyday inspired a tremendous degree of cultural anxiety—a kind of panic also seen in, say, early twentieth-century film censorship or recent discussions of the Internet, but unique in its intensity and effectiveness. More than any other American medium, the comic book has been obscured by the terms of its own success. To understand the recent move toward critical acceptance of comics as a literary form, we need to reexamine the development of this much-despised "comic book" as social object and market commodity.

Granted, this development ought to be crystal-clear by now. Numerous fan histories have traced the evolution of comic books, and, while quite a few have unfortunately slipped out of print, many remain available even to the casual browser. (For the most casual, many fan-authored websites give capsule histories of the medium, of varied dependability and usefulness.) For a model of fan history that excels within its limits, I would recommend Ron Goulart's detailed coffee table book, *Great American Comic Books* (2001); for a historical overview with academic cachet, Bradford Wright's *Comic Book Nation: The Transformation of Youth Culture in America* (2001). But neither of these books does quite the job I want to do here. Each is authoritative and valuable in its own way, yet each is structured by certain blind spots or exclusions: Goulart's work is an example par excellence of nostalgic reclamation, and as such privileges mainstream market genres; Wright's is a social history based on a self-styled "fun-house mirror" version of reflection theory, and by its own admission considers comic books "as a cultural representation, not as an art form" (xvii). (That there might be a productive dialogue or reconciliation between these two approaches is apparently beside the point; Wright has a different agenda.) Thus these two books embody dominant trends, and nagging lapses, in comics scholarship. Both books are most persuasive when dealing with comic books prior to 1960, but neither is literary-historical, that is, neither links its historical interests to the development of literary form. Robert C. Harvey's *The Art of the Comic Book* (1996) offers a more inclusive aesthetic history, but, rich as it is, its coverage of recent trends is fitful, its take on alternative comics narrow. As a complement to these and other notable studies, the following account focuses specially on a neglected aspect of comic book history (the "underground" comics movement), argues for its centrality, and, finally, makes a case for the continuing influence of the underground in today's alternative comics press. This account also seeks to demystify the commercial mechanism (direct sales) by which "underground" and "mainstream" comics gradually mingled, cross-pollinated, and gave birth to a new reading culture.

Let us begin, then, not at the beginning, but at a climax of sorts: the late 1960s to early 1970s, the era of underground comix (so-called). This era has at last been fittingly chronicled by Patrick Rosenkranz's *Rebel Visions* (2002), a long-gestating and stunningly detailed history (which readers are urged to seek out). Rosenkranz, however, focuses minutely on the biographies of key artists in the movement and only minimally on the way underground comix subsequently redefined the entire field. Though Rosenkranz makes a case for the movement's "legacy," and others have also gestured in this direction, little work has been done to substantiate claims for the underground's literary and artistic influence. Academically, the underground has been a period under near-erasure, with the exception of a very few studies such as Joseph Witek's *Comic Books as History* (1988). (Happily, though, this is finally starting to change: for example, the 2002 University of Florida Conference on Comics and Graphic Novels focused on the underground.) In what follows, then, I will make specific claims about the influence of the underground movement, arguing that comix above all were the catalyst for a radically new understanding of the art form.

During the underground period, the comic-book-as-social-object suffered a sea change. Comix, it is said, established the idea of comics as a form for adults (not "just" children), but this statement needs further qualification. If we look carefully at that era, what we find is something more specific: underground comix trumpeted the arrival of not simply comics for adults but *comic books* for adults. What's more, these comic books were most often for adults *only* (as the labels on so many comix covers baldly proclaimed). Underground comix did not single-handedly make comics reading safe for adults—after all, newspaper strips had long had an adult audience—but they did make comic *books* an adult commodity. Something about the act of purchasing an exclusively adult comic as an independent commodity (a "book" or magazine), as opposed to purchasing comics in the context of a newspaper, made these illicit publications novel and alluring. It was through the underground comix that comic books per se became an adult medium, and the self-contained nature of these "books," so unlike the comics in even underground newspapers, made the medium an ideal platform for kinds of expression that were outrageously personal and self-regarding, even by the standards of the radical press from which comix emerged.

The singular genius of the underground comic books was the way they transformed an object that was jejune and mechanical in origin into a radically new kind of expressive object, a vehicle for the most personal and unguarded of revelations. While prior comic books had featured some work that, in hindsight, appears quite personal and idiosyncratic, underground comix conveyed an unprecedented sense of intimacy, rivaling the scandalizing disclosures of confessional poetry but shot through with fantasy, burlesque, and self-satire. (Eventually the underground would give birth to a type of autobiographical comics comparable to literary confessionalism at its most nakedly personal, and this type would become central to alternative comics, as we shall see in chapter 4.) Thus the underground worked an alchemical change on what was basically an infelicitous medium, making this familiar class of object into the carrier of a new kind of meaning. In short, underground comix ironized the comic book medium itself: the package was inherently at odds with the sort of material the artists wanted to handle, and this tension gave the comix books their unique edge.

It is difficult to date the exact origins of underground comix, since they emerged from various sources (amateur 'zines, college humor magazines, underground newspapers, and psychedelic rock poster art) before coalescing into a distinct movement in the late sixties. It is not difficult, however, to pinpoint the birth of the underground *comic book* as a recognizable class of object; that distinction belongs to R. Crumb's *Zap Comix* No. 1, printed and sold in early 1968 (Rosenkranz 69–72; Harvey, *Comic Book* 193–95). Granted, a number of odd-sized booklets later recognized as "comix" had been produced before *Zap* in small (often very small) print runs, including pieces by artists who would go on to greater fame.[1] But it was not until Crumb's innovation that the idea of creating a sustainable underground comic book series took hold. Crumb would go on to create an anthology version of *Zap* featuring other artists, beginning with *Zap* No. 2 in mid-1968, and the series became the standard-bearer of the underground (Rosenkranz 87–88, 123).

Historian Robert C. Harvey has described Crumb's move to the comic book format as mere "happenstance"; yet others have testified to the significance of seeing Crumb's work published in precisely this form. Clay Geerdes, quoted by Harvey himself, declared, "It was the book [that is, *Zap*] that turned on all those light bulbs and taught people they did not have to submit to the East Coast comic book monopoly. . . . *Zap* taught them they could do their own" (*Comic Book* 210). Likewise, Les Daniels's *Comix: A History of Comic Books in America* (published in 1971) credits Crumb with "making the independent underground comic book a viable form," a development that would still have been recent at the time of Daniels's writing (169). Jay Lynch, cocreator of the seminal Chicago-based comix book *Bijou Funnies*, recalled that the development of *Bijou* was spurred by *Zap*, which Lynch and his collaborator Skip Williamson admired because it was a stand-alone publication (Rosenkranz 119). The two "figured Crumb really had balls to

publish something like that" (qtd. in Estren 52). Similarly, artist Victor Moscoso felt that *Zap*'s comic book format "opened the door," enough so that he accepted Crumb's invitation to join *Zap* with issue No. 2: "The form was perfect. A comic book, that size" (Rosenkranz 85). Though comix were crucially nurtured by a network of radical newspapers, such as the *East Village Other* and the *Berkeley Barb*, and early on gave rise to short-lived tabloids like *Yellow Dog* (in its first incarnation, 1968–69) and *Gothic Blimp Works* (1969), it was Crumb's subversive appropriation of the comic book that proved to be the decisive break with the past. As Bill Griffith remarked, Crumb "reinvented the comic book. Took it over just as other people of his generation took over music" (Rosenkranz 71). *Zap* became the catalyst for a whole new field of comix publishing because Crumb took back the comic book and redefined what it could do.

The reassessment of comics as a means of self-expression, then, began with the underground's usurpation of that commonplace object, the comic book. Again, by "comic book" I mean something quite particular: not just any publication consisting mostly of comics, but specifically the standard-format comics magazine as developed for the U.S. newsstand market in the early 1930s and formularized by the early 1940s. This comic book was obviously misnamed: not a book but a periodical, a cheap magazine printed on raunchy paper, descended from the foundering pulp magazines of the day and a cousin of the ephemeral strips found in newspapers. The underground comix artists of the late sixties seized this medium, hitherto associated with anonymous, industrialized entertainment, and transformed it into a vehicle for self-expression in a highly romanticized and radical way.

It may be objected that I have defined the "comic book" too narrowly, and, admittedly, it is tempting to apply the term to any stand-alone publication consisting of comic art (as some present-day authorities do). Yet the curious achievement of underground comix becomes much clearer when we acknowledge the term's historical specificity. The label "comic book," so rich with associations, belongs above all to a peculiar package born in Depression-era America, the offspring of industrial publicity and entrepreneurial zeal. Historian Ian Gordon's *Comic Strips and Consumer Culture, 1890–1945* reminds us that the earliest examples of this kind of comic book (as opposed to previous attempts to package comics in other formats) were promotional giveaways for industries otherwise unassociated with entertainment or art: oil companies, shoe manufacturers, and so on. Other historians have noted this practice, bemusedly, as a preface to the "real" business of making comic books, but Gordon wisely points out that these premium comics had a long reach: they were read by thousands, perhaps even hundreds of thousands, and were apparently quite popular (130). Such promotional magazines primed the pump, indeed established the conditions, for the sale of comics as self-contained commodities, independent of newspapers and general interest magazines. Thus the comic book was overwhelmingly a commercial proposition from the outset, and only later developed into a distinct artistic medium. Indeed, the years 1934 to 1945, from an aesthetic viewpoint, are about nothing so much as discovering that this low-rent format, originally adopted for purely mercenary reasons, could be used to create comics that looked and read very differently from their newspaper strip predecessors. This was a slow and inadvertent realization, hampered by the industry's fixation on minimal investment and maximum short-term profit. Only later would this format, generated by entrepreneurial scurrying around the fringes of large and impersonal industrial processes, become a fertile medium for self-expression. That's what the underground accomplished.

In hindsight, the peculiar format of American comic books seems a historic anomaly rather than a logical end development—which makes its reinvention and reification by the comix underground even more ironic. Early comic books, consisting mainly of reprinted strips bought from newspaper syndicates, were cranked out at great speed and minimal cost for a hungry audience of mostly juvenile readers; subsequent efforts to satisfy demand with new material, native to the comic book, had to compete with these formative, shoestring productions (Harvey, *Comic Book* 24–25). Thus the industry favored a highly

mechanical approach to creation from the outset—not as rationalized and routine as a Ford factory, but still artistically numbing. This was the "shop" or studio system of comics production, nearly an assembly-line affair, in which pages frequently changed hands and artists routinely finished each other's work. Various shops—such as Harry "A" Chesler's, the Eisner/Iger studio, and Funnies Incorporated, all famed in fan lore—sprang up to package complete comic book stories inexpensively for publishers looking to maximize profits (see, for example, Harvey, "Shop System"; Goulart, "Sweatshops"; Eisner, "Art and Commerce" 8–12). The issue at stake was how to create new comic book material in a format (and at a cost) established when the comic book was still primarily a promotional giveaway stuffed with newspaper reprints.

Even the unique physical dimensions of the comic book were the result of cost cutting. Comic books were originally half-tabloid-size; their dimensions came from folding a tabloid newspaper page in half to create roughly 8-by-10-inch pages. (The equivalent of sixteen tab-sized sheets could be laid out to create a pulpy 64-page booklet.) Comic books in this format—first as promotional giveaways, then as market commodities—were created by the Eastern Color Printing Company, a Connecticut-based printer, to wring more profits from occasionally idle presses. (For accounts of the comic book's origins, see, for example, Gordon, *Comic Strips* 129–31; Goulart, *Great* 12–15; Waugh 337–40.)

Cost-saving initiatives led to the flourishing studio system of the late 1930s, as well as to the practice (later standard) of publishers hiring staffs to produce or touch up comic books in-house. These economic conditions, inimical to reflection or revision, cemented the perception of the comic book as a shoddy, ephemeral diversion, a form of anonymous, relatively diluted, and industrialized pabulum. Production schedules necessitated the interchangeability of artists and the reliance on already-inbred story formulas. Positively, it might be argued that the shop system allowed energetic young amateurs to bootstrap themselves to a level of journeyman craftsmanship fairly quickly, and of course the shops did become seedbeds for some extraordinary talents. Yet the breakneck periodical scheduling and crass production values of most comic books from this era did much to tar the nascent medium with a reputation for amateurism, cynicism, and greed.

This was the so-called Golden Age of fan lore. Indeed it yielded some golden work, much of it either on the fringes of or entirely outside the shop system per se: for example, Will Eisner's *Spirit*, Jack Cole's *Plastic Man*, and the best of Joe Simon and Jack Kirby's studio (whose output was wildly inconsistent); Carl Barks's *Donald Duck* and *Uncle Scrooge* et al., John Stanley's *Little Lulu*, and, in the early fifties, work by Harvey Kurtzman (*Two-Fisted Tales*, *Frontline Combat*, *Mad*) and the rest of the E.C (Entertaining Comics) stable. Work of great vitality (as well as eccentricity, even flat-out weirdness) graced the burgeoning medium from the early forties onward, some of it in the various *Superman*-inspired "costume" comics, some of it in humor and "funny animal" titles, and some of it, as the forties waned, in the more controversial genres of crime, romance, and eventually horror comics.

Work of wretched quality was much more common, though in hindsight it too can be interesting. As Art Spiegelman has remarked, this was a Golden Age of comic books as "termite" art—a notion lifted from Manny Farber, whose seminal film criticism celebrated work produced "where the spotlight of culture is nowhere in evidence, so that the craftsman can be ornery, wasteful, stubbornly self-involved," creating hell-for-leather art that "eat[s] its own boundaries, and . . . leaves nothing in its path other than signs of eager, industrious unkempt activity" (Farber, qtd. in Spiegelman and Kidd 8). Such a cultural borderland can serve as a safe zone for play, a site where, as Roger Sabin puts it, " 'nobody is looking', [so that] it is possible to experiment and flex creative muscles" (*Comics, Comix* 9). In this embryonic period of frenzied, market-driven play, observes Spiegelman, comic books opened "a direct gateway into the unrestrained dream life of their creators" (Spiegelman and Kidd 8). Thus even the most abject stuff from the period may hold some retrospective fascination—and the best work, that in which orneriness and playfulness are abetted by skill, evokes vivid, dreamlike worlds that, once explored, are impossible to forget.

It is this imaginative ferocity that Michael Chabon captures in his Pulitzered novel on comic book history, *The Amazing Adventures of Kavalier & Clay* (2000), whose artist-hero, Joe Kavalier, imbues his comics with such passion, desperation, and skill. And it is this wildness that is so often celebrated in the glowing, sometimes apocryphal lore of fandom, rich with accounts of adolescent camaraderie and deadline-driven zeal: artists pulling all-nighters to crank out superhero tales; artists passing pages from hand to hand; artists jockeying for space in studios and apartments, or even drawing in bathtubs. (In this sense, the underground cartoonists of the 1960s were merely carrying on a tradition of freewheeling bohemianism.) Such stories are hard to resist, stuffed as they are with color and life, but they risk romanticizing what was at bottom a bluntly commercial and exploitative business, one that, with rare exceptions, produced work of flickering quality and slight ambition—eager, perhaps, but fitful and prone to burnout, despite its occasional incandescent bursts. In spite of the medium's considerable (millions-selling) popularity in the Golden Age, it did little to nurture or encourage its practitioners.

In sum, the early growth of long-form comics in the United States was dictated by the emergence of a conveniently exploitable medium, a product that proved cheap and accessible: the comic book as developed in the early to mid-thirties. This format proved successful where previous efforts had failed: first as a premium for other industries; then as an independent commodity nonetheless dependent on the syndicated newspaper strip industry; then, finally, as a commodity defined by its own original narrative material. The term "comic book" belongs specifically to this object, one that, by demonstrating the possibilities of comics in the long form, eventually opened the way for other packages that also contained long-form stories (for example, larger magazines, albums, and graphic novels). Yet it would take the singular intervention of the comix underground to awaken this great potential. In the meantime, this seemingly inauspicious medium defined the field of book-length comics in the United States for decades.

Perhaps it still does, to a degree. But things have gotten more complicated, for the comic book, despite its familiarity, has long since retreated from mass to niche medium. Since the early fifties, the medium's commercial peak, the comic book has faded to the margins of popular culture, from which it only occasionally sallies forth to trumpet some minor innovation or unexpected outrage. It is not easy to explain why comic books have been eclipsed this way—such happenings tend to evade explanation—but research suggests that several events coincided to hobble the growth of the industry at its moment of greatest commercial promise. These events included drastic realignments in American magazine distribution in the mid-fifties; increasing competition from television and other media; and, most notoriously, the tarring of comic books during the censorious public campaigns of the late 1940s and early 1950s.[2] Many comic book publishers acceded to criticism by publicly censoring themselves, that is, by adopting the onerous "Comics Code" in 1954, a surrender that effectively affirmed the general perception of the medium as juvenile pap;[3] then, throughout the latter 1950s and the 1960s, as if fearful of losing their juvenile readers, publishers resisted changing the format or cover prices of their publications, opting instead to decrease the amount of story and to boost advertising content. Prices remained static for an extended period, with few exceptions. (In 1961, Dell, a hugely successful publisher, hiked its cover price from ten to fifteen cents, and the result proved disastrous [Irving 26].) This price-fixing appears to have eaten away at profits, thus making the comic book an increasingly unrewarding venture for retailers and distributors, and further tipping the industry into decline—a long fall eased in the 1960s by the ironic, Marvel-led revival of the superhero genre and a nostalgic appreciation cultivated partly by Pop Art (see Sullivan; Varnedoe and Gopnik 213–26).

In any case, it was this format, so widely associated with faceless industrial entertainment, which underground cartoonists usurped and redefined in the late 1960s. Comix transformed the medium into a vehicle for a febrile romanticism in tune with the radical sensibilities of the Vietnam-era counterculture. The central irony of that most ironic of packages, the underground comix book, was the way it mimicked the very format of the corporatized comic

books of yore (at a time when comic books were declining from a mass medium to an acquired taste). The chief culprit in this was cartoonist Crumb: though his *Zap Comix* cannot truly be said to be the "first" entry in the comix underground, it was the first underground title by a lone cartoonist to be published in what was recognizably the traditional comic book format. Thus Crumb demonstrated that it was possible (though not easy) for one cartoonist to take complete control of a package whose very dimensions were designed with impersonal assembly-line production in mind. Crumb usurped what was then the most common vehicle for long-form comics, the newsstand-style comic book, and turned it into a deceptively friendly-looking container for stories that could hardly be carried on mainstream newsstands, due to their iconoclastic, sometimes scabrous, and indeed radical content.

In retrospect, this usurpation of the comic book seems perfect for Crumb's larger project in the late sixties, which was in effect to reclaim bygone images from American popular culture—from comics and animated cartooning in particular—and invest them with new, subversive meanings. Crumb's work from this period, while original in many respects, owes much to earlier comics and cartoons, particularly in its preference for rubbery, polymorphous characters (often anthropomorphized animals) and a broad, exaggerated style. In Crumb one can spot the influence of not only various newspaper cartoonists but also such comic book creators as funny animal master Carl Barks and grotesque humorist Basil Wolverton (*Powerhouse Pepper* and so forth). Crumb's characters, compounded of these influences, waver disturbingly between toothsome cuteness and parodic grotesqueness. The artist's originality lay in his use of such figures to express a vision at once self-regarding, almost solipsistic, yet socially aware, satirical, even politically astute. These figures, warped by a giddy desperation confessedly triggered by the artist's use of psychedelic drugs, had become part of his personal language, his way of expressing his haunted, questioning, radically skeptical view of American life and culture. Crumb colonized these received images (including virulent racist and sexist stereotypes against which he would push repeatedly and to which his work would often succumb) and made them ripe for adult treatment.

Crumb's efforts were inherently ironic, in a manner not unlike that of the Pop artists before him. Indeed this is his signal contribution to American comics: the ironizing of the comic book medium itself. With *Zap* Crumb achieved something that had eluded Pop Art: he ironically usurped not only the content of comics (that is, the characters and situations he had imbibed from childhood onward) but also the format (the periodical comic book), achieving a union of form and content that Pop Art, ensconced within the fine art world, could not. Crumb's *Zap* represented a reflexive, *comic-book* commentary on comic books unlike anything since the early days of *Mad* magazine (in its original comic book incarnation, 1952–55). Moreover, *Zap* was free of *Mad*'s bottom-line commercial ambitions.[4]

Crumb and many of his fellow comix artists—such as Lynch, Williamson, and Kim Deitch—were eclectic and drew inspiration from animation and especially newspaper strips in addition to vintage comic books. Indeed newspaper strips were crucial to enlarging their sense of comics beyond the generic confines of the comic book medium. Yet it was in comic book format that they advanced a pungent critique of American consumerism, turning the kitschy elements of the medium in on itself. Mock comic-book-style advertisements and parodic paratexts (logotypes, banners, indicia, and of course the hated Comics Code seal of approval) run rampant through the comix books; their insistent use invites readers to reconsider the relationships between text and reader implied in more conventional comic books. For instance, *Zap* No. 1 bears a mock Code seal on its cover, as well as a banner just beneath the logo that parodies the ingratiating hype of comic book publishers: *Zap Comics are Squinky Comics!!* (fig. 1). Its back cover is a comics-style advertisement extolling the wonders of "turning on," replete with "before" and "after" photos of frustrated bourgeois "hang-ups" who have shed their inhibitions through the wonders of getting stoned. (A similar full-page ad in the follow-up *Zap* No. 0 [sic] provides step-by-step instructions for smoking a joint.) The idea of

comic book readers as juvenile is stressed just as often as it is flouted: traditional, kid-friendly fillers, such as short gag strips and activity pages, are common in both *Zap* No. 1 and No. 0, as are references to "us kids." Most revealing is a mock editorial on the back of No. 0 that depicts an irate mother shredding her son's comic books, a spoof both of the medium's reputation as "cheap trash" and of the guilty pleasure that adults derive from indulging in it (fig. 2).

Aside from mocking the comic book format itself, Crumb's early stories spoof hippie claims to enlightenment and capitalist bromides in equal measure; they brim with capricious takeoffs of magazine advertising and knowing swipes at American consumerism. One vignette in *Zap* No. 1, for instance, refers to "Kool Kustomers," pokes fun at "Oscar Meyer," and claims to shrink "hemorhoids" [sic]. A story in *Zap* No. 0 introduces Crumb's guru/con man character, Mr. Natural, with this slogan: "Kids! Be sure to eat only Mr. Natural brand foods, and listen to him on WZAP Radio!" No. 0 also contains the satiric story "City of the Future," a bit of mock-utopian hype that perfectly undercuts the rhetoric of American progressivism ("Better worlds are being built!") while dreaming up more and more disturbing uses of technology. Such satiric thrusts, influenced by the gleeful cynicism of *Mad* and college humor magazines, were distilled by Crumb into a perfect comic book package, one that kept spiraling in on itself in vertiginous recursions, always aware of its comic book status. To say that *Zap* was a cynical package would be a bald understatement.

Crumb's contemporaries were quick to seize on such self-mocking elements, offering parodic takes on comic book conventions as well as barbed satires of the consumerist mentality. Often the comic book parodies were deliberately freighted with broader social concerns, turning spoof into a vehicle for cultural argument. For instance, the cover to *Wimmen's Comix* No. 1 (1972), by editor Patricia Moodian, distorts a clichéd scenario from romance comic books: a jilted woman looks enviously at a glamorous couple in a clinch, contrasting their picture-perfect features with her own comically exaggerated ugliness (fig. 3). *Wimmen's Comix*, created by an all-female collective

Figure 1. R. Crumb, *Zap Comix* No. 1 (front cover). © 2004 R. Crumb. Used with permission.

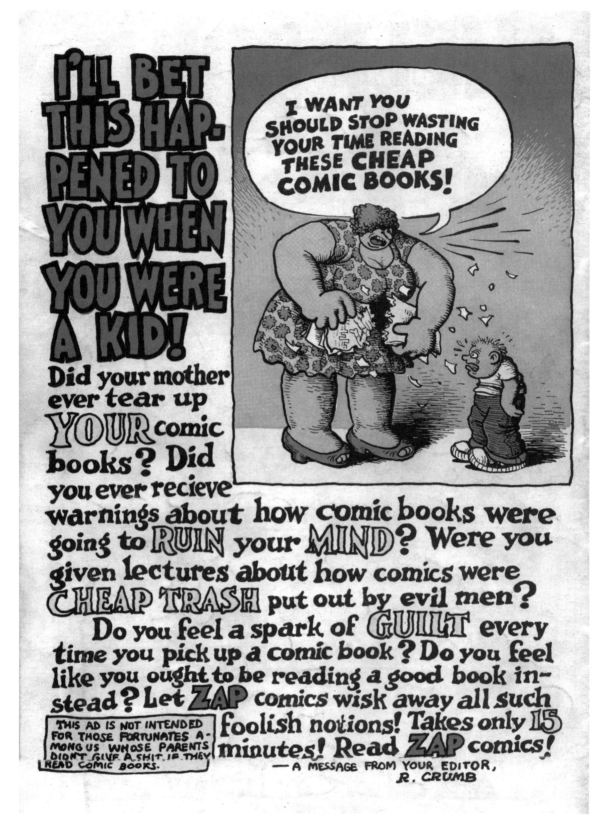

Figure 2. R. Crumb, *Zap Comix* No. 0 (back cover). © R. Crumb. Used with permission.

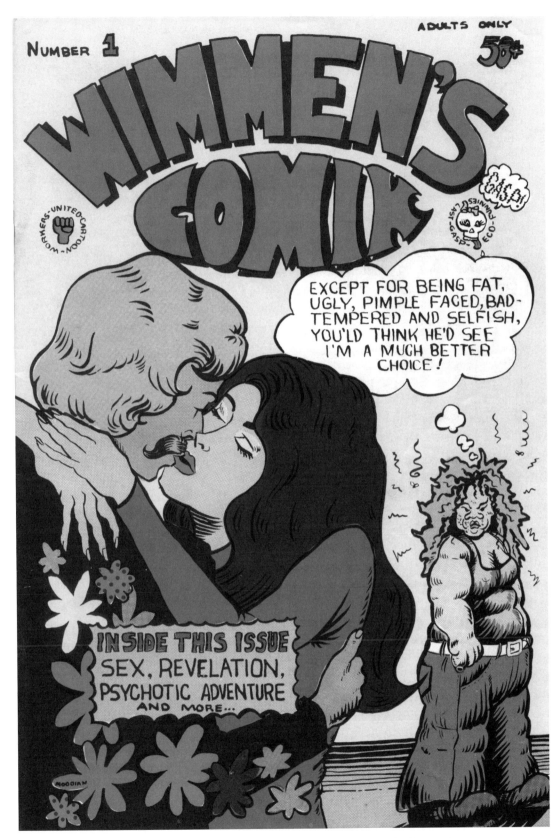

Figure 3. Patricia Moodian, *Wimmen's Comix* No. 1 (front cover). © Patricia Moodian-Pink. Used with permission.

in response to the masculine ethos of the comix scene, often deployed romance comic book tropes for subversive ends (as in, for instance, No. 1's story "A Teenage Abortion," by Lora Fountain, which uses a first-person narrative style typical of romance comics). Similarly charged parodic gestures distinguish the series *Young Lust* (launched in 1971 by Bill Griffith and Jay Kinney), which billed itself as "the underground romance comic": art styles and paratextual elements from mainstream romance are carefully parodied in stories about sexual threesomes, rock 'n' roll groupies, hippies, and GIs. *Young Lust*'s attention to detail was impressive: its cover elements and ersatz advertisements showed a keen eye for ludicrous minutiae (fig. 4). Many other comix books, from Denis Kitchen's *Mom's Homemade Comics* to Dan O'Neill's *Comics & Stories* (a nod to the classic *Walt Disney's Comics & Stories*), likewise played with such details—familiar but usually neglected aspects of the comic book reading experience.

Going beyond *Mad* and its imitators, the comix books at their most interesting transformed this received stuff into the rudiments of a highly personal language, one which might at any minute burst into startling lyric flights or retreat into obscurity and abstraction. Thus they were akin to the puckish thievings and reworkings of Pop Art. Yet, instead of seizing images from comic books and introducing them into art galleries, Crumb and his followers took such images, tore them loose from their traditional narrative moorings, and then injected them back into what appeared to be standard comic books—thereby intervening in an entirely different economy, one open to the grass-roots capitalism of the counterculture. While the comic books produced by Crumb and his fellow underground artists could not be offered for sale in the mainstream newsstand market, they did become mainstays of an alternative economy centered around the boutiques (or "head shops") of the so-called hippie movement.

Spurred by Crumb's seminal achievement, underground comix books shaped the growth of long-form comics in four crucial ways.

First, they demonstrated that it was possible to produce booklets of comics from outside the dominant comic book publishing establishment, which was hobbled by its rigid Code of self-censorship, a reactionary editorial culture, and debilitating economic practices. In so doing, comix opened the door to comic books that would be wholly owned by their creators; that could be kept in print over the long term (in theory and sometimes in practice), like books rather than "magazines"; and that could continue earning money for their creators in the form of royalties (unlike the "mainstream" comic books of the time, most of which were produced by artists working for a flat, per-page rate). Though few if any underground cartoonists could make a secure living solely from their profession, and royalties were sporadic at best, comix did pave the way for a radical reassessment of the relationships among publishers, creators, and intellectual properties, a reassessment that was to affect even mainstream comics in later years. Comix were the first movement of what came to be known among fans as "creator-owned" comic books—and creator ownership was prerequisite to the rise of alternative comics (see "Creators' Rights"; Wiater and Bissette xv–xviii).

Second, despite their adherence to the traditional format, comix books broke with standard periodical publishing: they were produced sporadically, with relatively few series and a large number of one-offs. As a corollary to creator ownership, comix were dominated not by series titles but by the names and reputations of their creators. Though there were a few long-lived series, mostly anthologies such as *Zap*, *Bijou*, *Yellow Dog*, and *Slow Death*, these were mostly published irregularly and were exceptions to the general rule. (Even the prolific Crumb gravitated toward one-shots, such as *Homegrown Funnies*, *People's Comix*, and *XYZ*.)

Third, comix introduced an "alternative" ethos that valued the productions of the lone cartoonist over collaborative or assembly-line work. In essence, comix made comic books safe for auteur theory: they established a poetic ethos of individual expression. By *poetic* I mean, not the literal sense, nor the vernacular sense of beautiful or elevated, but the idea that cartoonists were expected to express themselves singly, just as a poet is typically presumed to speak with a lone voice.

Figure 4. Bill Griffith, *Young Lust* No. 1 (front cover). © 1970 Bill Griffith. Used with permission.

This tendency was not absolute, as there were some collaborative comix (for instance, the *Zap* "jams," in which the artists challenged each other with improvisatory riffs). Such group efforts, however, were exceptions. Today the privileging of self-expression in alternative comic books is a very strong tendency—the rule rather than the exception—and alternative comics publishers favor the comic book as a "solo" vehicle for the individual cartoonist. These comic books are so much a product of the underground ethos, and so resistant to the mainstream model of production, that even their indicia and sporadic letter columns are often written in the artist's own distinctive hand.

Finally, many of the comix books were awash in irony, based on the appropriation of popular (or once-popular) characters, styles, genres, and tropes for radically personal and sometimes politically subversive ends. Not only Crumb but also many other underground cartoonists made themselves at home among shopworn ideas inherited from comics and cartoons past, using and redefining certain character types (for example, funny animals, such as in comix by Lynch, Deitch, and Bobby London) or genres (for example, horror comics, as in *Skull*, or superheroes, as in Gilbert Shelton's "Wonder Warthog" and Spain's "Trashman"). They pirated the past with subversive glee: Deitch's Waldo the Cat was an alcoholic's hallucination; Lynch's "Nard and Pat" were a human and cat pair in which the cat was more hip, socially adept, and sexually active than his human companion; and Spain's Trashman was an urban guerrilla fighting for the insurgent "6th International," a Marxist revolutionary group.

Taken together, the four above-listed factors would, paradoxically, serve to free long-form comics from complete dependence on the standard comic book package. These factors—sporadic publication, the emphasis on the author rather than established commercial properties, the development of an alternative economy, and the corrosive reexamination of familiar tropes—eventually coalesced into the alternative comics movement of the 1980s and 1990s, born within comics fandom but defined by its insistent, even strident, opposition to the normative

practices and narrative clichés of "mainstream" comic books. In time this resistance would make itself felt even at the level of packaging. Though the vehicle of choice was at first the familiar comic book, readers have since grown accustomed to seeing long-form comics in a greater variety of packages.

The liberatory potential of underground comix was most clearly realized by Spiegelman's *Maus*, perhaps the urtext of alternative comics. A personal, not to say poetic, tale, derived from oral history and lived experience, *Maus* invokes a familiar genre ("funny animals") to broach very difficult, politically supercharged material, and was produced outside the boundaries of conventional comic book publishing. Spiegelman's ironic use of animals to figure human beings (one of the most controversial elements in *Maus*) departs from R. Crumb's ironized funny animal figures such as Fritz the Cat; indeed, the germ of *Maus* was a three-page story titled "Maus" that Spiegelman produced in 1973 for an animal-themed underground comic book called *Funny Aminals* [sic]. In fact *Maus* represents the entry of the underground into the mainstream book trade, an achievement owed in part to the example of Crumb and other comix artists.

The history of long-form comics in English, then, owes much to the intervention of comix. In the formative *Zap* period, comix constituted a genuinely romantic, highly individualistic movement that sought to liberate the comic book as a vehicle for personal expression, while yet wallowing in the medium's reputation for lurid, rough-hewn, populist entertainment (its "termite" origins). Like the Beats, to whom many comix artists looked for inspiration, the pioneers of comix were self-styled hipsters and iconoclasts who both rejected and built on prior traditions; they too harbored subversive, in some cases revolutionary, political ideas and were to a degree associated with a radically democratic realignment of politics. As early nineteenth-century romanticism was informed by revolution (as utopian promise, bitter disappointment, and/or looming political threat), so the comix movement was sparked by the political energy of the late sixties counterculture, and reflected its demands for peace and political reform. The comix "underground" was spurred by a sense of possibility that was at least partly political in nature, and, like prior romantic movements, it looked forward to revolutionary realignments in the social order with a mix of overweening optimism and fearful ambivalence (the latter perhaps best seen in Crumb's uneasy blend of utopian and reactionary sentiment).

The comix movement eventually fell victim to crushing political disappointments. In 1973 the United States Supreme Court deferred the question of "obscenity" to local community standards (*Miller v. California*), a reversion that threatened national circulation of the often controversial comix. Meanwhile, the rise of antidrug (or more accurately antiparaphernalia) laws began to squeeze the so-called head shops out of existence, thus crippling underground distribution. These suppressive moves, in the context of political disaffection and the general enervation of the counterculture, proved devastating to comix (see Rosenkranz 215, 219–20; Estren 230; Sabin, *Adult* 174).

In this uncertain climate, the field became increasingly fractious, as participants fought for diminishing resources. Even as publishers wavered, reeling from the possibilities of legal repression, a mushroom growth of creators and titles had already filled their catalogs. A glut of new comix, many of them criticized as imitative and poorly produced, flooded the market (Beerbohm, "Origins" 120; Goodrick and Donahue 9; Rosenkranz 222–23). Boom turned to bust: by the mid-1970s the movement had succumbed to a sense of depletion at once economic and cultural. Paper costs soared while business dropped sharply (Sabin, *Adult* 174; Estren 8). At the same time, in the words of Art Spiegelman, "what had seemed like a revolution simply deflated into a lifestyle" (Spiegelman and Mouly, *Read* 6). Comix succumbed to their own clichés—sex, drugs and hedonism, sapped of political will—and withered, retreating to the margins of the culture.

This too is hard to understand, as documentation remains scant (though Rosenkranz's *Rebel Visions* has helped). A partial explanation might be found within the very terms of the underground's success. In hindsight, the movement's signal achievement

was the way it at once paid homage to the comic book as quintessential American kitsch *and* laid the groundwork for alternative approaches to comic art, approaches that would one day threaten the mainstream comic book with creative obsolescence. Central to this achievement was the way comix artists, spurred by Crumb, engaged the comic book medium itself as a vehicle for cultural subversion. Yet in this lies a deeper irony, for the medium appears to have subverted their radical impulses in turn. The shift among underground cartoonists toward comic books (as opposed to the college magazines and radical papers in which they first gained notice) paralleled the shift in mainstream comics history away from newspaper strips, toward comics magazines as independent commodities. Arguably, then, comix books urged the underground away from engagement in the radical press, thus in larger political issues, and toward a more reflexive involvement with "comix" as such. This is evident not only in the ubiquitous parodic gestures of the comix books, including their very packaging, but also in the brief, meteoric growth in comix as an entertainment industry in the early seventies. Though explicitly political work continued to appear in comix well after this period—indeed, some of the most explicitly political comix came after 1973—by the mid-seventies the comix had taken on more and more characteristics of their detested mainstream counterparts. Despite its radical potential, by 1975 the comix revolution ended up looking less political than stylistic in nature—and rather parochial at that.

In short the movement, once stretched, proved flaccid. As comix became entrenched, they lost their impetus and collective focus both politically and, eventually, aesthetically. Indeed the underground yielded a great many retrograde and poorly crafted publications, some hateful, others merely impenetrable. This cultural borderland, which had served as breeding ground for both radical and reactionary impulses, finally became a prison. The commodification of underground comic books diverted the energies of the movement into a narrow cul-de-sac, from which its reflexive cynicism offered no escape. As the underground developed an insular comic book industry of its own, the movement's empowering but double-edged embrace of amateurism combined with rapid and rapacious economic growth to create a flood of wretched material. By the mid-1970s many comix creators seemed ambivalent about that growth at best, and some began to redirect their satiric energy at comix themselves, seeing in the new market a reflection of the hated mainstream comic book industry (Estren 250–56; Rosenkranz 221–22).[5] To achieve escape velocity, some tried other kinds of publications—ultimately, this is where such seminal magazines as *Arcade*, *Raw* and *Weirdo* came from—while some faded to obscurity, weighted down by the new clichés.

Many comix remained volatile and subversive: witness for example the feminist commentary in *Wimmen's Comix*, or the ecologically themed horror of *Slow Death*. Yet their topical thrust was often blunted, or if not blunted then turned inward, by a preoccupation with their chosen medium. In that sense comix were truly products, and reflections, of comic book fandom, though superficially remote from fandom's celebratory, nostalgic ethos. Ultimately what was most "political" about them, most effective, was simply the freedom with which they approached the comics form. At their best they combined reflexive playfulness with an acute social vision, showing how much comics could do in the right hands; at their worst they were self-absorbed and self-defeating, as if prefiguring the counterculture's retrenchment—its decline from revolution to mere "lifestyle." By the late 1970s comix had come to symbolize the fecklessness and anomie of the fading counterculture, as effectively as they had symbolized its energy and political agency just a few years earlier. Today the books are simply artifacts, collectible symbols of yet another "lost" era that consumers can nostalgically long for, its political and cultural traumas safely blurred.

But from the promise of underground comix stemmed the alternative comic book and graphic novel of the eighties and nineties, a vision of long-form comics that allowed unprecedented aesthetic freedom and diversity, as well as a new sense of purpose. Even as the undergrounds per se retrenched, their influence spread, informing new kinds of comics in the United States and, ironically, abroad, even

where American-style comic books had never taken hold (see Gravett, "Euro-Comics"). After years in eclipse, the underground ethos would reemerge in a different context, again bracketed by comic book fandom but post-punk in outlook and responsive to new concerns. A reinvigorating, recombinant approach to comic art, international in character but inspired by the American underground, came to the fore in the eighties, labeled "alternative" or "the new comics" but clearly indebted to the comix of yesteryear.

With the advent of "the new comics" (a phrase much bandied about in the late 1980s), the traditional relationship between comics content and publishing format became unhinged, allowing for the experimental use of various packages. Today, even as the traditional comic book struggles for survival at the behest of an ever-attenuating fandom, the graphic novel, in its many shapes, has become the critical byword of the new comics. Yet, though the comic book per se no longer has a monopoly on the long form, it still exerts a powerful, not-to-be-underestimated tug on the imaginations of creators and fans—and, as we are about to see, the passions of mainstream comic book collectors have played their own crucial role in legitimizing the graphic novel and establishing a critical beachhead for alternative comics.

THE DIRECT MARKET AND THE CONSOLIDATION OF FANDOM

While inspired, indeed catalyzed, by the creative freedom of the undergrounds, alternative comics also owe much to subsequent practical changes in the distribution and exhibition of comic books as products—changes in which the underground played a vital but not exclusive role. Most of today's long-form comics are products of a specific, highly ritualized, and essentially commercial scene known as the *direct market* comic book shop—a scene at once rooted in the underground and insulated from its animating political and cultural concerns. The transformation of contemporary comics can be traced directly to this commercial environment, and because that environment has by turns both encouraged and stunted the art form, it requires careful analysis. This is not simply a case of underground iconoclasts invigorating the art form, then fans smothering it; nor is it simply a case of the lowly comic book being supplanted by more reputable forms. Rather, the influence of the market is a matter of encouraging and debilitating influences shrink-wrapped together.

Today's direct market represents a specialized hobby, a subculture that has grown from grassroots anarchy (the private and inchoate discourse of isolated fan conclaves) to a highly codified, in some sense disciplined and commodified practice—in short, an organized "fandom." This fandom revolves around comic shops, trade magazines, collectors' price guides, large- and small-scale conventions, and, now overwhelmingly, the rapid-fire discourses of the Internet. Instrumental in the rise of this fandom were such institutions as used bookstores, small-circulation amateur 'zines (fanzines), amateur press alliances (APAs), conventions, mail-order businesses, and "letterhacking" (that is, writing letters for publication in comic books and corresponding with other such writers, or letterhacks). Born out of science fiction fandom in the days of the hectographed and mimeographed fanzine, comic book fandom rose to prominence—to self-consciousness, anyway—with the advent of comics-specific fanzines and price guides in the early mid-sixties, followed shortly by the establishment of specialized conventions in 1964.[6] This fandom, increasingly aware of its buying power and creative influence, exerted significant pull on the content of superhero comic books from the early sixties onwards, a pull that major publishers Marvel and DC belatedly acknowledged in the late sixties and early seventies by hiring fans to critical editorial positions. By the early eighties, the accelerating decline of newsstand sales led these publishers to rely increasingly on the then newly emergent fan (that is, direct) market to stave off disaster (see, for example, news coverage in *The Comics Journal*, circa 1980–81). This situation led, albeit gradually, to an overwhelming emphasis on organized fandom as the comic book's core audience—and on the costumed superhero as its core genre.

The current market thus represents a paradox. It has roots both in the comix counterculture of the late sixties (in particular its distribution network, which prior to 1973 constituted a thriving alternative economy) and in the nostalgic interests of a minority of dedicated comic book collectors, particularly superhero collectors, who began to correspond and barter with each other during the late fifties, and more visibly from 1965 onwards (see Schelly 20–21, 89–97). This market, which now places such emphasis on the promotion of new mainstream comic books, originally grew out of two overlapping yet distinct fields, both considered marginal by mainstream publishers: a hobbyists' network concerned with bartering *old* comic books and the underground distribution methods established by comix. From this historic conflation, a loose network of retailers developed in the late sixties and early seventies, some of whom began to carry new mainstream comic books alongside underground publications. Many of these retail outlets were firmly rooted in the counterculture.

Despite overviews by scholars such as Roger Sabin (for example, *Adult Comics*) and Bradford Wright (*Comic Book Nation*), this crucial transitional period remains thinly documented. Because no book has yet emerged to provide a comprehensive, critical history of the direct market, it remains difficult to show precisely how much underground and mainstream comic books overlapped in these early shops.[7] Yet it is known that many comic shops did grow out of "head" shops, and as such routinely brought vintage comic books and new comix together within the same space. The Bay Area's "Comics & Comix," by all appearances the first comic book retail chain in the United States, made this commixing explicit in its very name and purchased entire lots of mainstream comic books from local newsstand distributors so that they could be racked alongside underground publications (Schelly 155; Beerbohm, "Origins" 125). Such underground-friendly shops were, arguably, the root of the direct market. Also, the antiestablishment ethos of comix appears to have influenced fanzines and the discourse of fandom in general. Comix challenged the dominantly conservative tone of early fanzines, and in their wake the amateur strips and critical commentary in some prominent 'zines showed a marked shift away from a hitherto overwhelming emphasis on the superhero (Schelly 115, 130–32). (Retrenchment would come later, with the co-optation of the direct market by superhero publishers.) In addition, the rhetoric of fandom began to reflect, however tentatively, underground cartoonists' attitudes toward intellectual property and creative freedom, even as comic book professionals began participating in "fan" publications (Schelly 137–39).

By the early mid-seventies, entrepreneurs, first among them New York comics convention organizer Phil Seuling, had formalized these arrangements by going "directly" to major publishers DC and Marvel and buying non-returnable comics at deep discounts. (The late Seuling, whose impact is a matter of record, has become a part of fan lore.) With this arrangement in place by 1975, a hobby hitherto centered on the trade of collectible old comics began to take in an increasing influx of new product. Yet the balance of trade in the shops continued to favor old comic books, the new output of the major publishers being fairly small and the underground having withered. This continued until the early eighties, at which point the major publishers, as noted, began to concentrate on this all-important fan market. The growing emphasis on fandom, among not only mainstream publishers but also upstart publishers adapted specifically to the new conditions, led to the growth of specialty shops so that by the early nineties there were thousands of such shops in existence, as opposed to perhaps two dozen twenty years earlier (hard figures are tough to find, but see, for example, Beerbohm, "Origins" 119; Sabin, *Comics, Comix* 157; "Comic Book Crisis"). Though crucially indebted to, indeed rooted in, the underground era, this burgeoning market was a far cry from the fervidly romantic counterculture of the early comix.

Today the direct market is decidedly postunderground in outlook. It consists of an international network of stores specializing in American comic books, including both mainstream and alternative titles but especially beholden to large-scale mainstream publishers. This network suffers from a high rate of attrition and so is in constant flux. A

predominantly American phenomenon, it has had much influence in other English-reading countries (most notably Canada and Great Britain). This market, because of its narrow demographics, strong sense of tradition, and efficient means of distribution, has nurtured the growth of fan-friendly products such as the graphic novel and the "limited" or mini-series, both significant departures in long-form comics narrative. It has also led to the unhinging of traditional work-for-hire arrangements between creators and publishers, and to stormy disputes over intellectual property (or "creator's rights"), as the economic and ideological lessons of the underground have rippled through fandom. The result is a cultural scene, international in scope but American in focus, in which iconophilia and iconoclasm, reaction and radicalism, clash and mingle. This is the sustaining yet problematic context for alternative comics.

This direct market, its terms codified by the early eighties, offers publishers the advantages of low entry costs and a high degree of predictability. It functions in essence as a subscription system, one in which the subscriber is not the individual consumer but rather the comic shop, which will in turn offer the product to consumers. (For brief accounts of how this market works, see Sabin, *Adult* 65–69, and McAllister, "Cultural Argument" 65–66.) To be more precise, the direct market offers publishers leverage in two crucial ways: First, orders are solicited from retailers in advance of publication so that the size of print runs can be adjusted according to anticipated demand. This helps avoid the wasteful and costly overprinting that typifies magazine publishing. It is in this sense that comic book publishing works by subscription: advance ordering underwrites the costs of printing, making the work possible in the first place. (Such subscription arrangements, of course, have also played a crucial role in the development of popular prose fiction, providing a practical, material foundation for the ascendancy of the novel.) Second, unlike regular newsstand sales, direct market orders are *non-returnable*. Whereas most magazine sales are handled on a de facto consignment basis, with unsold leftovers being returned to publishers or destroyed (to the vendor's credit), direct market comic books are owned outright by vendors and, with few exceptions, cannot be returned. This is why, in the eyes of publishers, it is shop owners rather than readers who are the ultimate customer: the publisher's concerns end with the retailer's order. This has the effect of softening the economic risk for publishers to a significant degree, for, without having to absorb the cost of returns, publishers are in a better position to experiment with new product. It is retailers who have to bear the brunt of unsold, unsuccessful comics.

Obviously, there is a fundamental asymmetry at work here, in that retailers are exposed to risk while publishers are relatively insulated from it. This arrangement, with minimal cost and maximal predictability for publishers, has encouraged the rise of small, alternative presses and even scores of self-publishing comics creators, some of whom are regarded as important figures within the industry (in comic books, self-publishing is *not* a sign of dilettantism). To a considerable degree, this growth in the alternative press has effectively unlocked the comic book's artistic potential. On the retailer's side, advantages to this system include a relatively loyal and extremely knowledgeable clientele, as well as substantial financial incentives (for example, volume discounts and plentiful in-store advertising). These advantages stoked the rapid growth of the comics retail network in the eighties, as the industry, spurred by collector investment in popular titles, seemed to grow from strength to strength.

Yet disadvantages to retailers are significant, in particular the financial drain caused by investment in poor-selling comics. Unlike vendors in the newsstand market, comic shop retailers have to keep everything that doesn't sell, which means that unsold comics not only fail to earn back their initial cost but also consume physical space and person-hours when they pass into inventory. The occasional appreciation of collectible comic books (caused by manufactured scarcity in the back-issue trade) only partly compensates for the fact that most unsold inventory does not grow significantly in value and simply eats up room, time, and money. This situation, only belatedly recognized as a major disadvantage, tends to discourage risk-taking by retailers, even as the economic

advantages for publishers encourage the production of a surfeit of new product. The result is an excess of comic books each month, shrilly marketed, of which most retailers can order only a small sample. The effects of this asymmetry have been most keenly felt in the wake of the euphoric comic-book speculation of the early 1990s, an economic binge that ended in the closing of thousands of shops and, eventually, the drastic consolidation of the market's distribution system (see *The Comics Journal*'s coverage of the industry 1994–97, especially "State of the Industry/ State of the Art Form" and "Comic Book Crisis"). In a climate such as this, retailers are intensely aware of the risks they face.

Nonetheless the direct market has stoked the development of long-form comics. Recent innovations in the long form, most notably the establishment of the graphic novel as a viable package, stem from the relative prosperity of the market in the 1980s, when direct-sales comic shops seemed a hotbed of entrepreneurship and the alternative press thrived. Mainstream comics had adopted underground distribution methods, and alternative comics basked in the increased exposure. This commercial high season excited a new enthusiasm for pushing back the artistic horizons of the form. Once again aesthetic developments were spurred by commercial developments (as had been the case during the medium's first flush of popularity, almost half a century before).

SHOPS AS TEXTS

To understand clearly this relationship between commercial and artistic growth, a historical analogy may help: consider the crucial, sustaining relationship that developed in eighteenth- and nineteenth-century Britain and America between popular fiction and the commercial "circulating libraries." Like comic shops, these so-called libraries had a pronounced impact on the history of a literary form, in that they nurtured the growth of fiction-by-parts, a trend that eventually hardened into the institution of the Victorian three-part (or "three-decker") novel. From the early-to-mid-eighteenth century through the late nineteenth, the growth of such circulating libraries, with their subscription arrangements, made long-form prose narrative affordable to middle-class readers, with of course significant structural and aesthetic consequences for the works in question. Literary historians have tended to gauze over the crucial importance of these commercial lending libraries; indeed, criticism has assumed the inevitability and desirability of the move *away* from commercial subscription, toward the primacy of the Novel as a freestanding and aesthetically self-sufficient, even monumental, form of expression. Yet the fact of the libraries' tremendous influence, on form and audience, and indeed on popular literacy, remains, a facet of print culture deserving further study.[8] In the field of comic books, the rise of the direct market has had a comparable, if scaled down, effect.

Like the commercial lending library, the comic book shop has in effect informed and *disciplined* its clientele. As Edward Jacobs has observed of lending libraries in the late eighteenth century, so too direct market comic shops have given readers "an unprecedented material basis for recognizing intertextual relationships, and for identifying generic conventions" (616). Jacobs links this emphasis on intertextuality with the physical layout of the shops (libraries) themselves, in which thematically similar books were grouped together, a practice that urged readers to see books as variations on particular genres rather than as singular expressions. Indeed, Jacobs argues that the physical ordering of the circulating libraries constituted an "institutional foregrounding of the genericism of all texts" (617–18). In other words, these libraries established a mutually reinforcing relationship between the organization of a commercial space and the content of the work exhibited in that space. In a sense this space/content relationship serves to discipline the consumer, making her or him a more sophisticated reader and fan.

Things are slightly different in comic shops, where the emphasis on genericism and intertextuality is less dependent on precise physical sorting by genre. Although many shops do rack comic books according to genre, others do not, preferring other methods (for example, sorting by publisher, or simply alphabetically by series). Thus they differ from bookshops or libraries in their layout. However, consumers' awareness of intertextuality is nonetheless stimulated by their total immersion in the shop environment, and, more important, by the periodical nature of most comic books, which keeps buyers coming back for more at regular intervals. The breakdown of comic book narrative into brief, relatively frequent installments (along with the concomitant emphasis on the hoarding of successive issues) provides a strong material basis for the fan's heightened sense of intertextuality. In contrast to the circulating libraries, which (like video stores today) stressed renting rather than buying, comic shops are about *getting* and *keeping*; possession is key. As Roger Sabin observes, buying "for investment" is endemic to the direct market, and indeed often defines the relationship between the industry and fandom (*Adult* 67). This crucial difference reflects fan culture's commodification of experience—a material practice admittedly remote from the ethos of the library.

Despite this core difference, circulating libraries and comic shops also invite comparison on the matter of advertising and publicity. Jacobs observes that the conventions of the Gothic romance, so popular within the circulating libraries, were used to promote the libraries themselves: their publicity ironically deployed diversion, misdirection, and mystery to stimulate the interest of seasoned readers in the genre. In this way the narrative properties of the Gothic reinforced, or, in Jacobs's apt phrase, "discursively co-operated" with, the physical strategies by which the libraries would isolate and exhibit the genre (617–18). In comparable fashion, comic book publishers in the 1980s developed print advertising and in-shop promotional gimmicks (often partly paid for by retailers) that emphasized distinctive graphic elements from the comics themselves, and, like the comics, depended on the effects of periodicity: the maintenance of suspense, the gradual unveiling of the new, and the resultant accretion of meaning. At its most forceful, this advertising was aggressively intertextual, complementing the promised comic books with posters, flyers, badges, toys, and even other comic books, thus creating a diverting, ever-changing retail environment—one in which the experience of reading and the experience of buying were effectively blurred. In short, the shop environment itself functioned as an elaborate paratext to the comic books; consumer rituals defined the margins, sometimes even the core content, of the reading experience.

Like the circulating libraries, comic shops narrowed the gap between audience and authors, establishing a space through which readers and prospective creators might have more direct access to the publishing industry. This was crucial for the development of small-press and alternative comics. The direct market, because of its low startup costs and relatively small (or predictable) economic risks, fostered the idea that fans might create their own comics, not simply at an amateur level, as in the early fanzines, but on a more or less level playing field with established professionals. Direct distribution meant dramatically increased access for self-publishing entrepreneurs, and the effacing of the once-rigid distinction between amateur and pro. Indeed the number and variety of self-published comic book projects—some extraordinarily well crafted, others dismal—has made that distinction rather porous (a phenomenon encouraged by the continual involvement of fans at all levels of the industry).

Other distinctions too are rather arbitrary. As in the circulating libraries, specialized distribution to comic shops has enabled distributors and retailers to delve sporadically into the business of publishing. A number of early direct market entrepreneurs (for example, Bud Plant) and companies (for example, Pacific Comics, Capital Comics) involved themselves in all phases of the industry, and some entrepreneurs continue to combine publishing, distributing, and retailing interests (though usually "separated" by corporate firewalls). In similar fashion, circulating library proprietors often went into publishing books themselves and evidently sought to recruit new, inexpensive talent (often female, very often anonymous) from among their patrons. To take the best-known example, William Lane, founder of the Minerva Library, also created his own publishing house, the Minerva Press, in addition to wholesaling complete, preexisting

circulating libraries to other entrepreneurs (Erickson 138). Thus he was involved in all phases of the trade.[9] Such multifaceted entrepreneurial endeavors have influenced the distribution, exhibition, and cultural influence of popular fiction and comic books alike.

Admittedly, the "circulating library" analogy fails insofar as it cannot account for comic book fandom's emphasis on collecting. The libraries were designed to make books accessible to a wider public at a time when book costs were relatively high and buying books outright was therefore thought to be the preserve of the wealthy. In contrast, the direct market was designed to appeal, with pinpoint accuracy, to a smaller, more committed audience that could be expected to spend a disproportionate share of its income on comic books. So, whereas the circulating libraries represented an opening out of popular print culture, the direct market represented in some sense a narrowing in: specialized hobby shops tend to be less responsive to demands for economy and accessibility. While circulating libraries fostered a new kind of popular narrative—its kernel the Gothic romance—comic shops seem inordinately dedicated to the nostalgic preservation of the old and outworn. (Of course there is another, perhaps related, difference to consider: whereas the circulating libraries were consistently condemned as encouragements to feminine frivolity, contemporary comic book shops are generally said to be grossly, overwhelmingly, male.) Yet the direct market, in spite of its debilitating emphasis on preservation and collection, gave birth to a new sense of aesthetic possibility, spurred by the example of the undergrounds. Just as the Victorian three-decker novel sprang from the lending libraries, the much-discussed "graphic novel" owed its very life to this new market.

THE EVOLUTION OF DIRECT MARKET COMIC BOOKS

Many of the alternative comics studied herein were born of the direct market during its 1980s heyday, when rising retail sales encouraged creative growth and, to a degree, diversification. While comic books in this period continued to be driven mainly by established genres such as the superhero (indeed superhero publishers sought to strengthen their grip on the market), the burgeoning alternative scene, rooted in the underground, urged the development of comic books that either sidestepped genre formulas or twisted them in novel ways. Gradually the tension between mainstream and underground aesthetics made itself felt in the conversations of fans: for some, the terms "independent" and "alternative," though seemingly near-synonymous, came to represent opposing aesthetic tendencies. Today the category "independent comics" may include, often does include, formula fiction inspired by the so-called mainstream, including much heroic fantasy; while "alternative" more often denotes satirical, political, and autobiographical elements inherited from underground comix. Yet, because the direct market continues to blend the two, drawing any hard distinction between them is difficult (notwithstanding the fierce position-taking of some fans).

The development in the 1980s of both "independent" and "alternative" positions owed much to the support of a growing fandom. The alternative comix of the eighties, despite their disdain for the mainstream and their invocation of the underground as forebears, were also indebted to a spate of fan-oriented, "ground-level" comic books of the mid-seventies, so called because they attempted to reconcile underground and mainstream attitudes. Such ground-level comics, though rooted in shopworn fantasy genres, testified to the influence of the undergrounds and represented a first, tentative turning toward more personal and innovative approaches. Among these quixotic publications were fantasy-adventure comics like Jack Katz's *The First Kingdom* (published by Comics & Comix/Bud Plant, 1974–86) and *Star*Reach* (published by Mike Friedrich's Star*Reach Productions, 1974–79). Such projects, marked by their use of mainstream comic book talent, appealed to mainstream readers while boasting an underground rationale and modus operandi. As they negotiated the new and as yet uncertain territory of the direct market, they in turn inspired comics that took the direct market for granted, published by new companies specially created for its unique conditions—companies like

Eclipse, Pacific, Capital, and, in Canada, Andromeda Publications and Vortex Comics. Some of these publishing companies, not surprisingly, grew out of successful retail and distribution businesses (for example, Pacific and Capital).

Notable publications from this second wave of ground-level comics (the late seventies to early eighties) included *Sabre*, a self-contained album by Don McGregor and Paul Gulacy (Eclipse, 1978); *Elfquest*, a serialized fantasy epic by Wendy and Richard Pini (self-published under the WaRP Graphics imprint, 1978); *Capt. Victory and the Galactic Rangers*, a traditional four-color series by mainstream veteran Jack Kirby (Pacific, 1981); and, in Canada, at least two titles: the SF anthology *Andromeda* (Andromeda Publications, 1977–79) and, in 1978, Dave Sim's series *Cerebus* (self-published under the Aardvark-Vanaheim imprint). Most of these comics were inexpensively produced in black and white, and all offered variants on traditional genres: science fiction, adventure, sword and sorcery, superheroics. These were the comic books that confirmed the efficacy of direct-only publishing and paved the way for the next host of independent publications.

Among the third wave were such seminal takeoffs of genre as Howard Chaykin's satirical SF series *American Flagg!* (First Comics, 1983–89) and Dean Motter et al.'s retro-futuristic *Mister X* (original series: Vortex, 1984–88). (Motter's *Mister X* collaborators originally included the Hernandez brothers of *Love & Rockets* fame, to be discussed in chapter 3.) These books, more graphically elaborate than their predecessors, were among many influenced by the newsstand success of *Heavy Metal*, the slick "magazine of adult illustrated fantasy" launched in 1977. *Heavy Metal* was adapted under license from the groundbreaking French series *Métal Hurlant* (1975–87), itself inspired by the free-spiritedness of the American undergrounds and known for extravagant, visionary artwork (Gravett, "Euro-Comics" 83; Sabin, *Adult Comics* 71–72). On a smaller scale, comic books like *Flagg!* and *Mister X* aimed for a similar graphic panache. They boasted dazzling design conceits incorporating architecture, fashion, and typography and were awash in eye-catching technique, expressive color, and improved production values in general. More important, they moved toward adult themes (again like *Heavy Metal*), more so than even the most eccentric mainstream comics of the day, and confirmed that familiar market genres could be put to the service of satirical and thought-provoking stories. These direct-only comic books thus fulfilled the promise of the earliest "ground-level" efforts. Some offered a breadth and complexity unprecedented in serialized comics, even as they sought solutions for the creative and economic problems caused by dependence on a serial readership.

Dave Sim's self-published series *Cerebus* (1978–2004) serves as an especially clear example of genre material blossoming in unexpected directions; it also demonstrates clearly the possibilities and problems engendered by the direct market. Indeed *Cerebus* is the *ur*-example of "independent" comics, informed by the underground's uncompromising stance on intellectual ownership yet disciplined by the publishing practices of the commercial mainstream. Launched in 1978 (dated Dec. 1977/Jan. 1978), *Cerebus* began as a slavish homage to/spoof of "sword and sorcery" fantasy, as popularized by Marvel's adaptation of Robert E. Howard's pulp hero *Conan*; in fact Sim swiped some images directly from the early issues of Marvel's *Conan the Barbarian* (drawn by Barry Smith). Yet within a few years Sim transformed *Cerebus* into a roving, uncategorizable and at times controversial vehicle for his ever-expanding interests in literature, religion, politics, and gender. As its visual canvas grew ever richer (thanks in part to the arrival of Sim's artistic collaborator/background artist, the single-named Gerhard), *Cerebus* evolved fitfully into a protean mix of epic fantasy, psychological drama, genre parody, and polemical treatise. The series grew to the point that it could embrace almost anything: electoral politics, apocalyptic visions, fictionalized lives of Oscar Wilde and Ernest Hemingway, the dreamlife of its title character (a very human "aardvark"), and Sim's increasingly antifeminist and politically conservative fulminations on the contemporary scene. Whatever it was, *Cerebus* was smart and ambitious, enough so that many came to regard it as (in the words of John

Bell) Canada's "greatest achievement in comic art" (*Canuck Comics* 40). In the process Sim became the ipso facto spokesman of a self-publishers' movement and of the direct market more generally.

Cerebus, a longtime staple of direct-only comic books, stands as a signal example of the medium's creative growth under direct market conditions. Long promoted as a 300-issue "limited series" designed to span a quarter century of its creator's life (the final issue appeared in Spring 2004), *Cerebus* cleaved strictly to the traditional comic book format and a monthly schedule, yet amassed one phonebook-sized compilation after another. These "phonebooks," with their extended plots and satirical themes, demonstrate that genre comic books can become vehicles for extended cultural argument and that, given an ongoing project like *Cerebus*, talented artists can successfully publish and republish their own work over the long term. As such, these volumes represent one of the seminal examples of "independent" comics within the direct market (a market that Sim has assiduously studied and promoted). Yet the curious achievement of *Cerebus* represents not only the potential but also the limitations inherent within comic shop culture. Because of Sim's indebtedness to that culture, his energetic riffing on topics familiar only to hobbyists, and his inattention to editing at the compiling stage, his books are at best problematic examples of the "graphic novel."

To be fair, the strongest satirical episodes in *Cerebus* (for example, the political maneuverings in the novel *High Society*) draw enlightening analogies between the seemingly parochial concerns of comic book fans and broader sociopolitical conflicts. Yet it is hard to imagine the uninitiated reader chuckling with glee over, for example, the dated broadsides against Marvel Comics that complicate the plot of Sim's *Church and State*, or the continual teasing of the monthly audience that interrupts and indeed arrests the narrative of Sim's *Reads*. By the author's own admission, the *Cerebus* series was as much about a process as about an end product (Interview 102–6), and its roots in serial publication complicated, at times undermined, its efforts toward novel-like coherence.

Cerebus thus represents an ambitious yet uneasy compromise between serial and novelistic aesthetics. Though the series' unruly accumulative quality accounts for much of its appeal, the critical reputation of *Cerebus* rests on its breakdown into discrete, novel-length stories, and, finally, on its claims to wholeness: for years Sim marketed the series by counting down toward its promised end, issue 300, and recent coverage of its ending has emphasized the complete and rounded-off nature of Sim's achievement. In fact Sim promoted *Cerebus* via a two-pronged attack: the promotion of the monthly as a limited, hence collectible, series of objects; and the promotion of the collected bookshelf editions as "finished" novels (despite the absence of substantial revision in these winding, often self-indulgent volumes). This dual emphasis accommodated the habits of comic book hobbyists while aiming toward a single, monumental saga. The tension thus created is evident in such stories as the two-volume *Church and State* (1983–88), which finds Sim switching restively from acute satire to broad farce, from deliberate plotting to abrupt parodic episodes that invoke superheroes and other comic book clichés.

Though promoted as a single epic tale, *Cerebus* reveled in being a comic book series, and indeed is most remarkable as an artifact of monthly publication. Its accumulated issues stand as the de facto journal of an industry veteran, known for his engagement with industry-wide economic concerns, his advocacy of independently owned and created work, and, increasingly, his broadsides against feminism, Marxism, and other political targets. Sim's essays, speeches and notes, published in *Cerebus* alongside the main narrative, constitute a vital part of his ethos as a comics professional. (In fannish conversation, "Dave Sim" is seldom simply a comic book author; he represents either a standard-bearer for artistic freedom, or a venomous crank, or both.) In fact Sim's attachment to the direct market, and to the relative freedom it offers the small press, became the conceptual bedrock of *Cerebus*, so much so that at certain points the series devolved into a roman à clef about the comic book industry. Sim's commitment to a traditional format and schedule was such an overriding concern that *Cerebus* often became a highly fraught

testimonial to its own process, revealing Sim's attitude toward the grueling demands, and personal rewards, of periodic self-publishing. (To this reader the series became increasingly oppressive in its later years, as its content became more nakedly autobiographical.) In short, *Cerebus* was, and remains, a product of the direct market, and its greatest appeal is to comic book fans.

Like *Cerebus*, most of the works discussed in the following chapters sprang from serial publication, and in some cases they too began as novel twists on familiar genre material. Gilbert Hernandez, studied in chapter 3, developed his complex "Heartbreak Soup" series from 1983 onwards through the periodic issues of *Love & Rockets* (which, though magazine-sized, was still supported by a loyal comic book audience). His early stories in *Love & Rockets*, and even on occasion his later work, show the formative influence of genre comics, often filtered through a satiric sensibility: superheroes and monsters battle; voluptuous women and well-muscled men pose and cavort; flying saucers and rockets sometimes buzz overhead. Yet, as Hernandez's work grew more confident, such elements were relegated to the background, and in time "Heartbreak Soup," a quintessential example of alternative comics, would generate a cycle of magic-realist short stories and novels that stand as some of the most provocative work in contemporary literature. Crucial to this growth was Hernandez's invocation of underground comix, vintage newspaper strips, and other points of reference, including film, canonical art, and, increasingly, his own heritage and social position as a Latino—all this in contrast to the mainstream comic book aesthetic invoked by *Cerebus*.

Like Sim, Hernandez started within generic bounds that he then tested. Unlike Sim, he gravitated toward an alternative aesthetic born of underground comix—in contrast to the "mainstream" approach of *Cerebus*, which favored an indefinitely sustained, strictly periodical structure and an emphasis on comic book in-joking (and, graphically, a classically illustrative style, notwithstanding Sim's penchant for caricature). Of course we should not exaggerate these differences: both of these artists belong to the same relatively small industry, and in fact Hernandez has recently done much work in mainstream comics (far different from his fully personal work). More to the point, both owed their early opportunities for growth to the direct market. Unlike Sim, however, artists like Hernandez have pursued sporadic rather than monthly publication—a testament to the influence of the undergrounds—and are allied with publishers who have sought wider distribution outside the hobby.

Sim's work has been the more amenable to the hobby's traditional emphases on strict periodicity and continuity: arguably, the monthly *Cerebus* succeeded in being a "comic book" in ways that *Love & Rockets* has not. Yet *Cerebus* is also more insular: though its stands as a pioneering example of extended comic book narrative, and thus represents the flowering of the medium under the aegis of direct sales, the terms of its success have thus far made it resistant to a wider critical appreciation. The ever-shifting and at times digressive nature of Sim's work suggests that there is something left behind when a strictly periodical series is reformatted as a "graphic novel." That "something," perhaps, is the comic book's investment in *being* a comic book, and the vitality of the series qua series. This is a tension faced by most of the long-form comics to be studied in the following chapters (including Hernandez's).

WHENCE CAME THE GRAPHIC NOVEL?

The above discussion raises a tough question: given the difficulty of serializing novels in comic book form, how did the idea of the *graphic novel* catch on?

This admittedly problematic term was popularized in the late 1970s by veteran cartoonist Will Eisner in an effort to attract a new audience to his book-length projects, beginning with *A Contract with God* (1978).[10] The term originally promised a way of promoting serious comics to the general book trade and a general readership: Eisner's aim was to break into bookstores, not comic shops. Yet, ironically, Eisner's term would eventually serve to legitimize a new, costlier way of selling comics to the initiated direct market fan. By the mid-eighties, the phrase "graphic novel" had become common currency in the comic

book publishing industry, as formerly newsstand-dependent publishers redirected their product to appeal more specifically to the direct market audience. That audience was increasingly self-conscious, relatively affluent, and eager for belated recognition of the comic book as "art," a hunger that made the upscale format of the graphic novel doubly attractive. For all that the graphic novel provided a new platform for alternative comics, it also became a kind of wish-fulfilling totem for mainstream comics.

Critics have lamented the vagueness of the term. Writing in 1988, Robert Fiore objected to "graphic novel" as a kind of semantic sleight-of-hand, designed to confer "unearned status" on comics that differ little from the standard output of mainstream comic book publishers (Groth and Fiore 5). Indeed, the term quickly became a way of simply designating a format, any format, with more heft than a standard comic book (Harvey, *Comic Book* 116). Marvel Comics and DC Comics, the leading publishers of traditional adventure fare, adopted the term to denote albums of unusual length (forty-eight pages or more), though those books typically offered a reading experience that fell well short of the novel, or even the literary short story, in terms of length and complexity. Granted, some early superhero "graphic novels" offered thematic elements that seldom made it into monthly comic books in such explicit form, but these books were relatively brief and continued to work in the hyperbolic idiom of the genre. They were scarcely "novels" in any sense that someone approaching them from outside the comics industry might recognize. Given the haphazard use of the term (even Eisner's seminal *Contract* was in fact a collection of short stories), Fiore's objection would seem reasonable. By now, however, the idea of the "graphic novel" has such force that we ignore the term at our peril (again, the currency of the term makes it irresistible).

When did the idea of the "graphic novel" move beyond comic shops and into the book trade? That intervention came not with Eisner's pioneering efforts but with the arrival in the late 1980s of several truly novel-length volumes that had originally been serialized: specifically, the first volume of Spiegelman's

Maus (1986); Frank Miller's darkly satiric superhero adventure *The Dark Knight Returns*, starring vigilante hero Batman (also 1986); and Alan Moore and Dave Gibbons's magisterial deconstruction of the super-hero, *Watchmen* (1987). All three of these had depended to some extent on serialization among comic book fans to underwrite their production; all had been parceled out in periodic form prior to col-lection and republication as volumes for the book trade. Yet *Maus*, first serialized in *Raw*, was the odd one out: the one least dependent on the direct mar-ket for its survival, and least reducible to comic book genres (though it invoked the anthropomorphic "funny animal" tradition to alarming effect). In con-trast, the comic book-derived *Dark Knight* and *Watchmen* were smash hits within the direct market, teasing loyal superhero readers with each new install-ment and each new revisionist spin on the familiar genre. Together these three volumes—really not very much alike—established a beachhead for "graphic novels" in the book trade and indeed expectations of success that for years went spectacularly unfulfilled (see Sabin, *Adult* 110–15, 245–48; DeHaven, "Comics").

Since then "graphic novel" has become not only a term of convenience within comic book fandom but also a label increasingly used by booksellers to bracket a dizzying range of disparate comics: from compilations of popular superhero comic book sto-ries, to translated volumes of Japanese *manga*, to the rare original graphic novel designed for a non-fan audience. Such works tend to be lumped together indiscriminately. Given the preponderance of super-hero and fantasy stories in comic books, the "Graphic Novel" section in bookstores often ends up next to Science Fiction, Horror, or other presumably related genre sections, though many comics (for example, Spiegelman's) look wildly out of place in such con-texts. But the format has at least gained a secure foothold within the book trade: graphic novels, despite the relative thinning of the comic book mar-ket, have at last become a recognizable commodity within bookstores.

Nonetheless the genre is an offspring of the comic book industry and owes its life to the direct market's specialized conditions. While the label *graphic novel* is by now used routinely in the less specialized (and less forgiving) book trade, it was the comic book shop that gave the genre its economic spark. The direct market, because of its low-risk terms, prompted the develop-ment of increasingly ambitious comics narratives (albeit still mostly within the constraints of serial form). Though the late 1990s saw a creative retrenchment, in response to economic crises within the industry, for a time the comic book market offered conditions encouraging to the creation of innovative work—and, in chastened and diminished form, it continues to do so, even as its most progressive publishers bid for attention in the larger book trade. The changes enabled by the direct market have so altered the perception of comics that the form has at last won commercial and critical attention as an emerging lit-erature. Alternative comic books and graphic novels are at the core of this development.

ALTERNATIVE COMICS ON THE CURRENT SCENE

In the wake of the graphic novel, today's direct mar-ket presents a bewildering clash of perspectives. On the one hand, major corporate publishers continue to exploit established properties through aggressively marketed, upscale comic books (for example, the number of new *Batman*- or *Spider-Man*-related items in a given month can be overwhelming). On the other, alternative publishers and creators continue to invoke the iconoclastic spirit and methods of under-ground comix, though they depend on the health of mainstream comics to keep the market afloat. These alternative comics-makers are caught in a bind: even as they struggle to cross over from comic shops to the larger possibilities of the book trade, they owe their continued livelihood to the direct market, which offers reassurances in terms of economic predictability and low risk. Because alternative comics de-emphasize heroic fantasy (the market's bedrock genre), they are unfortunately marginalized even within the marginal field of comic book fandom. By that field's peculiar standards, their core readership is considered highly specialized. The position of alternative comics is therefore fragile—though they continue to serve mainstream comics both practically, as a seedbed for new talent, and rhetorically, even ideologically, as an abiding and convenient Other.

The clash of perspectives within the direct market has been pronounced since the aggressive entry of Marvel and DC into direct-only publishing in the early 1980s. This clash has encouraged the persistent use of those admittedly imprecise and loaded terms, "mainstream" and "alternative," to distinguish between the various types of comics vying for fans' attention. While the origins of these terms are contestable, their continued relevance testifies to the field's unruliness: insular as it is, this market is crowded with different kinds of comics. Though mainstream superhero comics are the economic lifeblood for most direct market shops, alternative comics persist in challenging this state of affairs—hence the continuing reinforcement, the reification, of these contrasting terms. The challenge of alternative comics extends not only to style and thematic content but also, increasingly, to format, packaging, and frequency—a testament to the influence of the underground.

Comic shops may have reached a ceiling on their growth, not only because the direct market system poses disadvantages to retailers but also perhaps because comic book fandom is a generational phenomenon suffering from a lack of turnover. Certainly, faith in the commercial and artistic potential of comic books was hobbled in the late nineties by a traumatic decline from the boom years, pre-1993. Happily, though, optimism is in the air as of this writing, for the direct market has pulled well back from the brink

(since 2000 a period of readjustment and consolidation seems to have set in). Most encouraging, however, is that graphic novels are now pouring out of the direct market and into general bookstores, thanks to a revival of interest among book publishers (as well as recent partnerships between direct market companies and major book publishing/distributing houses). This influx of comics into bookstores offers some publishers and creators a real, if risky, alternative to dependence on fandom.

Today much of the creative promise of American comic art rests in the undercapitalized and therefore fragile microcosm of alternative comics. In fact, the creative heart of contemporary English-language comics can be found in the genres of the alternative comic book and graphic novel: heirs to the underground, born of the direct market's unique subculture and yet anxious to reach a wider, less insular audience. Such alternative comics have most forcefully demonstrated the complexity and potential of the art form; along the way, they have forged the strongest connections with avant-garde and art comics worldwide. From alternative comics has come a dramatic influx of work that challenges both the formal and cultural boundaries of comic art. While we should not make the mistake of simply dismissing strips or comic books based in mainstream market genres—they have been and remain crucial to the growth of the art, as the above history attests—it is alternative comics that have most compellingly extended, revitalized, and indeed redefined the form. Such alternative work will be this book's main focus, as we study productive tensions, and recent innovations, within comics.

CHAPTER TWO

AN ART OF TENSIONS

THE OTHERNESS OF COMICS READING

Of course we can now reach multitudes of children and semi-illiterate adults with images rather than with cultivated language. But should we? Any degradation of language is a potential threat to civilization.
—Fredric Wertham, "Comics in Education"

I've been writing all along and I've been doing it with pictures.
—Jack Kirby, Interview with Ben Schwartz

To posit comics as a literary form—and alternative comics in particular as a wellspring of notable literary work—may seem question-begging, given the traditional critical view of comics as a subliterary and juvenile diversion that anticipates or preempts the experience of "real" reading. Despite the recent groundswell in multidisciplinary word/image studies, this damaging view of comics is still alive and kicking in some quarters, where classist concerns about the cultural provenance of comics are reinforced by assumptions about essential "differences" between communication by text and communication by images. When doubts persist about the terms of readerly engagement with comics, and whether those terms are radically at odds with the teaching of traditional textual literacy, claims about the form's literary potential are bound to stir skepticism and resistance. Such doubts of course cannot be overborne by assertion, nor even by sheer weight of example—not everyone can be persuaded—but in the interest of clearing the air, it is worth asking, What kind of experience is reading comics? And to what extent does that experience resemble or diverge from the experience of reading traditional written text? How, if at all, might that experience affect the acquisition of print awareness and literacy?

These questions, though often unstated or taken as already answered, have bedeviled professional research since at least the 1940s and need to be addressed if we are to appreciate comics as a literary form. They are not the sort of questions one conventionally asks about visual art, but they are crucial to ask here, for they bear directly on the claim—my bedrock claim—that comic art is a form of *writing*.

This claim has increasingly found support among critics, as a reaction against the comparison of comics to cinema and other mechanically paced, hence comparatively "passive," forms of visual communication. Comics, in recent criticism, are not mere visual displays that encourage inert spectatorship but rather texts that require a reader's active engagement and collaboration in making meaning. Hence Will Eisner's critique of comics that too slavishly imitate the rapid pacing and narrative fragmentation of cinema (*Graphic Storytelling* 70–73) and Scott McCloud's insistence that the reader is always the author's active "accomplice" in constructing the meaning of a comics text (68). From invoking cinema as an upscale, hence flattering, analogy, comics scholars have decisively shifted toward recognizing the specificity of comics as a form, one distinguished from cinema by its own signifying codes and practices.

Comics theory, then, has tardily arrived at a crucial stage, that of dismantling the once-useful cinema/comics analogy.[1] The idea of comics as active *reading* has gained ground in critical conversation, and displaced the once-attractive comparison to film. This shift is politically loaded, of course, underplaying the complexity of audience participation in cinema (how *do* viewers read a film, anyway?) so as to stress the *difference* of comics—a strategy consistent with what Bart Beaty has called "the search for comics exceptionalism" ("Exceptionalism" 67). Crucial to this search is the (re)invocation of the written text as a more appropriate point of comparison.

Hence McCloud's grand summation in *Understanding Comics*: the form "offers range and versatility with all the potential imagery of film and painting plus the intimacy of the written word" (212). McCloud's invocation of *intimacy* and *writing* is no mere afterthought: though he seems unconcerned about the materiality of comics (that is, their physical construction as printed objects), McCloud clearly is concerned about their readability. Therefore he privileges their static nature—more precisely, the way they exploit the "juxtaposition" of still images. These are images that *stay*, unlike the successive moments in a film or video as it is being viewed. In that sense the images in comics read more like printed words or characters. A similar emphasis informs other recent formalist studies (e.g., Harvey's *Art of the Comic Book*, Eisner's *Graphic Storytelling*), which, along with McCloud, suggest a general critique of cinema as an explanatory template for comics.

Yet it is by no means clear that comics are universally regarded as a *reading* experience. Indeed, the recent insistence on comics-as-reading seems designed to counter a long-lived tradition of professional writing that links comics with illiteracy and the abdication of reading as a civilized (and civilizing) skill. This "anti-comics" tradition, or school, clearly gives vent to assumptions and anxieties about literacy acquisition among the very young (concerns shared with much popular and professional writing about children's literature). In fact anxiety over comics as an influence on reading, or as "competition" for real reading, dominates the earliest professional writing about the form. The first wave of American academic research about comics, from the 1940s to the mid-1950s, focused persistently on reading skills, reading habits and literacy acquisition (McAllister, "Research" 6–11; Nyberg 8–11; see also Lent, *Comic Strips*, and Zorbaugh). This critical wave resulted from the sudden popularity, indeed ubiquity, of comic books as juvenile entertainment, from the late thirties onward (though newspaper strips raised similar alarms in the popular press decades before—see, for example, Lent, *Pulp Demons* 9–10; Gordon, *Comic Strips* 41–42).

Mirroring popular concerns, the first wave of comic book research stressed the challenge comics posed to school curricula and to traditional notions of literature (both as reading matter and as a sacrosanct cultural patrimony). The field was shared by clinicians, sociologists, and educators, but it was the latter, especially librarians and English teachers, who dominated the discussion. Common among their writings were: concerns about the damage (optical as well as psychological) supposedly wrought by comics; invidious distinctions between the entrenched newspaper strip genre and the then less familiar, and certainly less reputable, comic book; assumptions about the *otherness* of comics vis-à-vis true art and culture (which were assumed to be nutritive and socially unifying); and specific suggestions of books that could serve as "substitutes" for, or alternatives to, comic book reading.

Because comic books were overwhelmingly associated with children, these first attempts to theorize about comics reading were inevitably urgent and instrumental in nature. Disinterest was impossible: academic and popular commentators alike (some served in both capacities) were spurred by the general controversy surrounding the medium. Popular and academic conversations about comic books necessarily overlapped and reinforced each other, and some of the most concerned parties—teachers and clinicians, for instance—were positioned so that they had no choice but to respond to arguments from all sides. Thus the early academic writings about comics were transparently political, part of a continuum of political activity that included professional symposia, public testimony, newspaper op-ed writing, mass book burnings, and the drafting of new laws. Because they were occasional in nature, most of these writings have dated badly. Yet, remote as they are, they represent the first kindling of academic interest in comic art. They should not be dismissed offhandedly, for they had lasting effects, both on the political treatment of the comic book medium and on the academic attitude toward comics as a form of writing and reading.

A full survey of this literature lies beyond our scope (therefore readers are referred to Amy Nyberg's *Seal of Approval* and John Lent et al.'s *Pulp Demons* for helpful overviews). Suffice to say that most academic studies from this period neglect to consider the appeal of the comics form per se, and conceive of it as, at best, a neutral or valueless carrier of themes and ideas better expressed in traditional books. While some writings of the period do acknowledge the hybrid, visual/verbal makeup of comics, this acknowledgment is usually pejorative: the "pictures" are held to be a detriment because they encourage a "lazy" or passive approach to reading. This position assumes that the verbal aspects of the hybrid text are of no consequence to the (presumably semi-literate) readers, who concentrate wholly on the pictures.

This argument is distilled in Fredric Wertham's famed *Seduction of the Innocent* (1954), which, besides asserting a causal connection between comics consumption and delinquency, also devotes a chapter to the impact of comics on reading skill. Wertham concludes that comics discourage or obstruct reading readiness, that they cause or exacerbate "reading disorders," and that most habitual comics readers are not "reading" at all but rather engaging in a lazier activity which he christens "picture reading," meaning "gazing at the successive pictures of the comic book with a minimal reading of printed letters" (126, 139). In Wertham's view, the ease of comics-gazing "seduces" children into mere picture reading, drawing them away from the more valuable activity of decoding written text. Wertham would later coin the phrase "linear dyslexia" to describe the "inability to sustain proper reading of whole lines . . . and of whole pages" that he believed followed inevitably from such extensive picture reading. He would also attack comics' visual/verbal nature by explicitly connecting written literacy with cultural inheritance, thusly: "[I]t took thousands of years to develop from communication by images to the abstract reading and writing process which is one of the foundations of civilization. . . . Any degradation of language is a potential threat . . ." ("Comics and Education" 19–20).

This view, so forcefully articulated by Wertham, still colors discussion of comics in the literary sphere, where, as Adam Gopnik has pointed out, comics continue to be regarded as an atavistic, indeed primitive and preliterate, form, despite evidence to the contrary ("Comics and Catastrophe" 29–30). Cartoonists' penchant for using nonstandard or distorted vocabulary, phrasing, and spelling—a habit that depends on the power of pictures to gloss and clarify—has often been adduced as evidence of this preliterate quality, though it arguably reveals quite the opposite: a sophisticated attitude toward language as a sign of character and context. Although Wertham derided the "faulty" spelling and peculiar "neologisms" of comics, as well as their reliance on "words that are not words at all," that is, onomatopoeia (*Seduction* 144), prior arguments had already established that word distortion in comics can be a source of meaning, and pleasure, for adult and child readers alike (see Hill 525). Indeed, the playful argot of such comics as George Herriman's *Krazy Kat* and Elzie Segar's *Popeye* marks a Modernist preoccupation with the fluid exchange between poetic and everyday speech—no less so, one is tempted to say, than *Finnegan's Wake*. Concern over such "degradation" of language continues to obstruct the critical reception of comics, even though, properly speaking, this anarchic approach to words should be seen as a creative asset rather than a liability. (As a student of mine once remarked, "I love the way the pictures make the dialogue so *free*.")

Academic critics of comics throughout the forties and fifties tended to ignore or to condemn the form's visual/verbal nature, viewing the radical fragmentation of the page and the nonstandard use of language as obstructive rather than enabling. Yet by the early seventies the overall emphasis of the professional literature had begun to shift, from censure to guarded endorsement of comics as an aid to literacy. Indeed the seventies saw a groundswell of interest in comics as instructional tools, a development summed up in 1983 with the appearance of a book titled *Cartoons and Comics in the Classroom*, edited by James L. Thomas. This book, subtitled *A Reference for Teachers and Librarians*, compiles thirty-two articles written by academics, school administrators, classroom teachers, and librarians between 1971 and 1981, articles culled from journals and magazines aimed primarily at educators (for example, *Elementary English*, *School Library Journal*, and *Reading Improvement*). Thomas's compilation urges the use of comics and instructional cartoons, while inadvertently testifying to the cultural anxieties still surrounding the form: several articles refer approvingly to the comic industry's self-censoring Code, and the full text of the Code is given as an appendix.

Articles of the sort collected in *Cartoons and Comics in the Classroom* register a tentative enthusiasm for comic art and share a common argument: the familiarity, accessibility and, in some cases, easy vocabulary of comics make them ideal tools for teaching reading, provided that teachers "focus the students' attention on the words, not the pictures" (Thomas 258). Comics are held to have a high "motivational value" (161), and articles extolling comics often invoke the popularity of the form, in some cases buttressing this claim with sales figures for comic books. Yet recognition of the unique properties of comics is scant. These studies tend to ignore the distinctive graphic qualities of the comics page in favor of an emphasis on verbal "readability" alone, and recommend classroom activities that focus on the isolation of key words or the analysis of prose, without attention to the visual context.[2]

Thomas's book confirmed a change in the prevailing attitude toward comics reading. This change can be traced to various overdetermined, indeed politically fraught, trends in American intellectual life, among them: shifts in academic attitudes toward mass culture, the displacement of media effects research from comics to television, and the entrenchment of holistic or "whole language" approaches to reading pedagogy. These trends conspired to quell anxieties about comics, and indeed to encourage the use of comics and other hybrid texts in reading instruction. Yet, still, the distinctiveness of comic art—its peculiar means of soliciting reader involvement and suggesting meaning—seldom came up for discussion. There remained an underlying consistency between the censorious writings of the forties and fifties and the guarded enthusiasm of the seventies and eighties. This consistency emerges repeatedly in certain rhetorical concessions: comics are designated as strictly utilitarian and are still regarded as distinctly *other* than "great literature." Yes, they are a time-honored part of American culture, and possibly an aid to reading, but as texts they are too impure, or too aesthetically fragile, to defend except on grounds of usefulness. Scholarship continued to resist comics and, more broadly, the commixing of image and text, except as a stopgap for the "reluctant" reader.

In sum, the professional literature reveals two schools of thought about comics reading, both founded on pragmatic concerns: either comics are effective aids to literacy, because they are "easy"; or comics are poor aids, perhaps even obstacles, to literacy, because they are "easy." Comics, in short, are either useful as stepping-stones or worse than useless. What both schools neglect is the *specificity* of the comics reading experience. Though comics may assist the acquisition of print literacy, they are by no means interchangeable with conventional reading; on this score the critics of comics as an instructional medium have a point. Yet these detractors err in assuming that the form impedes literacy acquisition because of its simplicity. Rather, we should say that comics are of only particular and limited use as reading aids because of their complexity.

Comics raise many questions about reading and its effects, yet the persistent claims for the form's simplicity and transparency make it impossible to address these questions productively. Criticism, whether formalist or sociocultural in emphasis, will remain at an impasse as long as comics are seen this way—that is, as long as they are rhetorically constructed as "easy." In fact comics can be a complex means of communication and are always characterized by a plurality of messages. They are heterogeneous in form, involving the co-presence and interaction of various codes. To the already daunting (and controversial) issue of reading, then, we must add several new complexities, if we are to understand what happens when we read comics.

From a reader's viewpoint, comics would seem to be radically fragmented and unstable. I submit that this is their great strength: comic art is composed of several kinds of *tension*, in which various ways of reading—various interpretive options and potentialities—must be played against each other. If this is so, then comics readers must call upon different reading strategies, or interpretive schema, than they would use in their reading of conventional written text.

The balance of this chapter will engage the fundamental tensions within comics, with emphasis on the kinds of judgment (or suspension of judgment) they demand of readers. I shall concentrate on questions of reader response, in the sense of participation and interpretation, rather than those underlying questions of reading process that properly belong to empirical study (for example, eye movement, working memory, or graphophonic competence). My aim is not to set forth an empirical model of comics reading but rather to establish the complexity of the form by broadly discussing the kinds of mixed messages it sends even to the most experienced of readers. This discussion will serve as a prospectus for the collective task of theorizing reader response in comics in a more general way.

Such theorizing, I will argue, must grapple with four tensions that are fundamental to the art form: between *codes* of signification; between the *single image* and the *image-in-series*; between narrative *sequence* and page *surface*; and, more broadly, between reading-as-*experience* and the text as material *object*. To demonstrate these tensions, I will draw on a range of examples, including alternative and mainstream, children's and adults', and European and American comics.

1. CODE VS. CODE ("WORD" VS. "IMAGE")

Definitions of comics commonly (though not universally) depend on the co-presence and interplay of image and written text. Some critics regard this interplay as a clash of opposites: the image's transparency versus the written text's complexity. McCloud, for instance, though his own definition deemphasizes words, insists on this contrast: he speaks of pictures as *received* information, in contrast to words, whose meanings must be *perceived* (49). Such a distinction posits a struggle between passive and active experience, that is, between inert spectatorship and committed reading. By this argument, comics depend on a dialectic between what is easily understood and what is less easily understood; pictures are open, easy, and solicitous, while words are coded, abstract, and remote.

Yet in comics word and image approach each other: words can be visually inflected, reading as pictures, while pictures can become as abstract and symbolic as words. In brief, the written text can function like images, and images like written text. Comics, like other hybrid texts, collapse the word/image dichotomy: visible language has the potential to be quite elaborate in appearance, forcing recognition of pictorial and material qualities that can be freighted with meaning (as in, for example, concrete poetry); conversely, images can be simplified and codified to function as a language (see Kannenberg, "Graphic Text" and especially "Chris Ware"). McCloud himself notes this, arguing for comic art in which word and image tend toward each other (47–49, 147–51). This recognition renders McCloud's larger argument incoherent, as it belies his earlier distinction between perceived and received information. The distinction does not hold in any case, for, as Perry Nodelman points out with regard to picture books, "All visual images, even the most apparently representational ones, . . . require a knowledge of learned competencies and cultural assumptions before they can be rightly understood" (17). Though the image is, as W. J. T. Mitchell says, "the sign that pretends not to be a sign" (*Iconology* 43), it remains a sign nonetheless, "as bound up with habit and convention as any text" (64). Pictures are not simply to be received; they must be decoded.

Still, responding to comics often depends on recognizing word and image as two "different" types of sign, whose implications can be played against each other—to gloss, to illustrate, to contradict or complicate or ironize the other. While the word/image dichotomy may be false or oversimple, learned assumptions about these different codes—written and pictorial—still exert a strong centripetal pull on the reading experience. We continue to distinguish between the function of words and the function of images, despite the fact that comics continually work to destabilize this very distinction. This tension between codes is fundamental to the art form.

A CASE STUDY: WARE'S "I GUESS"

If words can be *drawn*, and images *written*, then the tension between words and images can become quite complex. For example, in "I Guess" (*Raw* 2:3, 1991, reprinted in Ware, *Quimby*), alternative cartoonist Chris Ware experiments with a radically disjunctive form of verbal/visual interplay: a six-page story that sustains parallel verbal and pictorial

narratives throughout, never quite reconciling one to the other (figs. 5 and 6). In fact "I Guess" [a.k.a. "Thrilling Adventure Stories"] seems to tell two different tales. Its visuals pay homage to traditional superhero stories, in a slickly parodic style inspired by the 1930s and 1940s work of such artists as Joe Shuster (*Superman*) and C. C. Beck (*Captain Marvel*); its written text, on the other hand, consists of an ostensibly autobiographical reminiscence, in which a narrator recalls unsettling childhood experiences. Ware never subordinates one tale to the other, but instead juxtaposes word and image in suggestive counterpoint. The iconography of the superhero genre informs and deepens the autobiographical narrative, while the autobiography invests the clichés of the superhero with a peculiar resonance, inviting the reader to reconsider the genre's psychological appeal. Thus the interplay of the two suggests a third, more comprehensive meaning that the reader must construct through inference. As Gene Kannenberg Jr. argues, in a cogent and useful reading of Ware, this "third field of interpretation" captures the emotional conflict within the narrator himself, effectively "reproduc[ing] a psychological state upon the page" ("Ware" 185–86).

Ware's pictorial narrative, involving a conflict between a costumed superman and a mad scientist, parodies early superhero comics with some care, distilling many of the graphic and thematic hallmarks of the genre in its commercial heyday (its Golden Age, in fan parlance). Yet his coolly postmodern graphics exaggerate the cartoon simplicity of Shuster and Beck; he flattens the genre's fervid romanticism into rigid poses, embalming it. His meticulous rendering, lacking the roughhewn spontaneity of early comic books, pushes the visuals immediately into parody. Arch and overdetermined, the drawings defer to, yet remain crucially *different* from, a long line of predecessors. Hence they provide a ripe and suggestive context for the words.

In sharp contrast to the pictures, the written narration of "I Guess" explores a child's relationships with three different males: his grandfather, his "best friend," and his stepfather. The first-person narrator, rambling from one recollection to the next, speaks in a sort of blank parataxis, as if unable to draw conclusions from his own stories. His words, in their very blankness and simplicity, evoke the naiveté of childhood just as deliberately as do Ware's superhero visuals and capture the confusion of a child grappling with such perplexing issues as racial and sexual identity. For example: "he asked me if I felt weird that we were the only boys at the party. I said no, and then I asked him if he felt weird that we were the only white kids at the party. He said no, and then he asked me why I said that. I really didn't know and all of a sudden I felt gross so I rolled over and pretended to go to sleep" (78). Like the pictures, the words are essentially ironic: the narrator raises troubling questions but in a naive, unreflective way, thus cueing the reader to look further than the narrator himself can.

Ware's deployment of words in "I Guess" is radically disorienting, for, in defiance of convention, he weaves the written narrative freely, unpredictably, through the pictorial, creating what Kannenberg calls a "mutually reflective patterning" of verbal and visual themes (183). Narration appears within the drawings, not only in caption blocks, word balloons and thought balloons, but also in the guise of decorative titles, labels, sound effects, and even as parts of the diegesis, that is, as signs within the superhero's world itself. Ware practices a curious sort of enjambment: visual breaks in the text (between captions, balloons, and so forth) do not match syntactic or logical breaks in the narration. For instance, a sentence or clause may begin in a caption and continue in a dialogue balloon. Nor do changes in the relative size, shape, or boldness of the lettering always correspond to dramatic emphases in the narrated text. At times the visual emphasis seems comically inappropriate, as when, in the opening "splash" panel (fig. 5), the equivocal phrase "I GUESS" forms a bold masthead in giant letters, even as it starts a sentence that is completed in the caption underneath. Scraps of narration also appear as sound effects, as in the story's climax, where the highly fraught word "when" appears as an explosion: "*I liked things better / WHEN / it was just my mom and me, anyway*" (fig. 6).

More radical still is Ware's incorporation of the written narrative within the diegesis itself, in the form of banners, signs, and other word-bearing objects. Such

bewildering moments play with an ambiguity fundamental to comics: the verbal text (as Eisner reminds us) reads as an image, yet typically remains distinct from the narrative reality evoked by the drawings (*Comics & Sequential Art* 10; see also Abbott 156). Though the appearance of the text can inflect our reading, we assume that the printed words as such are not part of the fictional world we are experiencing. Rather, they represent or cue "sounds" within that world, or in some cases provide a gloss on that world, what might be called a nondiegetic amplification or commentary. Yet Ware destabilizes this convention by bringing fragments of the written text into the depicted world of the story (that is, into the diegesis). To the extent that this technique undercuts the verisimilitude of that world, it forces the reader to question actively the conventions of comic art. In stories that honor those conventions, printed sound effects and narration remain distinct from street signs, billboards and other objects bearing written messages within the diegesis; Ware, however, erases the distinction, thus disorienting the reader and encouraging critical awareness of those conventions. (Such conventions are the very things that make it possible for readers to construct meaning from comic art's plurality of codes.)

The story's intermixing of words and images enriches the first-person narrative, hinting at levels of oedipal conflict and psychological confusion unacknowledged in the words alone. At the same time, this verbal/visual tension compels the reader to consider critically the psychological undercurrents of the superhero genre, as suggested by certain recurrent character types and narrative tropes: the mad scientist, the imperiled woman, the hero's dual identity, the woman's rescue, the hero's gesture of mercy, the villain's convenient self-destruction. By mapping a confused, childlike narration onto these generic elements, Ware casts new light on the genre's structure and appeal.

Admittedly, "I Guess" represents a radical questioning of the way comics work; few comics test the limits of the form so rigorously. Yet, by destabilizing the conventions of visual/verbal interplay, Ware's six-page effort throws those conventions into relief, and encourages us to read even conventional comics

Figure 5. Chris Ware, "I Guess."
Raw Vol. 2, No. 3, page 76.
© 1990 Chris Ware. Used with
permission.

more attentively. Dismantling genre as well as form, Ware's experiment demonstrates the potential of comics to create challenging, multilayered texts: his simple, broadly representational drawings contribute to, rather than mitigate, the suggestive complexity of the narrative, while the blank, naive narratorial voice both amplifies and undercuts the appeal of the drawings. Moreover, the constant tension between the two forces us to take heed of the role the reader must play in constructing meaning. For it is only at the level of the reader's intervention that Ware's words and images can conjoin to suggest a meaning that subsumes both.

Ware's narrative strategy assumes a sophisticated reader, one who recognizes highly fraught parodic gestures as such, and whose confusion can be turned to advantage. In sum, "I Guess" illustrates the *interactive* nature of comics reading and the possibility of generating meaning through the manipulation of tensions inherent in the reading experience.

PICTOGRAPHIC LANGUAGE: CODE VS. CODE

Yet the tension between picturing and writing can exceed even what Ware's story offers. In fact

Figure 6. Ware, "I Guess."
81 (excerpt).
© 1990 Chris Ware.
Used with permission.

comics can exploit this tension without incorporating words per se, as the growing body of "mute" or "pantomime" (that is, wordless) comics attests (see Groensteen, "La bande dessinée muette"). Such comics often rely on diagrammatic symbols, such as panels, speed or vector lines, and ideograms, to gloss or reinforce what's going on in the pictures (see, for example, Fischer and Beronä). Nor does the "written" text within balloons or captions have to consist of words in a conventional sense. Indeed, in comics dialogue icons may take the place of words: the use of pictograms within balloons is a rich tradition, recently explored by such cartoonists as Hendrik Dorgathen and Eric Cartier. For example, Cartier's *Flip in Paradise* and *Mekong King*, told in miniature album format, use pictograms to suggest elaborate dialogues between the hapless picaro, Flip, and the inhabitants of the various lands he visits.

In *Flip in Paradise*, for instance, as the hero haggles over the price of a joint, his dialogue devolves into a cluster of visual non sequiturs—as if Flip is already beginning to succumb to the effects of dope (fig. 7). At first the pictograms in the balloons suggest bargaining, with ever-decreasing amounts of money, but as the balloons crowd together the dialogue's logic becomes harder and harder to grasp. Later in the same book a drunken Flip will teach a parrot some new words—all about killing and cooking the bird—as shown in a tête-à-tête in which man and bird spout the same pictograms. Cartier makes ingenious use of such visual symbols to dramatize Flip's struggles to communicate in strange lands

(ironic, as these symbols allow the cartoonist's work itself to cross national and cultural borders).[3]

Such visual "dialogue" may be drawn in a different style than the pictures used to establish the diegesis: typically, they are less particular, or more generic. Alternately, they may be of the very *same* style, just enclosed within balloons like regular dialogue. In François Avril and Philipe Petit-Roulet's *Soirs de Paris*, for example, the story "63 Rue de la Grange aux Belles" (fig. 8) uses elaborate pictograms to capture the conversations taking place at a cocktail party. The partygoers' dialogue balloons contain a range of pictures: from simple icons, as when a man asks a woman to dance; to cartoons in the same style as that used to depict the speakers (as when a would-be Romeo uses a series of balloons to itemize a woman's attractive features: her eyes, breasts, legs, and so on); to detailed swipes of images by such artists as Gaugain and Matisse, which indicate the topics of conversation among a group of cultured wallflowers. Such examples suggest that visual/verbal tension is not necessarily even a matter of playing words against pictures; it may be a matter of playing symbols against other symbols.

Such visual/verbal tension results from the juxtaposition of symbols that function diegetically and symbols that function non-diegetically—that is, the mingling of symbols that "show" and symbols that "tell." More precisely, we may say that *symbols that show* are symbols that purport to depict, in a literal way, figures and objects in the imagined world of the comic, while *symbols that tell* are those that offer a kind of diacritical commentary on the images or (to

40

Figure 7. Eric Cartier, *Flip in Paradise* (n. pag.). © Eric Cartier. Used with permission.

use another rough metaphor) a "soundtrack" for the images. In most comics, the symbols that show are representational drawings while the symbols that tell are words, balloons, and a few familiar icons. (These icons are nonalphabetic symbols of a sort that many word processors now make available to writers: arrows, dotted lines, lightbulbs, stars, and so forth.) But the potential exists for comics creators to push this tension much further, even to incorporate representational drawings as "dialogue" (as in Cartier, and Avril and Petit-Roulet) and to blur the difference between alphabetic symbols and pictures. At its broadest level, then, what we call visual/verbal tension may be characterized as the clash and collaboration of *different codes of signification*, whether or not written words are used. Again, the deployment of such devices assumes a knowing reader.

2. SINGLE IMAGE VS. IMAGE-IN-SERIES

Most definitions of comics stress the representation of time, that is, of temporal sequence, through multiple images in series. The process of dividing a narrative into such images—a process that necessarily entails omitting as well as including—can be called (à la Robert C. Harvey) *breakdown*, a word derived from "breakdowns," a term of art that refers to the rough drawings made in the process of planning out a comics story (*Art of the Funnies* 14–15). The reverse process, that of reading through such images and inferring connections between them, has been

dubbed (borrowing from gestalt psychology) "closure" by McCloud, in keeping with the reader-response emphasis of his *Understanding Comics*. In fact "breakdown" and "closure" are complementary terms, both describing the relationship between *sequence* and *series*: the author's task is to evoke an imagined sequence by creating a visual series (a breakdown), whereas the reader's task is to translate the given series into a narrative sequence by achieving closure. Again, the reader's role is crucial, and requires the invocation of learned competencies; the relationships between pictures are a matter of convention, not inherent connectedness.

At times this process of connecting, or closure, seems straightforward and unproblematic, as when strong visual repetition and/or verbal cueing make the connections between images immediate, or at least fairly obvious. For instance, Julie Doucet's self-referential vignette "The Artist" uses successive panels to capture the methodical, step-by-step provocation of a striptease (fig. 9). This striptease implicates the spectator in an unnerving way, for the artist ends by spilling her guts with a knife. The deliberate, incremental advances of the sequence, from one panel to the next, establish a rhythm and an expectation, and eventually this rhythm makes the unthinkable thinkable: the artist mutilates and literally *opens* herself before our eyes in calm, measured steps. This violent, self-destructive climax, accomplished through methodical breakdown, ultimately exceeds and beggars all expectations. (The technique reappears in

Figure 8. François Avril (drawings) & Philipe Petit-Roulet (scenario), "63 Rue de la Grange aux Belles" (selected panels). *Soirs de Paris* (n. pag.). © Les Humanoïdes Associés. Used by permission of François Avril and Philipe Petit-Roulet.

other early Doucet stories, such as "Heavy Flow" and "A Blow Job," with their gradual yet shocking transformations.)

At other times, closure may require more active effort on the part of the reader, as demonstrated repeatedly in Jason Lutes's novel *Jar of Fools*. A quarter of the way into the novel, a two-page sequence (36–37) depicts a day's work for Esther O'Dea, who serves customers at a coffee bar called the Saturn Café (fig. 10). In just twenty-four panels Lutes manages to evoke the tedium and sheer drudgery of seven hours on the job, showing both minute details and Esther's overall attitude toward her work. The breakdown of the action is characterized by several bold choices: for instance, Lutes challenges the reader by beginning from the inside out, with a close-up of Esther preparing a double espresso, rather than from the outside in, with an establishing shot of the café itself (here being introduced to readers for the first time). We see a larger image of the café interior only *after* Esther hands the espresso to a customer, and a shot of the exterior (specifying the location) only in the middle of the sequence. Thus Lutes

frames the entire day from Esther's point of view, sticking close to the minutiae of her clockwork routine. The repeated use of close-ups throughout the sequence reinforces the repetitive yet discontinuous nature of her work.

After showing the interior of the café, Lutes builds the rest of the sequence around Esther's query, "Can I help you?"—a phrase she mechanically repeats throughout the day. One customer responds to this with a suggestive sneer and a verbal come-on, "In more ways than one, sweetheart," an overture which Esther repays with stony silence even as she imagines belting the man with a left hook (36). That she *imagines* this, but does not do it, is something the reader must figure out for herself: Lutes suggests this both by the unvarying rhythm of the sequence and by the subtle variation in panel bordering around the imagined punch (the latter a technique used previously by Lutes to set off dreams and memories—by this point the reader presumably knows the code). Yet the moment comes as a shock nonetheless, due in part to the repeated use of a single, unvarying image—Esther's taciturn face—to

Figure 9. Julie Doucet, "The Artist." *Lève Ta Jambe Mon Poisson Est Mort!* (n. pag.). © Julie Doucet. Used with permission.

pace the sequence. We *see* her land a blow, yet nothing about her or around her changes to match this unexpected outburst. The reader must negotiate the larger context of Lutes's narrative to make this key distinction.

On the next page, as the hours crawl forward, Lutes repeats the image of a clock—along with Esther's "Can I help you?"—to suggest the slow, frustrating passage of time. Verbal and visual repetition (the clock, the coffee cups, Esther's face, *Can I help you?*) succeed in quickly evoking a sense of boredom and restiveness—no mean feat. The repeated close-up of the clock face, with changing times, finally *gives* way to the sight of Esther watching the clock from an oblique angle, as her spoken *Can I help you?* becomes an unspoken *Can I kill you?* (37). This is the moment when her shift ends, finally, and she can leave the café. In just a few panels, then, Lutes compresses a day's work into a montage of numbing, repetitive activity and emotional frustration. To follow this sequence, the reader must be mindful of Lutes's previously established habits as a storyteller—his approach to panel bordering, his

interpolations of dream and fantasy into mundane reality, and so on—and take an active part in constructing a flow of events from discontinuous images.

At times achieving closure can be quite difficult, as when images seem radically disjointed and verbal cues are scant. For example, Art Spiegelman's wordless "drawn over two weeks while on the phone" (from *Raw* No. 1, rpt. in Spiegelman and Mouly, *Read Yourself Raw*) presents a series of disconnected panels with recurrent character types and situations but no narrative per se. Generic conventions—nods to film noir, for instance—are repeatedly invoked but without a linear rationale; motific repetition suggests at best a vague connection between otherwise disjunct panels. Certain characters and symbols are repeated: geometric symbols, for instance, which serve as pictographic dialogue, as decorative effects, and, in a droll reversal, even as characters. But the sought-for "unity" of the piece, finally, rests on the reader's recognition of the author's formal playfulness rather than on any coherent narrative. It takes much knowledge and careful attention to read Spiegelman's series as a sequence.

43

Figure 10. Jason Lutes, *Jar of Fools* 36–37. © Jason Lutes. Used with permission.

The tension between single image and image-in-series is bound up with other formal issues, and therefore hard to codify. McCloud's *Understanding Comics* remains the strongest theoretical treatment (in English, that is) of comics sequencing; yet McCloud, perhaps because he does not consider visual/verbal interplay crucial to the form, neglects just how much the interaction of image and word can inform, indeed enable, the reading of sequences. Verbal cues do help to bridge the gaps within a sequence, as seen in common transitional captions such as "Later . . . " or "Meanwhile . . . " (devices that have fallen from favor as readers become more versed in reading comics, just as title cards, fades, irises, and other such transitional devices fell from favor in cinema). In fact verbal continuity can impose structure on even the most radically disjointed series. Witness, for instance, Spiegelman's oft-reprinted "Ace Hole, Midget Detective," in which the hero's nonstop narration (a spoof of hard-boiled fiction)

serves to structure an otherwise nonlinear barrage of non sequiturs, visual gags, and stylistic swipes.

To some extent, then, the process of transitioning, or closure, depends not only on the interplay between successive images but also on the interplay of different codes of signification: the verbal as well as the visual. In other words, how readers attempt to resolve one tension may depend on how they resolve another. Verbal/visual interplay often muddies the pristine categories of transition that McCloud tries to establish in *Understanding Comics* (moment to moment, action to action, scene to scene, and so on). Words can smooth over transitions and unobtrusively establish a dramatic continuity that belies the discontinuity of the images. Two contrasting examples from Harvey Pekar's *American Splendor*, both scripted by Pekar and illustrated by R. Crumb, illustrate this point:

In "The Harvey Pekar Name Story" (1977), the visuals pace and punctuate a verbal monologue, and the successive images are near-identical, so much so that a reader who held the book at arm's length and squinted would be hard-pressed to see any variation (fig. 11). (Lutes uses a similar strategy in the above example from *Jar of Fools*, but Pekar and Crumb use fewer variations and push the repetition much farther.) The story concerns the relationship between name and identity, and the near-sameness of the drawings both reinforces and subverts the speaker's preoccupation with self-definition. Here a man named "Harvey Pekar" (not to be confused with the author) addresses the reader in forty-eight equal-sized panels over four pages. His concern? His name—which, though unusual, turns out not to be unique, as he discovers by looking through the phone book, where he finds not one but two other "Harvey Pekar" listings. The deaths of these two other Pekars (Harvey Sr. and Harvey Jr., father and son) restore the narrator's sense of uniqueness, until a *third* Harvey Pekar appears in the directory, prompting the age-old question, "What's in a name?" On a more personal level, the narrator is left asking himself, and us, "Who is Harvey Pekar?"—a question he can answer only with silence, in the final, wordless panel.

Like Doucet's "The Artist," "The Harvey Pekar Name Story" relies on minute changes from panel to panel to convey a carefully timed sequence. Yet Pekar and Crumb take an even more deliberate approach, calling for a constant subject and point of view with only the minutest changes in gesture and nuance. Pekar's breakdowns invoke the rhythms of verbal storytelling or stand-up comedy, with occasional silent panels for pause and emphasis; the relationship between the speaker and the reader is everything, as the former confronts the latter in a frustrated attempt at self-affirmation. This attempt is fraught with irony: the consistent, even monotonous, point of view in every panel supplies the very appearance of stability that the narrator craves, but the serial repetition of his likeness (subtly varied by Crumb) erodes our sense of his uniqueness. Both the story's rhythm and its themes depend on the unvarying visuals, which force us to confront this "Harvey Pekar" in all his (thwarted) individuality even as they help us concentrate on the spoken text.

In contrast, Pekar and Crumb's "Hypothetical Quandary" (1984) merges words and pictures more dynamically, and asks more of the reader in her quest for closure (fig. 12). This story is inward-looking and nakedly autobiographical, focusing on thought rather than talk. Rendered in a bolder, brushed style, "Quandary" finds Harvey carrying on a dialogue with himself as he drives, then walks, to a bakery to buy bread: How would he react to success and fame? Would it blunt his writing by robbing him of his "working man's outlook on life"? Would it dilute his personal vision? This hypothetical dilemma (not entirely hypothetical, for Pekar *has* had brushes with fame, especially in the wake of the *American Splendor* film in 2003) occupies Harvey through his entire trip to the bakery; indeed, except for a single panel in which he buys the bread, all of Harvey's words occur in thought balloons, and the dark, lushly textured images position him within a fully realized world rather than vis-à-vis the reader in a full-on monologue. (For a thoughtful discussion of this story in a different context, see Witek, *Comic Books as History* 148–49.)

Propelled as much by Pekar's text as by the subtle authority of Crumb's pictures, "Hypothetical Quandary" moves Harvey (and the reader) over a great distance, telescoping his Sunday morning expedition into three pages. Like the above example from Lutes's *Jar of Fools*, this story relies on words as well as common visual cues for its pacing. Driving, walking, buying bread, walking again—all of these happen while Harvey's internal dialogue carries on without interruption, until the last two panels find him savoring the bread's fresh smell, his quandary forgotten. The continuity of the verbal text disguises the *discontinuity* of the visual: Pekar's ongoing words, exploring all the twists and turns of Harvey's thinking, elide the gaps in the visual sequence, making this stylized evocation of his world seem naturalistic and unforced. Whereas "The Harvey Pekar Name Story" weds the author's text to deliberately repetitive breakdowns and a single, static composition, "Hypothetical Quandary" uses text to carry the reader from one locale to the next without ever losing continuity of thought. These contrasting examples point up the possibility that

Figure 11. Harvey Pekar and R. Crumb, "The Harvey Pekar Name Story." *Bob and Harv's Comics* 4. © Harvey Pekar. Used with permission.

Figure 12. Harvey Pekar and R. Crumb, "Hypothetical Quandary." *Bob and Harv's Comics* 80. © Harvey Pekar. Used with permission.

breakdown may depend on mixing the verbal and the visual. Thus the two tensions named so far, *code vs. code* and *single image vs. image-in-series*, interact to create a yet more complex tension, soliciting the reader's active efforts at resolution.

3. SEQUENCE VS. SURFACE

In most cases, the successive images in a comic are laid out contiguously on a larger surface or surfaces (that is, a page or pages). Each surface organizes the images into a constellation of discrete units, or "panels." A single image within such a cluster typically functions in two ways at once: as a "moment" in an imagined sequence of events, and as a graphic element in an atemporal design. Some comics creators consciously play with this design aspect, commonly called *page layout*, while others remain more conscious of the individual image-as-moment. Most long-form comics maintain a tug-of-war between these different functions, encouraging a near-simultaneous apprehension of the single image as both moment-in-sequence and design element. The "page" (or *planche*, as French scholars have it, a term denoting the total design unit rather than the physical page on which it is printed) functions both as sequence and as object, to be seen and read in both linear and nonlinear, holistic fashion.

This tension has been described in various ways. For instance, French scholar Pierre Fresnault-Deruelle, in a seminal essay, proposed the terms "linear" and "tabular" to denote the sequential and nonsequential functions respectively ("Du linéare au tabulaire"; see also Peeters 39–40). "Tabular" perhaps conjures the traditional Western comics layout of a boxlike or gridlike enclosure, rather like a mathematical table, within which each panel acts as a discrete cell; potentially, though, it applies to any comics page, even one that abandons such rectilinear design. More generally, we can say that the single image functions as both a point on an imagined timeline—a self-contained moment substituting for the moment before it, and anticipating the moment to come—and an element of global page design. In other words, there is a tension between the concept of "breaking down" a story into constituent images and the concept of laying out those images together on an unbroken surface. This tension lies at the heart of comics design—and poses yet another challenge to the reader.

This tension can be illustrated through two contrasting examples from "Waiting," a series of single-page alternative comic book stories scripted by Linda Perkins and drawn by Dean Haspiel. The first in the series (from *Keyhole* No. 1, June 1996) uses a conventional design conceit, often called the "nine-panel grid" by comics readers, to suggest the repetitive, unvarying nature of a waitress's work (fig. 13). The strictly gridlike (3-by-3) configuration of the page imparts a constant, unyielding rhythm to the piece, one well suited to the patterns of repetition shown in the compositions. Of all the panels, only the middle one in each tier shows significant variation, as it depicts the face of yet another customer asking the same question (a question already answered in the menu). Panel four, showing the waitress outside (presumably outside the restaurant), implies seasonal variation through the use of snow, though, curiously, the waitress's outfit has not changed to suit the weather. The drastic elision of intervening time, and the static repetition of visual motifs—of exact images, in fact—emphasizes the numbing sameness of the waitress's work routine (not unlike the mood of the café scene in *Jar of Fools*). This routine is enlivened only by the comic grotesquerie of the customers. Here a rigid layout reinforces the air of tedium, frustration, and stasis (that is, of waiting, in two senses) conveyed in the repeated compositions.

If the first "Waiting" story conveys a sense of the tedium and repetition involved in waiting tables, the third (from *Keyhole* No. 3, January 1997) conveys a hectic, almost frantic impression of the hard work involved. Its more inventive and complicated layout reinforces the busyness and overwhelming sense of customer demand called for in the scenario: here the waitress is working very hard indeed, responding gamely to the simultaneous requests and comments of a large dining party (fig. 14). Perkins and Haspiel exploit the tension between page (*planche*) and panel to emphasize the stressful, even frenzied, quality of the dinner from the waitress's point of view.

Figure 13. Linda Perkins and Dean Haspiel, "Waiting." *Keyhole* No. 1. © Dean Haspiel and Linda Perkins. Used with permission.

Figure 14. Linda Perkins and Dean Haspiel, "Waiting." *Keyhole* No. 3. © Dean Haspiel and Linda Perkins. Used with permission.

The first three panels are page-wide oblongs, crowded with detail, which convey the entire dinner in synoptic fashion. Common questions and banal observations appear in tail-less word balloons, as if hovering over the party: *Where is the bathroom?*, *This would be the perfect place to bring Mom*, and so on. A man's request for "a wine glass" in the first panel leads to his cry for assistance in the second: "Hey!!! I spilled my drink!" (The waitress, intent on taking another customer's order, responds by handing him a towel, without even turning to look.) In the third panel, the waitress balances several steaming coffee cups on her arm while the customers look on in the background, barely visible over the cups. A full-figure image of the embattled waitress overlaps these three panels, linking them, her six arms spread Kali-like (roughly speaking) to imply her haste and efficiency. Each hand holds a common tool: a menu, a peppermill, and so on. This full shot of the waitress not only provides an irreverent bit of visual parody but also serves to unite these horizontal panels in a single graphic conceit without arresting the sequence of events depicted. What's more, we are able to see the events from multiple perspectives at once, for the first panel appears to show the dinner party from the waitress's viewpoint, while the second and third depict the waitress herself, in medium and close-up shots respectively. Her overlapping figure in these three panels frustrates any sense of linearity, allowing for an impossible and provocative at-onceness.

The last three panels on the page, forming the bottom tier, are stunted verticals of equal size, much smaller than the images above. They depict a briefer sequence of events: a final exchange between the waitress and the man paying the bill. In reply to the skimpy tip (just $5 for a bill of $295), the waitress asks the man, "Was there something wrong with the service?" His response is simple and unequivocal, though seemingly irrelevant: "Yes. My wife burned my toast this morning." His grotesque, comically exaggerated features contrast with the idealized close-up of the waitress immediately above, lending a spiteful certainty to his accusation. Here there are no outsized images to violate or overlap the bordered panels; only three simple images in a deliberate rhythm, reminiscent of the gridlike regularity in the first "Waiting" story. Whereas the top three panels convey the almost desperate efficiency of the waitress's efforts, and show her earning what by rights ought to be a generous tip, the last three show her comeuppance, as masculine spite holds her responsible, by proxy, for another woman's failure to please. It is largely through the ingenious layout of the page that Perkins and Haspiel underscore the unfairness of the man's response.

The page divides into two design units—the three horizontal panels and the three verticals—to contrast the waitress's efforts with her scant reward. In the top three panels, the temporal sequence is confused, even collapsed, by the full figure of the waitress, an overlapping design element that functions tabularly to stress the frantic nature of her activity. The overlapping of images suggests the overwhelming demands of her work. In the bottom three, the uniform, unbroken panels, shorn of any elaborate design elements, establish a rhythm that leads to the strip's bitter punch line.

Uniting these two design units, the final image of the man's face stares at the reader as if seen from the waitress's point of view, a visual echo of the story's first panel (in which the man turns to get her attention). Moreover, the final close-up of the man contrasts with the close-up of the waitress directly above: she looks left, intent on her work, while he seems to be moving right, as if to leave; her face, an unblemished white, contrasts with his darker, more detailed features. Yet the two are linked by a strong vertical down the right-hand side of the page: in a tabular reading, the last "cell" relates directly to the cell above it, while in a linear reading it supplies the climax for the entire six-panel story. Linearly, the incident progresses from dinner, through dessert, to the final payoff, while, tabularly, the figures of the waitress and the man vie for position on the page. The Kali-like waitress clearly dominates the surface, yet the man moves from right to center to right again, in an attempt to (re)assert his dominance. The layout of the entire page stresses the complete figure of the waitress, on the upper left, and the opposed close-ups of waitress and man, on the lower right. The fact that each panel functions both as a discrete part and within the larger context of the layout generates the tension that makes this vignette so effective.

From a reader's point of view, then, there is always the potential to choose: between seeing the single image as a moment in sequence and seeing it in more holistic fashion, as a design element that contributes to the overall balance (or in some cases the meaning-ful *im*balance) of the layout. The latter way of seeing privileges the dimensions of the total page/*planche*/surface, yet still invokes the meaning of the overall narrative sequence to explain why the page might be formatted as it is. Broadly, we may say that comics exploit *format* as a signifier in itself; more specifically, that comics involve a tension between the experience of reading in sequence and the format or shape of the object being read. In other words, the art of comics entails a tense relationship between perceived time and perceived space.

RE: TIMING, OR, SERIALITY VS. SYNCHRONISM

As the above discussion reveals, the representation of time in comics can vary considerably: from precise breakdowns that depict a sequence of events in minute detail to single drawings that conflate a whole series of events in one panel. In our second "Waiting" example, for instance, the horizontal pan-els, sprinkled with disembodied word balloons, repre-sent a kind of synchronism, a distillation of time in which the implied duration of the sequence is rather ambiguous, enough so as to cover an entire meal. In contrast, the vertical panels at the bottom of the page are precisely timed to depict a brief sequence succinctly and unambiguously. Thus a single page can move from a vague evocation of passing time to a precise, incremental depiction of single incident (in this case a momentary exchange of dialogue: brief, clipped, even brusque). Such changes in rhythm occur so often in comics as to be almost invisible.

In the case of "Waiting" this effect is, again, partly the result of an ingenious layout. It is also partly the result of the unconventional use of float-ing balloons to convey snippets of banal, dinner-table conversation. As McCloud observes, the use of words "introduce[s] time by representing that which can only exist in time—sound" (95). But this effect also depends to some extent on the composition of each drawing: in this case, Haspiel draws many diners in the horizontal panels, in order to evoke the confusion of a large gathering. Words, images, graphic design—all conjoin to create a three-panel sequence that covers an extended period of time. In fact the composition of an image and the use of words within it can create a radical synchronism by which the single image represents a lengthy interval (see McCloud 95–97; Abbott 162–65). In other words, time elapses not only between the panels but also *within* them. While images in series (break-downs) may convey the passage of time through explicit inter-panel transitions, time is also conveyed within the confines of the single panel, thanks to composition and verbal/visual tension.

Here we have two contrasting approaches to what McCloud (108) calls "the systematic decompo-sition of moving images in a static medium": on the one hand, seriality, that is, breakdown, in which a sequence is represented through a series of contigu-ous panels; on the other, synchronism, in which a single panel represents a sequence of events occur-ring at different "times." While seriality may encour-age a facile comparison between comics and cinematic montage, synchronism demonstrates the limits of the comparison, offering images that can make sense only within a static medium. Examples of synchro-nism in comics include the diagrammatic "motion lines" and other types of ideographic shorthand that denote movement, and the use of multiple, some-times overlapping images of a single subject within a given panel (McCloud 110–12).

One example of multiple images in a single panel would be the common "take," in which a character's sudden reaction—typically, one of surprise or alarm—is shown through the partial overlapping of different facial expressions. A more elaborate technique is what McCloud calls the "polyptych," in which sev-eral distinct images of a single figure (or set of fig-ures) are laid over a single continuous background (fig. 15). That background may be (as in McCloud's example) explicitly divided into smaller units by

Figure 15. Scott McCloud, *Understanding Comics* 115 (excerpt). © 2004 Scott McCloud. Used with permission.

panel borders, which serve to reinforce the break-down of the larger image into successive moments of "time." In cartoonists' parlance, such divided polyptychs are called *split panels*. They dramatically exploit the tension between linear and tabular readings of the image by creating a series of panels that also acts as a single unit—what Eisner calls a "metapanel" (*Comics & Sequential Art* 63). Such "split" panels are often used to emphasize precise sequencing or deliberate rhythms. In contrast, an *un*divided polyptych (that is, a single, undivided frame that represents an extended span of time synchronistically) tends to stress haste, intensity, near-simultaneity—or, oddly enough, the opposite: stillness and inertia.

Whether divided or not, the polyptych blurs comics' equation of time with space. It invokes the tensions established above, *single image vs. image-in-series* and *sequence vs. surface*, to generate tension of another order: between serial and sychronic readings of a single panel. This is what I would call a second-degree tension (one that presupposes the reader's awareness of the other basic tensions). Exploiting this second-degree tension assumes a sophisticated reader, because it requires that reader both to choose and to defer choosing: *I can, indeed*

must, read this image or set of images in more than one way. This demand calls attention to the ways comics negotiate time and space, which is why polyptychs tend to be used when time or space become the thematic concerns of narrative itself. Polyptychs are powerful tools for timing, or, alternately, for suggesting a character's timeless immersion in a rich, diverting space.

Bill Watterson demonstrates the potential of the synchronistic panel in a *Calvin and Hobbes* Sunday page (reprinted in *Weirdos from Another Planet!*, 1990) that succeeds in evoking both speed and environment (fig. 16). This single-panel outing depicts the title characters in a typically frenetic yet contemplative mood, as they race along in their wagon to make the most of the last days of summer. Watterson suggests their haste by directing the eye across the continuous background, as Calvin and Hobbes careen over hill and dale, describing an arc that brings them closer to the reader, then takes them further away. Both the word balloons and the tree trunks in the foreground (which serve as de facto panel borders) parse this scene into successive moments, introducing the time element, yet the unbroken background blurs our sense of time, conveying at once the characters' deep immersion in this scene of natural beauty and the headlong urgency

53

Figure 16. Bill Watterson, "Calvin & Hobbes." *Weirdos from Another Planet!* 89. "Calvin and Hobbes" © 1988 Watterson. Reprinted with permission of Universal Press Syndicate. All rights reserved.

of their ride (a trope familiar from previous *Calvin* strips). Synchronism allows Watterson to linger on the vividness of the scene, while honoring the restless, energetic nature of his characters. For the boy and his tiger, nature is an arena of frantic activity—one in which "lingering" is usually done at full speed. The extraordinary thing about this page is the way it conjures up both the impatience of childhood and the timeless, still quality of the child's surroundings.

Synchronism can take other, less obvious forms, such as in the characteristic "splash" pages or spreads by the celebrated comic book artist Jack Kirby, known for his attempts to render motion in static form: multiplane compositions, slashing diagonals, drastic foreshortening and extreme distortion of the human figure. This style, regarded as "cinematic" by many (apparently including Kirby himself) in fact represents a distinctly *un*cinematic way of evoking movement in static form, a way much more suggestive than literal. Though influenced by the

classicism of adventure strip illustrators such as Alex Raymond (*Flash Gordon*), Kirby's cartooning recalls Futurism in its decomposition of movement and Cubism in its simultaneous depiction of different points of view. Though Kirby's crowded spreads seem to capture discrete and explosive moments of action, in fact they represent extended spans of time in synoptic fashion.

Take, for instance, the scene-setting image of warfare (fig. 17) found at the beginning of Kirby's *New Gods* No. 9 (July 1972, reprinted 1998). Figures loom in the extreme foreground and middle distance; figures dot the deep background as well. Motion lines give lingering physical presence to temporal phenomena, such as the squirting of acid and the leaping of bodies, while the posing of every figure suggests a vast surge toward the right-hand margin. Figures affront the viewer in drastic close-up and recede into the background along sharp diagonals, while the reading order of the word balloons guides

Figure 17. Jack Kirby (inked by Mike Royer), "The Bug." *Jack Kirby's New Gods* 198–99. © 1972 DC Comics. Used with permission. All rights reserved.

the eye from left to right, top to bottom. Tension between word and image contributes to our sense of elapsed time: one balloon notes that the attackers, the so-called "bugs," have disabled the first line of defense, while the next balloon promises to open a breach in the wall that surrounds the enemy. The leader of the charge, "Forager," stands on the far right, his words urging movement, his hand beckoning the bugs toward the margin: "Forward! Forward! Keep going!" Overall, the characters exhibit a peculiar angularity that shades toward geometric abstraction yet suggests fierce activity (swarming) and directionality (forward!). Through composition and verbal/visual interplay, Kirby captures successive moments simultaneously; this is not a snapshot but a tableau.

Such synchronic images need not be confined to the hyperbolic vocabulary of adventure comics. They can depict more mundane types of activity as well. For instance, the climactic full-page image from Mary Fleener's autobiographical "Rock Bottom" depicts

what appears to be (the story equivocates, forcing the reader to suspend judgment) a drug-addled sexual imbroglio between Mary, her occasional lover Face, and a glamorous woman named Roxanne (fig. 18). Fleener's trademark "cubismo" style, a dizzying blend of Picasso and her own sharp-edged technique, offers a radically disorienting minefield of interpretive choices for the reader, as figures blend in a sexually suggestive synchrony. Is this a dream, as Mary's sleepy expression on the top left implies? Provoking and humorous imagery—in particular, Mary's startled reaction to the (clitoral? phallic?) guitar-playing figure that emerges, erect, from a vagina—suggests her sexual encounter with Roxanne, an encounter which belies her own homophobic anxieties (shown earlier in the story when Mary worries about playing a musical gig in a lesbian bar). The overlapping images imply an entire sequence of activities that Mary cannot remember upon waking the next morning. Like Kirby, Fleener uses a single composition to suggest successive stages

Figure 18. Mary Fleener, "Rock Bottom." *Life of the Party* 46. © Mary Fleener. Used with permission.

of action. (That two such different cartoonists, divided thematically, ideologically, and historically, both exploit the ambiguity of timing suggests that this is an area ripe for study.)

In contrast to the temporally ambiguous pages of Kirby, Fleener, and Watterson, the split panel tends to stress strong rhythms and the systematic analysis of movement. For example, in the war comics of cartoonist-editor Harvey Kurtzman (published by EC in the early 1950s), split panels serve to capture the broken rhythms of warfare, alternately slow and lightning-fast, as long intervals of torpor are punctuated by sudden fits of frantic, violent activity. At times Kurtzman's split panels emphasize the painful slowness of war and the numbing sameness of the action, which threaten to make the participants indistinct and, in fact, interchangeable; at other times, his split panels provide a precise, almost stroboscopic, breakdown of rapid movement. Often these split panels are true polyptychs, showing a single figure moving against a continuous background; at other times, they are a means of parsing *simultaneous*

Figure 19. Harvey Kurtzman, John Severin, and Will Elder, "Campaign," page 5 (excerpt). *Two-Fisted Tales*, Vol. 3. © William M. Gaines, Agent, Inc. Used with permission.

actions into successive frames—effectively turning one moment, one panel, into a sequence of two or more. Though the split panel's function depends on context, in every case it presents the reader with an ambiguity: should it be read as simultaneous or as successive, as a moment or moments?

Consider, for instance, the Civil War story "Campaign" (originally from *Two-Fisted Tales* No. 31, Jan./Feb. 1953) drawn by John Severin and Will Elder over Kurtzman's breakdowns. Here much of the action depends on waiting for things to happen: Kurtzman focuses on the peninsular campaign of 1862, as Federal troops advance on Richmond, Virginia, but the "action," so eagerly anticipated by the new recruits, mostly involves digging in, waiting, and marching. In mid-tale, a split panel (fig. 19) shows the Federals marching through Seven Pines toward Richmond, their advance punctuated by the sounds of cannon fire in the woods: "KLAK KLIKITY CRASH" (5). The weary soldiers, bent with the weight of their packs and rifles, are divided into three panels but on closer examination comprise a single composition, in which the individual figures are hardly distinguishable from each other.

Are these three different sets of soldiers, or three successive images of the same soldiers? The soldiers' complaint—that their delay in Yorktown has cost them

the advantage in Richmond—is voiced by more than one man, but the faces and personalities of the men are indistinct. Though the breakdown of the image into three successive panels punctuates the soldiers' speech and reinforces the numbing rhythms of the march, it does not single out the speakers. This indifference to individuality serves the story's larger argument, which stresses the confusion, grinding tedium, facelessness, and futility of war. In the end, the nameless sergeant, called simply "Sarge," will succumb to fever (ironically, not to wounds suffered in battle) and will be replaced by one of the recent recruits, called simply "Boy." This replacement assumes not only the sergeant's rank but also his demeanor, even his appearance. The split panel in mid-story, implying the monotony and impersonality of war, anticipates this final irony, reinforcing the ideological thrust of this characteristic Kurtzman story: warfare is meaningless and numbing. This split panel, unlike the examples above, is clearly divided into discrete blocks, but, like them, depends on a sense of temporal ambiguity.

A similar device appears, but to opposite effect, at the beginning of "Enemy Contact!" (*Two-Fisted Tales* No. 22, July/Aug. 1951), illustrated by Jack Davis—one of many Korean War tales penned by Kurtzman while that war was still being fought. This tale, which concerns an attempt, in the midst of battle, to save the life of a soldier with acute appendicitis, begins with brutal images of death, as three American soldiers are mowed down in quick succession by "an enemy machine gun" (fig. 20). The opening splash panel shows a soldier against a stone wall, falling, contorted with pain, the POK POK POK of the machine gun driving holes into the wall behind him. The four panels beneath, taken together, form a single image, tracing the line of machine gun fire as it sweeps across the wall, felling two more soldiers and almost claiming another. The breakdown of the moment into four shorter intervals—merest fractions of a second, one imagines—isolates each victim, stressing the wantonness of the attack. These are events; these are individual deaths. Yet, while the panel borders parse the event into microseconds, the weaving of the sound effects over the images in an unbroken line (POK POK KRAK) turns this rapid-fire breakdown into a single, shocking tableau. (The next page will show us this same wall, in a single, oblong panel, with three corpses in front of it.)

Kurtzman's control of reading rhythm is methodical, and radical. He went as far as using the split panel to stretch out the reading of single moment in time (the antithesis of the synchronic approach seen above in Kirby and Fleener). He would break a moment down to suggest the way the eye might (almost instantaneously) sweep over it and take it in—that is, "read" it. For instance, in the Korean War story "Air Burst" (*Frontline Combat* No. 4, Jan./Feb. 1952), a final split panel stresses the story's ultimate irony (fig. 21). The Chinese soldier "Big Feet" is killed by a booby trap set by his own companion, "Lee," whose body Big Feet carries toward the American line in the hope of surrendering. The split panel depicts the moment after, as American troops on the advance (for whom the trap was intended) discover the scene. Directing our eye across the page, the three subpanels are keyed to Kurtzman's captions, above; his emphatic prose isolates each part of the picture for our perusal. In order: the long-dead body of Lee "sprawls on the path"; Big Feet lies dead next to him, a tripwire tangled around his foot; and the wire connects to the grenade which has just taken Big Feet's life. The split panel allows Kurtzman to zero in on each important element in his story (Lee, Big Feet, and the trap), while placing Big Feet (the victim of Kurtzman's tragic irony) in dead center. The American soldiers, on whose advance the entire plot depends, approach cautiously in the background.

Time-wise, Kurtzman's "Air Burst" may be said to represent the opposite of the approach shown in, for instance, Fleener's "Rock Bottom." While Fleener overlaps images in a single synchronistic panel, creating a dizzying and suggestive simultaneity, Kurtzman uses three discrete panels to direct the reading of a single, highly charged moment. In "Rock Bottom," as in our Watterson and Kirby examples, timing is vague but evocative—open—while in "Air Burst" the timing is overdetermined, precisely controlled, almost metronomic. From these examples, we can see that the image-series alone does not determine timing in comics, for it is possible to have a series of panels in which no time seems to pass, as well as a single panel into which moments, hours, even days, are compressed. There is no single prescription for how the tensions of image/series or sequence/surface are to be resolved; rather, there is always an underlying tension between different possible ways of reading, between serial and synchronistic timing. Understanding comics conventions only heightens that tension. The reader must invoke what she knows of comics, including image/series and sequence/surface, to entertain and ultimately to reconcile different understandings of time.

4. TEXT AS EXPERIENCE VS. TEXT AS OBJECT

At a higher level of generalization, the tension *sequence vs. surface* is but one example of a larger relationship between (a) experience over time and (b) the dimensions of comics as material objects. The latter aspect, comics' materiality, includes not only the design or layout of the page but also the physical makeup of the text, including its size, shape, binding, paper, and printing. Like traditional books, but perhaps more obviously, long-form comics can exploit both design and material qualities to communicate

Figure 20. Harvey Kurtzman and Jack Davis, "Enemy Contact," page 1. *Two-Fisted Tales*, Vol. 1. © William M. Gaines, Agent, Inc. Used with permission.

THE MORTAR SQUAD IS NO MORE!
LEE SPRAWLS ON THE PATH...
TWICE KILLED. LONG DEAD!

POOR, CLUMSY 'BIG FEET' LIES
WITH HIS FACE IN THE BLOODY
DIRT, HIS BIG FOOT CAUGHT ON A WIRE!

THE WIRE TRAILS TO THE RING OF A
PULL CORD DANGLING BENEATH
THE REMAINS OF A HAND GRENADE!

Figure 21. Harvey Kurtzman, "Air Burst," page 6 (excerpt). *Frontline Combat*, Vol. 1. © William M. Gaines, Agent, Inc. Used with permission.

or underscore the meaning(s) available in the text. Indeed, many comics make it impossible to distinguish between text per se and secondary aspects such as design and the physical package, because they continually invoke said aspects to influence the reader's participation in meaning-making.

Material considerations influence not only the total design and packaging of a publication but also matters of style and technique. The delineation of images, for instance, is always affected by the materiality of the text, for, as Eisner observes, comic art is necessarily rendered "in response to the method of its reproduction" (*Comics & Sequential Art* 153). In fact style in comics is often profoundly influenced by technological and economic means, and many cartoonists develop highly self-conscious relationships with those means, relationships that, from a reader's point of view, can become fraught with significance. For instance, the European *Klare Lijn* or *Ligne Claire* ("Clear Line") tradition of cartooning, popularized in the much-loved *Tintin* series by Belgian master Hergé, privileges smooth, continuous linework, simplified contours and bright, solid colors, while avoiding frayed lines, exploded forms, and expressionistic rendering. A style of drawing linked with the flat color of *Tintin* and similar series, the *Klare Lijn* (so labeled by the Dutch cartoonist Joost Swarte) is marked by its traditional association with children's comics, yet has grown to embrace or at least influence a whole school of alternative cartoonists who work for adults as well as, or instead of, children (see

Gravett, "Hergé"). These cartoonists often treat its associations ironically, as if to question Hergé's ideal union of style and subject (among many others: Swarte, Ever Meulen, Daniel Torres, the late Yves Chaland, and, in perhaps less obvious but still significant ways, Jacques Tardi, Vittorio Giardino, and the United States' Jason Lutes). In the work of such cartoonists as Swarte and Torres, the Clear Line carries an obvious ideological as well as stylistic burden: their comics not only parody racist stereotypes redolent of *Tintin*'s late-colonial ethos but also reveal a fascination with blurring the distinction between organic and inorganic form, a tendency perfectly realized in Swarte's cool, ironic work for both children and adults (see Heller).

Often the Clear Line seems to deny the materiality of the comics page, relying on precise linework and flat colors to create pristine and detailed settings into which simply drawn characters are inserted. Though the settings are often much more complex than the characters, the two are equated through an unerring evenness of line: like the characters, the settings tend to be without shadow, except in the most diagrammatic sense, and also relatively textureless. The resultant tendency toward flatness produces what McCloud calls a "democracy of form," in which each shape has the same clarity and value, conferring the same authority on cartoon figures as it does on meticulous scenic detail (190). This tendency can of course be undercut, as in Swarte's strip "Torn Together" ("Samen gescheurd" in Dutch), which spoofs the democracy of forms and calls attention to the materiality of the page (fig. 22). Beginning with a panel whose upper left corner has deliberately been torn off, "Torn Together" goes on to depict a contretemps in which one man tears off the lapels of another's jacket, then tears off his ear, to which the other responds by tearing out the first man's right arm.[4] (The dripping blood looks particularly incongruous in the *Klare Lijn*.) The second man proceeds to stuff the disembodied arm and ear into a vase to create a decoration, which he waters like a plant. This is an especially clear example of Swarte's interest in the confusion of living and unliving form: the flat coloring and pristine linework create an Hergé-like scenario that ironically equates the tearing of paper with the tearing of people's bodies. The style is inextricably part of, and prerequisite to, the story's meaning.

In contrast to the Clear Line are more expressionistic styles that revel in the texture of the page, insisting on the materiality of the print medium. Gary Panter, for instance, hailed as "the Father of Punk Comics," has pioneered a raw, "ratty-line" approach at odds with the pristine illusionism of the clear line (Callahan 10, 93; Spiegelman and Mouly, *Read* 8). Panter himself views his work in terms of "marks" rather than lines, a distinction that privileges expressiveness over clarity or precision (Groth and Fiore 231–32). In contrast to the school of Hergé, which epitomizes the use of line as a means of definition and verisimilitude, Panter's mark-making emphasizes texture as a means of immediate, visceral expression (fig. 23). He privileges the raw gestural qualities of a drawing, as a record of physical activity, over its iconic or referential function. Panter's work—notably his occasional series *Jimbo*, which follows a punk everyman through various bizarre and fragmented episodes (for example, *Cola Madness*, *Jimbo in Purgatory*)—boasts a disorienting variety of graphic techniques, as well as an oblique and disjointed approach to language. The result is a ragged cartoon surrealism, often narrative in only the loosest sense, fusing the iconography of comics and animation with a painterly, fine-arts sensibility and the aggressive energy of punk. Indeed the humor of Panter's

work depends in part on his use of rough, energetic marks to reconfigure characters lifted from television cartooning and children's comics, characters usually rendered with a slick consistency befitting industrialized cel animation. The approach recalls R. Crumb's anxious reinvention of cartoon icons in the late 1960s (see chapter 1), but with an even greater emphasis on pure mark-making rather than figuration. (The dark texturing also recalls other underground pioneers such as Aline Kominsky-Crumb and Rory Hayes, as well as Panter's British contemporary Savage Pencil.)

Many alternative comic artists, both in the United States and abroad, have followed in Panter's wake, drawing on the ironic tension between simplified cartoon vocabulary and roughhewn graphic technique. (Such disparate artists as David Sandlin, Jonathon Rosen, Julie Doucet, and Lloyd Dangle all qualify, as do such Europeans as M. S. Bastian of Switzerland and Max Andersson of Denmark.) This tension often serves to express a violent and absurdist worldview colored by apocalyptic anxieties, as in much of Panter's own work (see McKenna; Panter, Interview with John Kelly). In general, the post-Panter ratty-line (or "ugly art" or "comix brut") school subverts the cultural and ideological reassurances proffered by the Clear Line, and as such represents a visual argument about the implications of style. This argument foregrounds the active role of the reader in constructing meaning.

Beyond the bald ironies of punk, many other recent comics invoke the materiality of print by using suggestive styles based on tone and texture, just as the *ligne claire* is based on the precise delineation of form. Such styles (especially evident in the European avant-garde, with its objet d'art approach) tend to explore the relationship between figure and ground. For instance, French artist Yvan Alagbé (fig. 24) often approaches figuration in a sparse, open, almost gestural way, despite a finely nuanced realism of expression; his pages pose indistinct or half-completed figures against blank, undifferentiated backgrounds, exploring the tension between positive and negative space. Simply put, Alagbé's characters seem constantly on the verge of dissolving into the page itself.

Figure 22. Joost Swarte, "Torn Together." *Raw* No. 7, page 2 (inside front cover). © Joost Swarte. Used with permission.

Figure 23. Gary Panter, "Jimbo is 'Running Sore.'" *Read Yourself Raw* 53 (excerpt). © Gary Panter. Used with permission.

His work thus reveals a profound faith in the reader's capacity for visual closure, as it calls on our ability to complete a process of figuration only begun by the artist. In such works as *Nègres Jaunes* (1995) Alagbé turns this daring graphic technique to cultural argument, thematizing the blackness and whiteness of ink and paper as signs of ethnic and cultural difference (see Beaty, "AMOK"; Pollman).

While Alagbé's work relies on traditional grid-like paneling to enclose and delimit its open spaces, German artist Anna Sommer (*Remue-Ménage/Damen Dramen*) allows series of images to spill freely across the undivided expanse of the page (fig. 25). She too displays great confidence in the reader's ability to construct meaning from fragments. Her fluid approach to *sequence vs. surface* mirrors her thematic interest in openness and surprise, in particular her exploration (as here) of the mutability of gender. This method goes beyond questions of layout to the interrogation of the physical page as surface and ground. Indeed, artists like Alagbé and Sommer call for a materialist criticism, one in which print-specific qualities such as drawing technique, tone, and surface can be interrogated for their

narrative significance. Ditto those artists known for their painterly manipulation of texture, such as France's Jean-Claude Götting (who creates dense, dark imagery with a lithograph-like grain); Italy's Stefano Ricci (who sculpts thick, almost palpable tones by alternating drawing, erasing, and painting on fragile paper); the United States' Debbie Drechsler (who balances contour and texture through the mesmerizing buildup of delicate lines); and Switzerland's Thomas Ott (whose grim, often horrific fables are carved out of scratchboard, white on black—a perfect union of technique and subject). All of these artists are characterized by a keen grasp not only of comics as a narrative form but also of the relationship between narrative content and physical medium, that is, between the experience of reading and the material object. Calling attention to that relationship, these creators highlight the distance between text and reader, and foreground the reader's creative intervention in meaning-making. Their works bear out Pascal Lefèvre's dictum that "the materiality of a comic is essential. . . . The form of a drawing draws attention to the object represented in a way that deviates from ordinary perception" ("Recovering Sensuality" 142).

63

Figure 24. Yvan Alagbé, "Etoile d'Orient."
Le Cheval sans Tête, Vol. 5: *Nous sommes
les Maures* 38. © Yvan Alagbé. Used with
permission.

The above examples may seem exotic to American readers—but one need not look far afield to find invocations of the page-as-object. In Art Spiegelman's celebrated *Maus*, for instance, the page repeatedly refers to itself, as "objects" overlap the panels, creating at once an illusion of volume and a sense of intimacy (as if these found objects have been mounted in a diary or scrapbook). Maps, tickets, photographs—these commonplace items appear to have been laid "on top" of the page, as if to ratify the book's documentary nature as a family auto/biography. Early on, for example, Spiegelman conveys a key moment in the courtship between his father Vladek and his mother Anja by drawing a photograph of Anja into, and *on*to, the page (1:17). Anja's "photo" dominates the page, suggesting both the factualness of Spiegelman's account and Anja's growing importance in Vladek's reminiscence (see chapter 5, fig. 56). This ironic appeal to the book's status as a physical object is complex and heavily fraught, as we shall see later on. Suffice to say here that the reader's awareness is called to the materiality of the book itself (albeit through an illusion), in such a way as to inflect her understanding

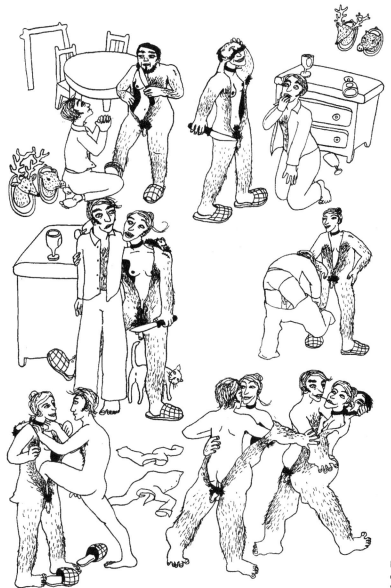

Figure 25. Anna Sommer, "La femme du chasseur." *Remue Ménage* (n. pag.). © Anna Sommer. Used with permission.

of the narrative. This gambit is characteristic of Spiegelman, an artist for whom print is a privileged point of reference. (*Maus*, notwithstanding its subsequent reformatting for an archival CD-ROM, is first and foremost a *book*.) Such self-reflexive commentary is in fact quite common in comics: beyond questions of texture and volume, the materiality of texts is often highlighted through embedded visual references to books, other comics, and picture-making in general—things and activities inevitably fraught with special significance for cartoonists and their readers.

CONCLUSION: TOWARD THE HABIT OF QUESTIONING

Comics *are* complex objects. In light of the above discussion, the experience of reading them would seem to call for negotiation among various possible meanings. Despite the codification of techniques designed to ease this negotiation—for example, the use of overdetermined transitions (*Meanwhile . . .*), rigid gridlines, and various pictographic conventions—there is no one "right" way to read the comics page, nor any stable, Platonic conception of that page.

65

There is simply no consistent formula for resolving the tensions intrinsic to the experience. In fact awareness of these tensions, an awareness expected of the prepared or "sophisticated" reader, may multiply the number of choices available to the reader and can result in an even more intensive questioning of the page (as the above discussion of timing, for instance, makes clear). The foregoing analysis, then, cannot tell us How to Read Comics; it can only suggest certain heretofore neglected aspects of the experience.

Some may yet object that the form needs no instruction manual, no "how to" book to get between readers and their pleasure. Admittedly, there is much in comics that seems intuitive, much that seems naively pleasurable; the form's reliance on pictures can make it (or certain aspects of it) immediately accessible, even to many readers who have not mastered all the disciplines that formal literacy demands. I have seen evidence of this among the children in my own life. Yet, as the above discussion shows, the form uses diverse means to solicit and guide reader participation and always involves *choosing* among different options—different strategies of interpretation, different ways of understanding. There may be much more going on than mere "picture reading": comic art is characterized by plurality, instability, and tension, so much so that no single formula for interpreting the page can reliably unlock *every* comic. Far from being too simple to warrant analysis, comic art is complex enough to frustrate any attempt at an airtight analytical scheme.

In fact comic art is growing more complex all the time. The form is in flux, becoming more self-conscious in its explorations as creators increasingly recognize the knowledge and sophistication of readers. Ploys once deemed necessary to relieve formal tensions and to settle ambiguities (overdetermined transitions, word/image redundancy, predictable layouts, and so forth) have become less common, as authors have come to expect readers who are experienced, playful, and tolerant of discontinuity. This vision of a knowing readership has changed the art form, for an author's imagining of her audience profoundly influences her sense of form and her willingness to take chances, just as, conversely, the reader's awareness

of form enables her to become the kind of audience the author envisions. As comics readers have become more experienced, comics have traced an arc of development similar to other cultural forms, such as the novel and cinema: away from presentational devices designed to ease audience adjustment and toward a more confident and thorough exploration of the form's peculiar tensions, potentialities, and limits.

This is not to say that today's comics are uniformly more sophisticated than the comics of yesteryear. Indeed, one would be hard-pressed to find a more thoroughgoing exploration of the comics page than the Sundays in George Herriman's *Krazy Kat* (1916–44), which playfully poke at every convention without ever compromising the strip's blend of wry lyricism and thematic depth. Likewise, in the work of the form's pioneers—for example, in Rodolphe Töpffer's epochal series of comics albums (c. 1827–46)—we find continual, and ever-surprising, experimentation. But the interrogation of comics form has recently become more widespread, intensive, and self-conscious. This is true even in the tightly controlled precincts of American newspaper strips, where, for example, Bill Watterson's use of breakdown to juxtapose reality and fantasy (in *Calvin and Hobbes*) has led to comparable moves in many other strips. Yet it is especially true of alternative comics and graphic novels in the wake of Spiegelman's *Maus*. In the alternative comics avant-garde, we find radical reexaminations of form from such respected cartoonists as Chris Ware, whose *ACME Novelty Library* brings a post-Spiegelman rigor to the manipulation of design and color, and France's Marc-Antoine Mathieu (*Julius Corentin Acquefacques, prisonnier des rêves*), who has experimented, dizzyingly, with the design and material packaging of comics-as-books (see Beaty, "Compelling Experimentation"). All of these works point to a growing awareness of "the audience" as experienced, knowledgeable, and eager to recognize its own role in making meaning.

We cannot acknowledge the scope and sophistication of that role as long as we insist on the ease and simplicity of comics. The notion of *ease*, so often mobilized in criticism (even appreciative criticism) of the form, overlooks the complexity and complicity involved in reading comics, reducing this interactive process to the passive registration of a few highly-charged impressions. This is why criticism in English, until very recently, has been unable to distinguish between *skimming* comics and *reading* comics, with the result that critical discussion of the form has been generally impoverished and, at times, irresponsible. My hope is that the above discussion, though it stops short of trying to construct a universal critical scheme, will inspire readers to ask probing questions of the comics they read, questions such as:

• What can I glean from the different codes (images, words, symbols) invoked here? What can I learn from their interaction? How do words and images relate to or approach each other?

• Does the appearance of the written text seem to influence or inflect my reading of it, and if so, how?

• Does there seem to be one unified "message" here, reinforced by the overlapping of codes, or instead a conflict and contradiction between messages?

• How am I to understand this sequence of images, based on what I have to do to connect one image to the next? What is included, and what excluded, from the sequence? How do words and symbols assist, or complicate, my efforts to read this sequence as such?

• How does the layout of this page or surface—the relative size, shape, and positioning of its images—inflect my understanding of the narrative? When I look at this page, am I conscious of its overall design, or of the way I move from one design element to the next? Are there moments at which it helps to be aware of both? How are the boundaries, or margins, of the page used? How are the successive images delimited and juxtaposed?

• What relationship does this page create between time and space? Am I ever in doubt about that relationship?

• How does the design of this publication reinforce or work against its content? Does reading this text feel like witnessing a story, or handling an object, or both?

Such questions, while perhaps impressionistic, provide lenses through which we can more fully appreciate, and more pointedly critique, the comics text.

In fact addressing such questions is a must, not only for the discussion of comics as literature but also for sociological and ideological analyses of comics as artifacts of mass culture. For it is the reader's effort to resolve such questions that positions her vis-à-vis the text, indeed that defines her as "the reader," calling on her to assume a particular role. If reading is an act of reimagining oneself in response to the demands of a text, then we need to consider how comics present their "demands," that is, how they reach out to their readers and urge them to fulfill certain tasks. Comics demand a different order of literacy: they are never transparent, but beckon their readers in specific, often complex ways, by generating tension among their formal elements. Recognition of this complex relationship is prerequisite to grappling with the literary, sociohistorical and ideological aspects of the form—and such a recognition lies behind and indeed motivates the remainder of this study, as we turn our attention to groundbreaking examples of alternative comics.

CHAPTER THREE

A BROADER CANVAS

GILBERT HERNANDEZ'S *HEARTBREAK SOUP*

Between its launch in 1981 and its fissioning into separate projects in 1996, the anthology *Love & Rockets* broke new ground for comics in terms of both content and form. Created by brothers Gilbert, Jaime, and (occasionally) Mario Hernandez,[1] *Love & Rockets* fused underground and mainstream traditions, in the process reaching new audiences for whom such distinctions were moot. Though it at first built on such shopworn genres as superheroics and romance, *Love & Rockets* transcended these conventions, revitalizing long-form comics with new themes, new types of characters, and fresh approaches to narrative technique. In so doing, it became the quintessential alternative comic, indeed gained the status of a brand—so much so that, in 2001, after a five-year hiatus, the Hernandez brothers yielded to reader demand and once again brought their work together under the *Love & Rockets* banner. (Volume 2 of the series continues as of this writing.)

The thematic and formal innovations of *Love & Rockets* were of a piece: *what* the series had to say and *how* it went about saying it were knotted together. This interrelation of theme and form stands out most clearly in Gilbert's cycle of stories about the fictional Central American village of Palomar, a series most often referred to as *Heartbreak Soup*. Over its thirteen years (1983–96), *Heartbreak Soup* yielded a wealth of stories and achieved a novelistic breadth and complexity to which few comics aspire. (Of course it did not do so alone: Jaime's *Locas* series, the "other half" of *Love & Rockets*, is gutsy, complex, and heart-rendingly beautiful—also beyond our present scope, alas.) The Palomar tales demonstrated, bountifully, the art form's potential to evoke complex settings and characters—and to address thorny sociopolitical issues. Indeed *Heartbreak Soup*, at its height, seems nothing less than a profound meditation on the social responsibility and political efficacy of comics.

Happily, readers can now discover the whole of Palomar in one monumental volume, titled simply *Palomar: The Heartbreak Soup Stories* (published in 2003). This single, definitive volume is the best way to dive into Gilbert Hernandez's work. Yet the collected *Palomar* in effect denies its own origins, for it hides the way serialization both enabled and constrained Hernandez's creative process. The growth and eventual contraction of *Heartbreak Soup*, the series, epitomize the challenges faced by long-form comics. Though Hernandez successfully exploited serial publication to give his stories a broader canvas, and in the process developed radical new ways of evoking space and time in comics, serialization also curbed and directed his work, forcing him to confront, in the novel *Poison River* and subsequent efforts, the limits of periodical publishing. The story of *Heartbreak Soup*, in short, is the richest, also one of the most complex and problematic, examples of alternative comics in the long form.

BREAKING NEW GROUND

Love & Rockets announced its difference from the outset: in magazine (roughly 8.5-by-11-inch) rather than comic book form, it introduced themes and characters hitherto unknown in American comics. Specifically, Jaime and Gilbert evoked Southern California's punk rock scene, capturing its rough-and-tumble nature while applying its DIY (do-it-yourself) aesthetic to their own work. (Rock 'n' roll remains a constant reference point throughout *L&R*.) At the same time, Los Bros Hernandez (as they became known) pushed back the horizons of U.S. comics by portraying Mexican-American culture with sensitivity and candor, thus bringing to comics a new sense of (multi)cultural diversity, vitality, and tension. Social and political life in California's barrios, and in the provincial villages of Latin America, became their abiding concerns, indeed the wellsprings of most of their work. In addition, Los Bros defied the long-standing masculine bias of comic books by focusing

on distinctive and complex female characters. These characters, as they matured, mixed caricature, low-key realism, and a refreshingly inclusive sense of beauty. As such, they broke with the fetishism of both mainstream adventure comics, with their feverish celebration of the disciplined, superheroic body, and most underground comix, with their scabrous, at times misogynistic sexual satire. The brothers' thematic innovations—the punk milieu, their eagerness to explore their Latino roots, and their regard for women—inspired fierce loyalty among their readers. For many, alternative comics began with *Love & Rockets*.

Letters from fans in early issues of *L&R* (1983–86) testify to this loyalty. For example, in issue No. 12 (July 1985) a self-styled "hard-core" punk applauds the book for portraying punks "as human beings with gen-yoo-wine personalities rather than the switchblade-wielding Nazi vermin we [are] in the mainstream publications." Similarly, a correspondent in No. 14 (Nov. 1985) praises Jaime's depiction of the hard-core scene, which, he says, contributes to the book's "almost realistic" view of young people, in contrast to the aseptic, "Hardy boys-type" of characterization found in most comic books. In No. 13 (Sept. 1985), one reader lauds the multicultural cast of *Love & Rockets*, calling the book "the first real '*All-American*' comic, in which the viewers find themselves totally immersed in the lives of different racial groups" (a point echoed years later by *The Nation*'s Patrick Markee, who, in a rave review, recognized the world of *L&R* as "the kind of new American place that is almost never identified on our cultural road map" [25–26]). In No. 18 (Sept. 1986), a woman from El Salvador writes, "I am extremely proud of the way you're representing our idiosyncrasy to the rest of the world. . . . You are vindicating our culture and introducing it better than any 'fine' artist."

Regarding gender, in No. 13 a female reader praises Los Bros' positive treatment of women, saying, "I absolutely love the strength of the females you've created. . . . It's about time some comic-book women were strong and human at the same time." In No. 14, likewise, a woman writes of female characters who, at last, "aren't portrayed as meek mouses who hold their men in God-like regard . . . or radical men-haters." Such letters, often from people writing to a comic "for the first time," pepper the early issues of *Love & Rockets*, as do accolades for Los Bros' portrayals of "real life" and "real people." These letters reveal a faithful core readership, one that recognized itself in the brothers' new brand of comics.[2]

Yet this loyalty was sorely tested by the brothers' innovative approach to long-form narrative. As it evolved, *Love & Rockets* demanded much of its audience, as its storylines were often serialized over many issues, creating long, sometimes novel-length, narratives of unprecedented depth and scope. In fact the stories grew in length and complexity throughout the eighties, climaxing between 1990 and 1993 as *Love & Rockets* ran no less than three serialized graphic novels at once—a period Gilbert has described in hindsight as "crazy" (Gaiman, Interview 96). Such extended stories added new layers of meaning and complication to the brothers' respective series: Jaime's open-ended *Locas*, based on the lives of several young women in "Hoppers" (a barrio modeled on the brothers' own hometown of Oxnard, California); and Gilbert's *Heartbreak Soup*, based in Palomar but including various other locales in Latin America and California. These vast, densely populated cycles, built up over the fifty issues of *Love & Rockets*, represent long-form comics at their most ambitious.

This ambition was a matter, not simply of scale, but also of formal daring. If *Love & Rockets*, with its cultural scope and novelistic ambitions, extended the thematic reach of American comics, it also, necessarily, reexamined the formal tensions that constitute comics as such. In particular, *Love & Rockets* explored the tension between the single image and the image-in-series, taking a bold approach to breakdown that enabled Los Bros to work on a wider scale with extraordinary freedom and economy. While in some respects both Gilbert and Jaime cleave to traditional storytelling strategies—for instance, both favor the rectilinear or "grid" layout followed by most Western comics—they nonetheless take a drastic approach to narrative elision, leaping freely between

story elements: characters, locales, and events past and present. Such radical breakdowns demand greater inferential effort from readers. Like the excerpt from Lutes's *Jar of Fools* studied in chapter 2 (fig. 10), Gilbert and Jaime freely manipulate time, space, and point of view, collapsing hours or even years into abrupt transitions, splicing together reality and fantasy, and discerning patterns in widely separated events. Relying on the cohesiveness of the total page (and the familiarity of *L&R* as a series) to guide and reassure their readers, Los Bros pushed the tension between single image and image-in-series to the extreme, transitioning from one element to the next without warning.

This technique, what Joseph Witek (1996) has termed (after McCloud) "uncued closure," pits image, image-series, and page surface against each other. Trusting the wholeness of page and of story to clear up abrupt, nonlinear transitions, Los Bros practice the kind of breakdown demonstrated in, for example, Spiegelman's avant-garde "drawn over two weeks while on the phone," but with more traditional narrative aims. This technique opens up new potentialities in terms of shifting viewpoint, narrative recursion, symbolic juxtaposition, and, above all, the reader's active engagement in interpretation. Los Bros did not adopt this habit simply to exhibit their skill, but to pack as much hard content into their work as possible: over the course of *Love & Rockets* their use of uncued breakdowns responded to, and grew more and more audacious with, the growing complexity of their stories. The thematic thrust of their work encouraged, even demanded, such formal sophistication—again, the form and content of *Love & Rockets* are inseparable.

This is especially true of Gilbert's *Heartbreak Soup*, which emphasizes, first, the town of Palomar as a complex social arena or space; and second, the psychological development of a single family (Palomar's resident matriarch Luba and her domestic lineage) over a span of decades. Palomar's teeming emotional landscape, then, allows Gilbert to explore the possibilities of comics as both a spatial and a temporal art. These seemingly opposite emphases, on space and time, demand much from both creator and reader; yet *Heartbreak Soup*, for all its formal gymnastics, maintains a strong narrative momentum and, always, a visceral urgency. Gilbert's synoptic understanding of space and time, once shared by the reader, allows a tremendous depth of characterization and feeling with a minimum of exposition. Narratively, *Heartbreak Soup* demands a complex evocation of place and history; formally, it cuts to the heart of a paradox essential to comics: that time, in a literal sense, *is* space (again, see chapter 2).

In fact the history of *Heartbreak Soup* shows two overlapping arcs of development. First, Hernandez achieves a thorough understanding of the myriad social relationships within Palomar—a movement that climaxes with the novel *Human Diastrophism* (created 1987–89), an interrogation of individual and social responsibilities within a densely populated "space." Second, Hernandez moves toward an in-depth awareness of historical time and the individual's place in it, an arc that climaxes with the novel *Poison River* (1989–93), a sprawling look at the intertwining of the personal and the political over a span of many years. While *Heartbreak Soup* is by no means the mere sum of these developments, these two foci—space and time—reveal both Hernandez's deep understanding of comics form *and* his determination to use the form for the sake of provocative cultural argument.

FORMAL HABITS AND WHY THEY MATTER

Heartbreak Soup is about a place and the people who inhabit it. As such, it focuses on the development of the community as well as the individual, in contrast to the agonistic individualism that has traditionally dominated comic book fantasy. Whereas most comic books favor lone protagonists who have been clearly set apart from society, Gilbert's stories acknowledge, even depend upon, the energy and variousness of communal interaction. More specifically, they emphasize the always complex relationship between personal anxieties and desires and the constraints, opportunities, and frictions of social life. For Gilbert, individual psychology and communal

interplay go hand in hand: insofar as *Heartbreak Soup* is about desire and disappointment (as its title suggests), it argues that such feelings are gregarious. The social whirl of Palomar arises from, and sparks, individual passions. Indeed, individual depth and social breadth, held in balance, account for much of the series' appeal. No other series in contemporary American comics features a cast as rich, or as complexly interrelated, and few focus so resolutely on the complications of life among family, friends, and community. The beauty of *Heartbreak Soup* (as of brother Jaime's *Locas* series, but to an even greater degree) lies not simply in its colorful individual characters but also in the depth and unpredictability of their interaction.

Given this emphasis on social life, *Heartbreak Soup* presented a formal challenge, namely, how to focus on subtle, often unspoken emotions and relationships without sacrificing the energy of social interaction or freighting the page heavily with exposition. This is not to insist that exposition has no place in comics, or that all comics should move quickly; in fact Hernandez has sometimes resorted to extensive narration (for example, "For the Love of Carmen"). But in general *Heartbreak Soup* depicts life lived on the run and catches its characters in medias res; readers are expected to pick up insights on the fly, as they eavesdrop for a moment here, a moment there. Life in Palomar, after all, is not ruminative; the stories demand brisk movement as well as emotional clarity. These demands had a salutary effect on Hernandez as a cartoonist, for, impelled by the complexity of Palomar, he synthesized a novel approach to comics storytelling, drawing on the raw materials of comic books, comic strips, folklore, literature, and film. Spurred by—and in turn spurring—brother Jaime's efforts, Gilbert developed a distinctive repertoire of techniques suited to the kind of stories he wanted to tell.

Building up such a repertoire, I submit, is what comic artists do to harness the tensions inherent in the form and turn them to advantage. The experienced cartoonist continually develops, or seeks to develop, distinctive ways to organize this inherently unstable form; in other words, each artist strives toward his or her own formal habits, or *protocols*. Such protocols are ways of seeking fitness: habitual means of balancing the disparate elements of comics, so as to insure the harmony and mutual reinforcement of form and content.

Faced with the challenge of evoking a complex social world, Hernandez developed distinctive protocols in three areas: one, his approach to drawing characters, which, while often broadly stylized, nonetheless captures subtle nuances of expression and body language; two, his panel compositions, which often position characters visually within a dynamic social context; and three, his interpanel transitions, often abrupt and uncued, which, again, allow him to cover long distances (spatially and temporally) without sacrificing either energy or coherence. While none of these strategies is unique to Hernandez, his combination of them is radical, a quirky and original response to the narrative problems he has set out to solve.

The first of these three areas, his approach to drawing characters, concerns both *style*, that is, the degree of abstractness, and *technique* in the strict sense, that is, the finesse of the rendering (see Eisner, *Comics and Sequential Art* 151, 157). These qualities are notoriously difficult to write about, the more so when faced by styles as polymorphous as those of the Hernandez brothers. Los Bros' distinctive ways of drawing, at once naturalistic and broadly comic, were synthesized from a wide range of graphic influences, most notably, the rough-hewn fabulism of classic Marvel artists Steve Ditko and Jack Kirby; the coy sex appeal of *Archie* comics, under artists Harry Lucey and Dan DeCarlo; the understated humor of Charles Schulz and Hank Ketcham; and the ironic, angst-filled cartooning of R. Crumb. (Such eclecticism has since become one of the hallmarks of alternative comics.) Jaime, for his part, is known as a master of stark, chiaroscuro technique, and has achieved a startling degree of realism; Gilbert, on the other hand, has developed a wilder, more expressionistic approach, strongly influenced by the comic distortions of such artists as Ditko, Crumb, and *Mad*'s Harvey Kurtzman (Fiore, Groth, and Powers 98–105; Knowles 51).

In fact Gilbert's style, though superficially plain, is complex insofar as it reconciles naturalism with caricatural abstraction. He employs a sliding scale of realism, drawing some characters (for example, children) broadly and wildly, but others (for example, prominent adult characters) in a more restrained, naturalistic way. Such inconsistency is of course native to the art of cartooning, but Gilbert goes further, at times drawing even his most realistic characters with cartoony abandon, especially when they are in the grip of strong feelings like fear or rage (a technique common in Japanese *manga* but less so in American comics).

However, it is the second and third points, Hernandez's compositions and interpanel transitions, that most demand study. Here film theory provides an apt language for analysis—notwithstanding the problems presented by importing the argot of one discipline to another. Recent studies of comics (as noted in chapter 2) have resisted the comparison to film, so as to underline the specificity of the art form; yet, as Robert C. Harvey has argued, the language of film can be a useful, albeit limited, tool for discussing the arrangement of elements within a comics panel (*Art of the Funnies* 17). Indeed the intuitive use of film terms has been a hallmark of much comics criticism. This comics/cinema analogy, admittedly inexact, has a special urgency in the case of Hernandez, because he has often cited film as a major, perhaps *the* major, influence on his methods (see Fiore, Groth, and Powers 87–88, and Groth's preface to Hernandez, *Chelo's Burden*). Though careful to point out that he is "not a frustrated filmmaker," Hernandez ranks his artistic influences as "films, other comics and then novels . . . , in that order" (Hernandez to the author, 22 Mar. 2000).

The inevitability of the comics/cinema comparison, and its insufficiency, raises a larger point. Cartoonists, as they work their way toward their own distinctive protocols, draw inspiration from (at times consciously invoke) other objects, media, and art forms, such as film. For instance, Spiegelman's *Maus* (as remarked in chapter 2) invokes the materiality of found objects in order to stress the diaristic nature of his story: images of tickets, notebook pages, and other printed artifacts are superimposed over Spiegelman's characters, as if he were assembling a family album or scrapbook. Spiegelman is one of many comic artists for whom layout, typography, and the physical design of books are important signifiers in themselves—artists for whom print and paper are privileged reference points, and the tension between experience and object is paramount. In contrast, Gilbert Hernandez (with rare exceptions) downplays the idea of the object itself and indeed draws much of his inspiration from the language of movies. Despite his immersion in comics, his protocols have been shaped by the signifying practices of film.

Indeed, as William Anthony Nericcio observes, Hernandez repeatedly uses and comments on "the dynamics of cinema" ("Artif[r]acture" 95). His work recalls traditional narrative cinema in specific ways, mimicking the movie camera's capacity for naturalism, intimacy, and movement. The artist himself, while distinguishing between film and comics, acknowledges his reliance on movies as "the best visual reference as far as capturing a scene" (Hernandez to author), an admission that sheds light on his habits of panel composition. In fact Hernandez's panels favor certain filmic devices, which he uses to pose characters in close relation both to the reader and to each other: extreme close-ups, close two-shots, foreground framing, and deep focus, that is, extreme depth of field. These protocols insure that the relationships among characters (and between each character and the whole of Palomar) are established and upheld with absolute clarity.

Individual *close-ups* and *two-shots* enable Hernandez to capture his characters' most intense emotions, whether openly displayed or barely concealed behind carefully composed façades. The individual close-up allows such recurrent devices as direct asides to the reader (used sparingly early on, later abandoned) and blank, silent panels revealing lone characters in unguarded moments of reaction or contemplation. In a strip whose principals are usually shown in motion, such still moments serve as dramatic punctuation, offering revealing snapshots of individual character. Similarly, the two-shot

captures intimate exchanges, whether fierce, gentle, humorous, or erotic. In particular, what I call the *vis-à-vis shot* (that is, a close-up of two facing characters in profile) stresses the mutuality of the exchange by giving equal emphasis to both parties.

Foreground framing reinforces this sense of intimacy and serves the added purpose of strengthening our sense of continuity during exchanges that extend over several panels. In each panel, the "framing" of one figure by another (or part of another) in the near foreground reminds us of the physical relationship between the characters and implies a larger space or world "outside" the panels (for example, figs. 27, 28). This protocol evokes the shot/reverse shot convention of classical film editing, though without its restrictive emphasis on a single, consistent axis of movement (the so-called 180° rule). Clearly, this is post-cinematic cartooning: the looming figures in the foreground affront the picture plane in the same way that foregrounded figures may affront a camera's lens. Instead of ordering his fictive world around the reader's omniscient eye, Hernandez thrusts readers into the midst of intimate exchanges, as if we were eavesdropping. In such exchanges, he frequently uses silhouetting, filling the outline of the foreground character with black to simplify the composition and direct the reader's eye to the main figure. Like the close two-shot, such foreground framing insists on the relationship, at once spatial and emotional, between the characters, and lends variety to what could otherwise become repetitive, numbing sequences full of talking heads.

Likewise, Hernandez's *depth of field* emphasizes the complexity of the larger social milieu of Palomar. In "deep focus"—I am using the photographic term metaphorically, of course—interactions can take place across wide distances; the "space" between foreground and background characters can establish the complexity of a setting, or underscore the emotions of an interchange (for example, characters shouting angrily across a distance, or keeping their distance from each other). In fact *Heartbreak Soup* is filled with such "deep" images, panels in which elements on different planes are unobtrusively combined, sometimes to score a specific narrative point, often simply to evoke the variety and unpredictability of Palomar as a place (for example, fig. 26). This habitual use of deep focus helps to create not only a spatial but also a social context. If Palomar does come to life as a place, as a thoroughly imagined and imaginable world, it is partly because Hernandez's multiplane compositions provide a perfect graphic setting for his interest in community.

In short, Hernandez's panel compositions reflect his themes. Yet, in addition, his focus on community influences the way he breaks down stories *into* panels, that is, the way he handles the tensions between image and image-series and between sequence and page surface. An analogy to cinema may again prove useful, but in this case it is the failure of the analogy that helps: while breakdown is roughly comparable to cinematic editing or montage, it differs insofar as the page gathers multiple images into a single surface, a static unit of meaning through which the reader can move at will. As *Heartbreak Soup* progresses, Hernandez capitalizes more and more on this static, *readable* quality, relying on the integrity of the overall page to clarify drastic "cutting" or ellipsis. Though powerfully influenced by cinema, he trumps traditional narrative film by favoring abrupt, unsignaled cuts and interpolations between images. On screen, such jarring cuts (though increasingly common) are still most often used for the sake of visceral shock; they conjure sudden, disorienting flashbacks or visions, momentarily jeopardizing clarity and coherence. Yet such transitions make perfect sense in the printed medium of the comics page, for print, as McCloud points out, allows *before* and *after* to remain ever-visible, ever-present, elements (104). The static nature of comics permits a self-paced reading, slow or fast according to the reader's desires, even recursive if need be, which allows Hernandez to make sudden cuts between panels without sacrificing the continuity or the easy, unassuming naturalism of his stories. This technique, Witek's "uncued closure," responds to and becomes bolder with the growing complexity of Hernandez's story cycle. Combined with the compositional strategies described above, such abrupt breakdowns

enable Hernandez to keep track of the overlapping relationships within his ever-expanding repertory company of characters.

BUILDING UP PALOMAR

Heartbreak Soup's emphasis on these relationships is evident from the very first story in the cycle, "Sopa de Gran Pena" (*Love & Rockets* No. 3–4, 1983; *Palomar* 13–57).[3] While "Sopa" hinges on a tragic love triangle between Manuel, Soledad, and Pipo, it also introduces the mysterious *bañadora* (bathgiver) Luba, and highlights the friendship between "the guys," a group of adolescent boys composed of Vicente, Satch, Israel, Jesus, and the newcomer Heraclio. The adult lives of these men, covered in such later tales as "The Laughing Sun," will account for much of *Heartbreak Soup*'s continuity; in "Sopa," however, the relationships that bind the five together are as yet tentative and only part of a larger web of social connections. This larger context includes many relationships (for example, Carmen and Pipo, Luba and Chelo) that will figure more prominently in the stories ahead.

The complexity of such interlocking relationships becomes clear in the story "Ecce Homo" (*Love & Rockets* No. 10, 1984; *Palomar* 145–60). "Ecce Homo" takes place at a town picnic or similar gathering and shows Hernandez's secure grasp of Palomar as a community. Here Borro, the ex-sheriff of Palomar, reappears, virtually reinvented since his early appearance in "Sopa"; here Tonantzin Villaseñor, only briefly glimpsed before, is reintroduced and deepened, her promiscuity and desperate need for self-affirmation revealed. The relationship between Pipo and her abusive husband Gato (an ironic reversal of his unrequited longings in "Sopa") brings added tension and complexity. The coterie of male friends established in "Sopa" remains more or less intact, apart from Jesus (now a convict), but their relationships have grown and changed, and Heraclio's role has become more central. "Ecce Homo" is a pageant of Palomar's citizenry, driven not by any particular plot or crisis but rather by the various

Figure 26. Gilbert Hernandez, selected pages from "Ecce Homo." *Palomar* 151, 154. © 2004 Gilbert Hernandez. Used with permission.

relationships that Hernandez wants to establish, re-establish, or underline. As such, the story exploits Hernandez's arsenal of narrative techniques to the fullest (fig. 26).

Reading "Ecce Homo," one has the feeling of roving through a large party, encountering and later re-encountering various characters whose ties to each other are just beginning to come to light. Blending the many elements of *Heartbreak Soup*'s continuity into an organic whole, "Ecce" solidifies our sense of the town's collective identity. The story allows us to "stroll" through the scene, taking in relationships that connect the various characters to each other. Indeed, "Ecce" contains playful elements that suggest that Hernandez is not only taking roll but taking stock of all that has happened in *Love and Rockets* thus far. Besides the casts of *Heartbreak Soup* and other Gilbert stories, various characters drawn by brothers Jaime and Mario make cameos. (In fact most of Jaime's major characters appear, as

do a number of non-*Love and Rockets* "characters"—for example, Frida Kahlo, R. Crumb, Gilbert Hernandez and his wife, Carol Kovinick-Hernandez, and several skeletons inspired by Jose Guadalupe Posada.) Thus, as we wander through the Palomar scene, eavesdropping on its featured players, we also glimpse other visitors to this fictive world, fanciful visitors who remind us that we too are merely peeking into something larger and more complex. At once we are swept into the life of Palomar, yet reminded of our visitor status.

"Ecce Homo" tells much that we must know if we are to understand the relationships and issues at stake in later stories. Here for the first time Luba's eldest daughter, Maricela, emerges as a distinct character, and we learn, albeit indirectly, that Luba abuses her. Here we witness Tonantzin falling prey to male flattery and in effect prostituting herself to shore up her uncertain sense of self-worth. Here too we see Borro's crude advances on Luba and his willingness to strike out violently when his desires are thwarted. Beneath the apparent frivolity of the cameos and the drunken good humor of characters like Heraclio are undercurrents of tension—dark and disturbing elements that will emerge most fully in later tales. (As in Posada, so here: light and darkness, vitality and death, not only coexist but join hands.)

"Ecce Homo" represents a stretch for Hernandez the cartoonist, as it packs an entire town into sixteen pages. Here his compositional and breakdown techniques are in constant practice, choreographing the interplay between at least two dozen established characters (again, see fig. 26). The approach is cinematic, yes, but also succinct, graphically playful, and, as ever, wonderfully cartoony. Two-shots, foreground framing, silhouetting, shot/reverse shot exchanges, and deep-focus compositions depict the complex social workings of Palomar, with its mingled friendships, loves, lusts, antagonisms, and misunderstandings. Throughout "Ecce," Hernandez maintains continuity of action, yet achieves a startling graphic repleteness and variety, as well as subtle emotional nuances—all the while positioning foreground and background details to suggest an impinging social context.

If "Ecce Homo" romps through Hernandez's imaginary world, then the two-part story "Duck Feet" (*Love & Rockets* Nos. 17–18, 1986; *Palomar* 259–86) shakes this world to its foundations. Struck by an epidemic brought on by the wrath of a disgruntled *bruja* (witch), the Palomar of "Duck Feet" reveals a heretofore unknown potential for violence: Sheriff Chelo inadvertently kills the fugitive Roberto, and the headstrong Tonantzin, acting as Chelo's deputy, is later assaulted by Roberto's gun-wielding cousin Geraldo. Meanwhile, Luba remains stuck in the bottom of a hole, despite her daughter Guadalupe's anxious efforts to free her. As the epidemic sweeps the town, many characters are physically transformed, their features grotesquely mottled, even distorted, by the symptoms of the disease. Several scenes take on a frankly nightmarish quality, as Guadalupe stumbles through the streets, retching and hallucinating. Hernandez's breakdowns seamlessly blend reality, memory, and vision, as when, for example, Guadalupe's fond memories of her mother give way to a more frightening vision of Luba, which in turn gives way to the reality of Tonantzin shaking the bleary, vomiting child (281). Again, Hernandez's handling of form responds to the dramatic demands of his narrative. As the scattered members of his cast converge on the same moment of confrontation (fig. 27), his breakdowns grow more ambitious, the transitions more abrupt, leaping unexpectedly from (in McCloudian terms) subject to subject and action to action. The breakdown of action and the design of the entire page reinforce each other: narrow panels crowd together, creating a staccato rhythm, which climaxes with discovery, violence, deliverance, and relief.

The final page of "Duck Feet" (fig. 28), a quiet dénouement after a frantic tale, is as radical a move as anything that has come before. An even grid of nine wordless panels, each one showing a different subject, suggests the apparent calm that has settled over Palomar in the wake of the epidemic, and tells us what has become of all of the featured characters in the story. Disconnected as the images are, they reveal what we need to know about each character and the town as a whole. In the first panel, for instance, we see the outside of Luba's house, where, we know, Luba and Guadalupe are convalescing, while in the second and third panels we see the rest of her family at work. Panels four and seven, one right above the other, show the sisters, Tonantzin and Diana, respectively: Tonantzin has been changed most by recent events, and seems lost in thought, unconcerned with the masculine brawl going on (no doubt for her favor) behind her; Diana, below, seems to be running to escape from thinking. In the penultimate panel we see Geraldo, confined to prison, his bandaged arm a reminder of the tale's violence, while the last panel shows the retreat of the mysterious bruja, ending the story on a question mark. Here transitioning from image to image (that is, resolving the tension between single image and image-series) requires divining a pattern from a string of apparent non sequiturs, silent and open to interpretation.

Figure 27. The climax of "Duck Feet." *Palomar* 283. © 2004 Gilbert Hernandez. Used with permission.

Figure 28. The dénouement of "Duck Feet." *Palomar* 286. © 2004 Gilbert Hernandez. Used with permission.

THE COMMUNITY IN CRISIS: HUMAN DIASTROPHISM

Thematically and formally, the novel-length *Human Diastrophism* (*Love & Rockets* Nos. 21–26, 1987–88; *Palomar* 320–424) trumps "Duck Feet" by placing the town in the grips of an even greater crisis. This genuine graphic novel, subsequently revised and collected in the book *Blood of Palomar* (1989), tested the serial magazine form of *Love & Rockets* as never before, summing up and extending *Heartbreak Soup* with few expository concessions to its core periodical readership. Sharp, unsentimental, and complex, *Human Diastrophism* represents a milestone in Hernandez's depiction of Palomar as social space and a pivotal moment of self-reflexive examination, as he interrogates the social and political effectiveness of comic art. The novel stands as one of the signal examples of alternative comics from the 1980s.

Diastrophism echoes "Sopa de Gran Pena" in many ways, recalling or reworking some of its basic themes and motifs. However, unlike the bucolic setting of "Sopa," the Palomar of *Diastrophism* seethes with anxiety, its fragile community jeopardized by violence, political terror, and disintegrating relationships. Here Hernandez creates his most complex network of interactions, pushing his techniques to the utmost to capture the way individual behavior affects the social dynamic. Indeed the crux of *Diastrophism* is the question of personal responsibility for the social good, yet ironically much of its dramatic tension stems from characters who remain unaware of, or unmoved by, the needs of the community as a whole.

Broadly speaking, *Diastrophism* depicts traumatic changes that overtake Palomar and its citizens, changes triggered by the intrusion of the outside world into the previously cloistered village. The most obvious public crisis in the novel is the search for a serial murderer at large in the town, whose random attacks strike up a panic in Palomar's intimate population. As the search for the killer gathers steam, and the panic escalates, a horde of mischievous monkeys appears out of nowhere and sweeps the town like an epidemic, attacking people and vandalizing houses. As omens of the encroaching modern world, the monkeys symbolize the townspeople's fears, yet also provide a cathartic outlet for, and welcome distraction from, those fears. Hence the townspeople set about killing and cremating them in earnest. The resulting mayhem, at once risibly comic and brutally graphic, underscores the novel's prevailing tone of violence and hysteria.

Within this climate of terror, many of Palomar's individual citizens undergo diastrophic (roughly, "earth-shaking") changes in their own lives. Most notably, Luba (by now familiar as a single mother of four and the proprietor of the local bathhouse) pursues her own fleeting youth in the person of Khamo, an old lover and the father of two of her children. Khamo has returned to town unexpectedly as a worker in an archaeological dig—ironically, the same dig that has brought the killer to town (though, unlike Khamo, the killer is a returning Palomar native). Luba's family, already strained by her neglect, begins to unravel as her affair with Khamo revives, then falters, shattering her confidence and driving her into a series of aimless sexual encounters. In particular, Luba's daughter Maricela, driven by her mother's violent abuse, plots to leave Palomar with

Riri, with whom she has been pursuing a clandestine lesbian affair. Luba, oblivious to all but her own need for affirmation, remains aloof to Palomar's social crisis, unaware of the very complexities on which Hernandez's narrative technique insists.

Meanwhile, Tonantzin worries her family and friends with prophetic talk of an impending holocaust. Set off by the paranoiac writings of the convict Geraldo (the very man who assaulted her in "Duck Feet"), Tonantzin sees Palomar as a fragile pawn in a struggle between global superpowers, and her mind is filled with images of the apocalypse. Despite the well-meaning interference of friends and family, Tonantzin adopts the traditional garb of her Indian ancestors in a vain effort to make a "political statement" (352). Inadvertently, she too provides the townspeople with much-needed distraction, a bitter irony given her lone commitment to meaningful social action.

Tonantzin's sudden politicization underlines her long-established naiveté. Named for the Aztec mother goddess, Tonantzin ("Revered Mother") is nonetheless an object of gossip and ridicule in the town. She bears the onus of a scandalous past, including, ironically enough, a series of abortions resulting from her prodigal sexuality. As vendor of the local dietary staple, fried *babosas* (slugs), Tonantzin provides for her people much like her mythic namesake; yet, as established in "Ecce Homo" and later stories such as "An American in Palomar" and "Duck Feet," her character has a tragic dimension. Ill-educated and lacking both confidence and purpose, she is credulous, rash, and easily manipulated. *Diastrophism* finds her seeking a new purpose in life but at the behest of Geraldo, a millenarian religious zealot. The very inadequacy of Tonantzin's would-be "political statement" makes it almost unbearably poignant.

In contrast to Tonantzin, Humberto (a new character) rejects direct social action, seeking instead to take part in the life of the town obliquely, through the medium of his art. An aspiring young artist, Humberto struggles to educate himself, and indeed redefine himself, by mastering the craft of drawing. He becomes a vehicle for Hernandez's own searching self-examination. Thus, as Nericcio has argued, the novel becomes partly "a *Bildungsroman* of a strug-gling neophyte artist—Goethe's *Wilhelm Meister* re-imagined pen in hand south of the border" (99–100). Thanks to the patronage of Heraclio, Palomar's resident teacher, Humberto is suddenly immersed in the work of his artistic forebears (Van Gogh, Picasso, Munch, Modigliani, and others), a dunking that proves at once inspiring and intimidat-ing. "I had no idea they had gone this far . . . that you *could* go this far," he muses. "What have I been doing?" (336). Thus immersed, Humberto must grapple with a particularly acute case of the anxiety of influence. Galvanized *and* frightened, he now sees everything through the lens of his art.

It is Humberto and Luba, both emotionally iso-lated characters, who serve as focal points for Her-nandez's exploration of social responsibility. Neither seems aware of the ripples of consequence spread-ing from his/her actions. Luba struggles to salvage her confidence after losing her hold on Khamo, heedless of the town's disintegration. Just so, Humberto tries desperately to improve his art and to define its social place and value, regardless of the chaos erupting around him. As Luba puts herself and her family at risk through her random sexual liaisons (including one with the killer), so Humberto puts himself and others at risk through his single-minded dedication to his art.

"MY WORK SPEAKS FOR ITSELF"

Humberto's desire to improve is prompted not only by the well-meaning patronage of Heraclio but also by his desperate need to learn how to draw "for real"—that is, to improve his craft—before he breaks the rules. This need is impressed on him by his occasional companion Augustin, who insists that Humberto's work is "fast and sloppy and fake" (344). Spurred by Augustin's criticisms, Humberto resolves that he must learn to draw realistically, from life, before he can do "stuff as good and wild as them *real* artists" (346). Unfortunately, Humberto's quest to draw "for real" exposes him to a third influence, one that forever alters his life and his art.

While eavesdropping with his drawing tablet in hand, he witnesses the killer Tomaso's attempted murder of the young woman Chancla (fig. 29). Haunted by images of the stabbing, Humberto does not come forward to testify as to what he has seen, but instead withdraws into a world of his own, in which he compulsively replays the event over and over by drawing it. In one panel, we see him lying naked, arms spread as if he is being crucified; the light from a window above casts a shadowy cross over his body, as he lies on what appear to be pages from his drawing tablet (fig. 30). Zooming in for a close-up, Hernandez emphasizes Humberto's eyes, which are now sunken, shadowed, and staring, as if fixed on a single object. From here on, Humberto's eyes, often shaded or distorted, will be his most promi-nent characteristic. A later panel, thrust between two scenes without explanation, underscores this, showing Humberto retching into a toilet, his sunken, bloodshot eyes revealing a nausea as much psycho-logical as physical (357). Still later pages emphasize the likeness between Humberto's eyes and the eyes of the monkeys terrorizing the town (368, 375). Thus the artist's eyes, his means of observing the world, also become the outward sign of his trauma. Humberto is scarred by his own attempt to play the role of dispassionate observer.

From this point on, Humberto creates disturbed and violent images that suggest a struggle to assimi-late the events in Palomar into his art. Now town characters such as Luba and Tonantzin are even more wildly distorted than usual in his drawings (367); now he sketches the killer with an angelic halo, or a beatific smile (364, 398). As he grapples with the anxiety of influence, fanned by knowledge of his artistic forebears, Humberto also grapples with the violence that threatens to tear his world apart. This double confrontation unleashes a flood of frightening imagery from his pencil.

Hernandez incorporates Humberto's images into his own, many of them homages to such famed artists as Picasso and Munch (for example, 343, 367). At the same time, Hernandez himself swipes liberally from these artists (for example, 396). These homages conflate Hernandez and Humberto, author

Figure 29. "Human Diastrophism." *Palomar* 347 (excerpt). © 2004 Gilbert Hernandez. Used with permission.

and character. For example, a Picassoesque, Cubist rendering of Luba on the cover of *Love & Rockets* No. 21 (also the back cover of the collected *Blood of Palomar*) serves as both an introduction to Hernandez's opus and a suggestive sample of Humberto's work, underlining the ambitions of both (fig. 31). These intelligent swipes suggest a complex relationship between, in T. S. Eliot's Modernist formulation, tradition and the individual talent, while the narrative itself probes the social consequences of that relationship (consequences so often neglected in Modernist orthodoxy).

Through Humberto, Hernandez reasserts those consequences. More precisely, he questions the power of art to intervene in social and political crises,

and probes the issue of the artist's social liability. Indeed, if *Human Diastrophism* were to have an epigraph, it might well be Susan Sontag's dictum, "The person who intervenes cannot record; the person who is recording cannot intervene" (*On Photography* 12). This potent aphorism, culled from Sontag's watershed critique of photos and photo-making, implicitly calls into question the efficacy of *all* artistic media. Sontag redefines the camera, not as a window open to the world but as a *screen* that can shield its user from direct contact with, and responsibility for, the world. More broadly, her argument challenges us to think about the responsibilities of artists to the world they strive to document.

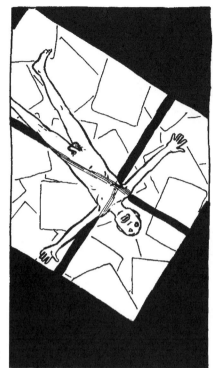

Figure 30. "Human Diastrophism."
Palomar 351 (excerpt). © 2004 Gilbert
Hernandez. Used with permission.

This question of art's political accountability stems from the inevitable conflict between activism and aestheticism: Can an artist give plastic form to political concerns, without aestheticizing and thus neutralizing those concerns? Can art usefully intervene in social crises? With characteristic audacity, Hernandez delivers this challenge via the unexpected vehicle of the comics magazine, a mass-produced, collectible artifact. More explicitly than his previous stories, *Diastrophism* examines the social responsibilities of all artists (implicitly including comic artists) and presages a growing self-consciousness in his work. Thus the novel takes a pivotal position in that work.

Humberto himself is self-conscious to a fault. His art becomes his world—and it is an ugly world indeed, as we see when Luba, stood up by Khamo, ducks into Humberto's house to escape from the drizzling rain. When Luba remarks that his art is "ugly as hell," Humberto replies curtly, "How else do you expect someone to draw hell." Goaded by her intrusion, he claims not to care about anyone, thus rejecting any form of human connection, any

personal responsibility for the townspeople, the unknowing subjects of his art (362). By this point he has completely withdrawn from social contact.

His withdrawal has a dire effect on himself and the community. Though Humberto alone possesses the secret of the killer's identity, he cannot or at least does not divulge it, choosing instead to paper the town with drawings of the killer, in hopes that his work will testify for him. Obsessed with becoming a great artist, Humberto cannot intervene directly in the public crisis but tries to influence events through his drawings alone, guided by his belief that "great art reveals the deepest truths" (390). When confronted with his drawings, he refuses to explicitly identify the culprit, claiming, "My work speaks for itself" (386). Unfortunately, his refusal to testify verbally allows Tomaso to go free, and to kill others; thus his art proves not enough to stem the chaos and social collapse taking place around him. Ultimately, Humberto becomes a pariah, cast out of Hernandez's carefully constructed society for his refusal to act. Through Humberto, then, Hernandez attacks the artist's traditional presumptive role as a

Figure 31. Front cover, *Love & Rockets* No. 21. © 2004 Gilbert Hernandez. Used with permission.

marginal or elevated social observer, and questions the social efficacy of art itself.

This question grows even more urgent as the novel reaches its end (reader be warned: a big spoiler follows). On the final page, Humberto and Augustin meet again, and once again the talk is about art (fig. 32). Humberto, despised and forlorn, despairs of drawing ever again, but Augustin, unpretentious as ever, urges him to help paint a mural that, as Augustin puts it, will "kick everybody's ass" (424). Symbolically, the prospect of the mural suggests

Humberto's potential to turn necessity to advantage and once again challenge his community through his art, this time freed of any social constraints or "expectations." The proposed mural (implicitly, a graphic narrative, like comics) not only reminds us of Humberto's sketches of the killer but also recalls, first, the revolutionary political *muralismo* of such Mexican artists as Siqueiros and Rivera, both of whom are mentioned early in the novel (325), and second, the comic book form itself, which has traditionally been unburdened by high expectations. By

Figure 32. The final page of "Human Diastrophism." *Palomar* 424. © 2004 Gilbert Hernandez. Used with permission.

suggesting such a public and narrative form, Augustin holds out the possibility that art can still rock the world, can still challenge and change the status quo. Humberto is intrigued by his friend's offer, but their conversation is suddenly interrupted by a snowstorm of white ash that falls from the heavens, blanketing the town. This ash, prophesied earlier in the novel, symbolizes an act of sacrifice that tries to go beyond talk or art—a sacrifice that has already happened, though Humberto and Augustin know nothing about it.

"TALK OR ART OR PROPAGANDA JUST ISN'T ENOUGH"

It is the now-politicized Tonantzin who offers up this sacrifice, in witness to an unspecified cause. Three pages before the novel's end, Tonantzin is glimpsed beneath a tree that the townspeople call Pintor's Tree, under which ghosts are believed to gather (as shown as far back as "Sopa de Gran Pena"). Yet she has already left Palomar with Luba's erstwhile lover, Khamo. The reader, thus alerted, begins to suspect that something has happened to Tonantzin out there in the larger world (421). Yet Hernandez, in a telling comment on our media-dependence, reveals her actual fate only indirectly, through a television screen as seen by American eyes. The transition is sudden, unexpected:

Somewhere north of the border, photojournalist Howard Miller steps from his darkroom (fig. 33). His girlfriend, Cathy, watching TV news, recounts with horror the self-immolation of "this girl" involved in "this protest in front of some embassy somewhere" (422). Pointing to the screen, Cathy retells the event, her voiceover commentary serving as soundtrack for a series of panels that reveal the girl's sacrifice. Code versus code, image versus word—Cathy's uncomprehending monologue accompanies successive images of Tonantzin's burning (we see Khamo trying to save her). Miller, ugly-American protagonist of the earlier story, "An American in Palomar," has no idea that "this girl" is a girl he once wooed and exploited: Tonantzin.

Cathy's position as spectator is our own. Shocked by televised images of real-life violence, she doesn't know how to respond. Revealingly, she likens "this girl" to "monks" burning themselves in some of Howard's photographs (an allusion, presumably, to Malcolm Browne's photos of a Vietnamese *bonze* burning himself in protest against the Diem regime in June 1963—a defining example of the relationship between photojournalist and subject). Cathy then tries to distance herself from the event, wondering if the girl was "crazy" to do something so "extreme." In reply, Howard suggests that she may simply have been someone "deeply hurt from seeing the world around them go to shit," but confesses that, in this girl's case, "he wouldn't know" (423). (Though he *should* know, in this girl's case.) Then he argues that, based on what he has seen with his own eyes, there are times when "talk or art or propaganda just isn't enough," when love motivates people to make such sacrifices for the sake of change. His words have the air of sincerity, and his simple statement, "that's just the way I feel," seems sympathetic.

Yet, in the final panel of the novel's penultimate page, Howard Miller slips effortlessly from these feelings to the question that has really been occupying his thoughts: the success of a new photographic "effect" that he has been trying out. In other words, *Art* is still his immediate concern. He asks Cathy's opinion but receives no immediate reply. Cathy is disturbed by what she has just seen, as her faraway expression suggests, whereas Howard is inured to it all and able to segue easily from appalling tragedy to questions of technique. Thus Howard's dialogue in the preceding panels rings false, his concern as insubstantial and inconstant as a fleeting TV image. Far from connecting him with the tragedy of what Cathy has witnessed (and what he himself, presumably, has witnessed time and again), Howard's camera—his window on the world—has shielded him from feeling.

This brutal coda resonates with Humberto's earlier abdication of responsibility and gives the novel a shattering thematic punch. Hernandez implies that, while art may open up new worlds to our appreciation, it can also insulate us from tragedy by aestheticizing

Figure 33. The climax of "Human Diastrophism." *Palomar* 423. © 2004 Gilbert Hernandez. Used with permission.

it, turning it into a series of images and objects for our consumption. This is precisely the dilemma outlined by Sontag, when she refers to taking photographs as a way of *refusing* as well as certifying experience (9); it is precisely the problem dramatized by Humberto's art. Can images, removed from experience, wake us up to what is happening in the world, or do they merely inoculate us, deadening our sensibilities and numbing our empathy?

The last page of the book, again, suggests the revolutionary potential of art, but threatens to smother that hope under a blizzard of ash, a symbolic reminder of Tonantzin's seemingly futile sacrifice (424). As the clouded sky fills with flecks of ash, the word "FIN," superimposed over the last panel, gives the novel an apocalyptic finality—no less devastating for the knowledge that, yes, okay, there will be future Palomar stories. (In fact some of my students, unfamiliar with the larger arc of *Heartbreak Soup*, have interpreted this apocalypse quite literally as the end of the world.) The ending reeks of despair. Despite this, *Human Diastrophism* leaves room to hope for an ambitious, socially responsive comic art, one that can indeed "kick everybody's ass." In fact, *Diastrophism* seems to have energized Hernandez, daring him to push even harder: having violated the sheltered world of Palomar this way, he pressed on without flinching. After a brief respite from long-form work,[4] his next novels, *Poison River* and *Love and Rockets X*, continued to explore the political turmoil and social unease confronted in *Diastrophism*. Thus Hernandez challenged his fellow comic artists to seek greater cultural and political relevance.

ACCELERATING FORMAL RHYTHMS

If *Human Diastrophism* is, in the end, a meditation on the power or impotence of art as a social instrument, it is also, not coincidentally, a rigorous test of comic art's ability to depict complex social interaction—not to mention a bravura exercise of Hernandez's narrative skills. In fact its very form insists on the social connectedness that Humberto tries to deny. Thus, as the novel progresses, its formal rhythms become more intense, its breakdowns bolder and more elaborate, in response to the town's mounting hysteria. In the novel's last third, having established the overlapping relationships among the characters, Hernandez shifts gears rapidly, jumping from one relationship or plotline to the next. As in "Ecce Homo" and "Duck Feet," again, the community of Palomar takes on a life of its own, growing ever more frenzied and complex.

Early in the novel, Hernandez uses fluid and unsurprising transitions from panel to panel and subject to subject, in order to show the essential connectedness of all the goings-on in Palomar. Economy and restraint are the bywords here, as Hernandez minimizes the tension between single image and image-series. For instance, in a three-page sequence early in the novel (324–26), Hernandez quietly reintroduces a number of significant characters, establishes several relationships and plotlines that will propel the story, and underlines some of the essential themes that will give it its peculiar resonance. He does all this without once making a sudden shift from scene to scene; rather, he follows several characters through the streets of Palomar, easing the reader from one encounter to the next by changing depth and perspective and by repositioning key characters vis-à-vis each other. This sequence is remarkably smooth, knit together by exchanges of angle that mimic the shot/reverse shot continuity of traditional cinema, as well as shifts from foreground to background figures, variations in distance (long, medium, and close-up shots), and even spoken cues from off-panel characters. Transitions are subtly reinforced by such devices as foreground framing and silhouetting (for detailed discussion, see Hatfield).

In contrast, key sequences later in the novel shift from subject to subject with daring abruptness, reflecting the town's growing panic and the story's surging momentum. In particular, an extraordinary sequence two-thirds into the novel (383–85) ratchets up the tension between single image and image-series to the extreme, capturing the growing frenzy of activity in the town. Starting with an aerial view of Palomar, labeled "ground zero," Hernandez moves the reader rapidly through a fragmented three-page sequence that pushes several plotlines to the breaking point (Hatfield). This frenetic passage effectively translates Hernandez's fascination with film into print; indeed the novel's accelerating rhythms call to mind the struggle, in classical film theory, between the aesthetics of the fluid shot (*mis-en-scene*, à la Bazin) and the aesthetics of montage (editing, à la Eisenstein). Such sequences, not simply grandstanding displays of technique, respond to Hernandez's abiding interest in the complexity and simultaneity of communal life, whether in peace or in crisis. Their formal ingenuity serves his overarching themes.

Conversely, Hernandez's thematic interests reflect, and evidently were shaped by, his mastery of comics form: Gradually the stories in *Heartbreak Soup* responded to his growing fluency in the form, as notions of time, memory, and repetition became thematically central. In short, the influence of content and form proved reciprocal. As the above-mentioned techniques enabled characters to interact on a vast scale, without sacrificing the vivid singularity of each, they prompted ever larger and more complex narrative structures, culminating in the demanding multigenerational epic *Poison River* (*Love & Rockets* Nos. 29–40, 1989–93) and subsequent stories, where non-chronological inserts and indeed non-linear sequences are common. *Poison River*, not coincidentally, exceeded the limits of Palomar, giving Hernandez a much wider geographical and cultural stage on which to play out his increasingly baroque narrative gambits. (Therefore it does not appear in the single-volume *Palomar*.) *River*'s scope and complexity, as we shall see, enabled him to extend the searching self-criticism begun in *Diastrophism* and to sharpen his satiric political vision. Unfortunately its complexity also undermined its success as a serial, forcing Hernandez into a period of artistic and commercial crisis.

POISON RIVER: IT'S A MAN'S MAN'S MAN'S WORLD

Poison River represents the apogee of Hernandez's art to date, a dense, aggressive, and disturbing novel that weds formal complexity to thematic ambition. (Collected in 1994, it remains notorious among fans as his most tangled and difficult work.) Set outside Palomar, the novel covers not only a wide geographical area but also a span of at least nineteen years in the life of Luba, from infancy to young womanhood. Thus it trumps Hernandez's bold use of time throughout *Heartbreak Soup*, intensifying his use of abrupt shifts and narrative fragmentation, but now with a new focus. Here Hernandez concentrates less on the life of a community, more on the complex interweaving of past and present circumstances (familial, cultural, and political) in a single life. Time is *Poison River*'s chief variable, and conveying its passage becomes the supreme test of Hernandez's skill.

By this time, Luba has clearly emerged as *Heartbreak Soup*'s most complexly developed female character, thus the central character in Hernandez's woman-centered universe. Whereas *Human Diastrophism* captures a crucial moment in Luba's public transformation from disreputable *bañadora* to mayor, *Poison River* fills in the harrowing story of her early life and thus compels the cartoonist to shuttle back and forth through history. In this case, Hernandez's aim seems not so much a broad social canvas as a psychological depth-sounding. *River* is "Luba's story."

Or is it? In fact, the novel does not really force a choice between breadth and depth; it does not insist on an either/or. *Poison River*, for all its emphasis on Luba, takes place in a minutely detailed political environment, one that continually impinges on Luba's life. This looming sense of context prevents Hernandez (and his readers) from focusing too narrowly on Luba's psyche. Indeed *Poison River* refuses to settle on Luba exclusively and often pushes her to the periphery of the action. Her psychological growth occurs in a tense, crowded milieu, geographically vast, shaped by both petty personal concerns and the huge, transpersonal forces of history. Both Luba and her world are in flux. Moreover, Hernandez uses radical shifts in time to insist on the intermingling of the personal and political.

In this sense *Poison River* marks the climax of a developmental arc that starts much earlier, for Hernandez's fluid sense of time began as far back as the second *Heartbreak Soup* story, "Act of Contrition" (*Love & Rockets* Nos. 5–7, 1984; *Palomar* 71–103). Chronologically, "Act" takes place years after the first tale, "Sopa de Gran Pena," and the vague span of time between them includes Luba's move from a van to a more permanent home, her establishment of Palomar's one and only cinema, and the births of three of her daughters (whose fathers remain a mystery until much later). "Act" also introduces telling details about Luba's past, such as her habit of nightclubbing during her teens—an allusion to Luba's jaunts with her friends Lucy and Pepa, as later recounted in *Poison River*. (Indeed, a picture of the three women in "Act" anticipates precisely a panel from *River* drawn some seven to eight years later.) By opening such gaps between stories, Hernandez was able to sketch in the history of his characters gradually through interpolated flashbacks, a technique that became central to his work. Starting with "Act," he moved with growing confidence between the "present" and the "past," tracing what in hindsight seems a clear progress: from the overdetermined transitions in "The Reticent Heart" (*Love & Rockets* No. 12, 1985; *Palomar* 165–75), a tale that bluntly labels its flashback as such, to the fluid mingling of memory, dream, and reality in "Holidays in the Sun" (*Love & Rockets* No. 15, 1986; *Palomar* 215–28). In the course of these few stories, Hernandez learned to manipulate time with greater elegance and freedom, and developed the habit of interpolating memories and visions sans verbal cues. By *Poison River* he had achieved a narrative economy in which past and present interpenetrate to a startling degree.

If *Heartbreak Soup* is marked by Hernandez's ability to age his characters believably—to capture them at different times in their lives—then *River* represents his most complex achievement along these lines. Here he fills in Luba's life prior to settling in Palomar, beginning in infancy, and at last brings her (and her daughter Maricela and cousin Ofelia) to the outskirts of Palomar, just prior to the events of "Sopa de Gran Pena." What's more, every featured player in *Poison River* emerges as a complex character with his/her own past and individual strengths and weaknesses. In the revised, collected edition of the novel, the title page of each chapter shows one

key character (for example, Luba's cousin Ofelia; her father, Eduardo; her father-in-law, Fermin) at several different points in his/her life: in childhood, adolescence, middle age, and various points in between. Luba herself is spotlighted twice, first as the youthful "Lubita," a diminutive nickname given by her husband (chapter 6), and later as the older "Luba" (chapter 17). This fluid sense of time affects the entire narrative: sudden shifts in time occur frequently, and, two-thirds of the way in, an abrupt, sixteen-page flashback (not signaled as such) crucially replays some of the earlier events in the novel from a new perspective.

Poison River, in short, is a tangle—just as Luba's life is confused, complicated, and dangerous. To explain *why*, Hernandez ultimately focuses on the enigma of her mother's identity. Luba's mother Maria, seen in *Poison River* for the first time, turns out to be a beautiful cipher—a voluptuous feminine trophy who, strangely, becomes the key to two generations of intrigue involving a cadre of Latin gangsters. Young Luba, who has never known her mother, unwittingly becomes linked to the gangsters by marrying one of Maria's former lovers, the gangster/musician Peter Rio (whose surname, of course, means "river"). Thus Luba is burdened by her mother's past liaisons. Just so, all the novel's characters are connected by a chain of circumstances, a *rio venono* (poison river) of consequences.

Poison River is notable not only for its nonlinear structure but also for its overall tone. The novel is harsh, often brutal, and in some ways hardly seems a part of *Heartbreak Soup*. Though focused on Luba, it takes place outside Palomar and builds a vast network of new, carefully shaded but generally corrupt characters, centered on Peter Rio. Peter is at the heart of a whirlwind of criminal and political activity, which spans two generations and affects the lives of Maria and Luba in complex ways. His world is shockingly different from the matriarchal retreat of Palomar, for *Poison River* surveys the political landscape of postcolonial Latin America in general, offering a dauntingly complex critique of the intersections between crime, political counterinsurgency, sex, and sexism. A harrowing story, *River* echoes the real-life tales of conspiracy, terrorism, and drug trafficking that by now infect our view of Latin America's relationship to the United States (tales in which the United States is very much implicated, as Hernandez reminds us).

Though ostensibly Luba's biography, *Poison River* takes place in a man's world, in which women are to be protected and excluded from the vicissitudes of "business." Luba herself, as in "Duck Feet" and *Human Diastrophism*, remains largely unaware of what's going on. Paternalistic chauvinism runs rampant through the novel, with Luba's husband, Peter, determined to shield her in every way from knowledge of (and the consequences of) his business affairs. Women are at once idealized and held in contempt by the men who dominate the novel's sociopolitical world. At one point, for instance, the gangster Javier curtly dismisses the idea of a woman having input into the affairs of business, "as if her say could ever matter," to which his partner replies, "Right. If we ever let a woman have any say in business, we're all through" (140–41). Such sentiments are the foundation of *Poison River*'s androcentric world.

Peter maintains that political and commercial affairs are no concern of Luba's. For example, in reference to "the abortion and birth control controversy," of which Luba has suddenly learned by watching television, Peter remarks that "such matters should never even be discussed in front of someone as young as you, much less in the house, Luba." Indeed Peter rejects the very idea of having TV in his home, though Luba refuses to part with it (91). His emphasis on the house as a place of refuge is symptomatic: for Peter, home is an idealized sphere, to be kept apart from the complications and ever-looming violence of the business. The house, with Luba in it, should be entirely insulated from the outside world. Yet this cannot be, for the violent repercussions of the business seep even into the domestic sphere, undermining the very home life that Peter holds sacred. Specifically, Luba and her friends Lucy and Pepa, housewives all, begin combating the isolation and boredom of their lives by shooting up with a drug (heroin, presumably) supplied by gangsters who run drugs for Peter's boss,

Salas. Luba, fearful of discovery by Peter, only takes the needle between her toes, but nonetheless becomes a regular user. In fact her drug-using episodes with Lucy and Pepa erupt in a kind of bacchanalian excess, as the women cavort through Peter's home in the nude, their bodies painted with words and symbols, Pepa brandishing the needle like a dagger (90). Thus they enliven their everyday lives as prisoners of a domestic ideal that forces them into dependence and ignorance. Terrified that Peter will discover her drug use, Luba abandons the needle for a time and begins boozing heavily, but then shoots up again late in her pregnancy; indeed a botched injection precipitates her labor, and later we are told that Luba's child has died of heart failure, presumably because of her drug abuse (139). Thus the fruits of Peter's business poison even his house, his wife, and his child, a symbolic demolition of the wall he has tried to build between "business" and home.

The subversive effects of "business" on home and family go even further: According to an old business transaction (rather like the conditions imposed in many fairy tales), Peter must yield up his firstborn son to a black market trade in children run by gangsters at the Jardin de Paz, that is, *Garden of Peace*, a burlesque club. (The babies are supplied by a doctor and nurse who use their black market gains to finance the expansion of their hospital.) Even before his death, Luba's newborn son is whisked away, so that Luba is never allowed to see him but simply told that he has died. Peter, caught in this tangle because he once *bought* a child from the black market for his then-mistress, the transsexual Isobel, is compromised by "the business" even before meeting Luba (and further compromised by the belly dancers at the Jardin, who appeal to his sexual fetish and keep him firmly in the pocket of the black marketers). Even Peter's most private affairs and passions are caught up in a logic of calculation, exchange, and payoff: the cold language of the business deal. As the chief of the gangsters tells him, "one day we *will* consummate this transaction" (134). Though Peter fails to see it, the "business" completely undermines his idealized conception of the home.

Ultimately, *Poison River* argues that the "business" can never be bracketed off from the emotional foundations of our lives; both professional and domestic spheres are united in a chain of complicity and consequence. Just as the novel's drug traffic is tangled in sexual politics, law enforcement, and the political struggle between revolutionary and counterrevolutionary factions, so this confluence of forces poisons even the private lives of Hernandez's characters. This is revealed in a shockingly offhand way late in the novel, when a scrap of dialogue implies that the terrorist attack that left Luba's cousin Ofelia with a damaged spine, and left Ofelia's friends Gina and Ruben dead, was anonymously engineered by the rightist gangster Garza and the club owner Salas the elder—both linked to Luba's husband, Peter, through the "business" (120). This same attack forces Ofelia; her mother, Hilda; and Luba (then a small child) to flee the town of Isleta, and Ofelia to take refuge in a distant part of the country. Thus it also sets in motion the chain of events that will lead Luba to Peter and her life with him. *Everything* is connected in *Poison River*, though not one single character realizes this: to movers and shakers like Garza, Salas, and Peter, the identities of such victims as Gina, Ruben, and Ofelia are beneath notice.

Poison River, then, differs from prior *Heartbreak Soup* stories in that it engages more directly with the sociopolitical realities and myths of modern-day Latin America. It seems more embedded in the traumas of history than the tales that take place in Palomar's frankly synthetic locale. Whereas the early *Heartbreak Soup* tales refer only obliquely to the political struggles going on in the outside world, *Poison River* extends the aggressive cultural critique of *Human Diastrophism*, placing Luba's life firmly within the context of the Cold War and examining the profound repercussions of that war within Latin American culture. The terrors of revolutionary and counterrevolutionary violence lie like a shadow across the novel and at times take center stage. *River*'s landscape is fraught with echoes of military and ideological conflicts, which, though they rise to the surface only occasionally, inform the entire narrative.

These political tensions are deadly. "Leftists" are targeted for extermination by the self-styled patriots who inhabit the gangsters' circle, most notably by Garza. A complex but wholly unpleasant character, Garza sanctions murder, yet takes pains to distinguish himself from the "criminal element" of Communists and Communist sympathizers (89). To him, political loyalty and commerce are of a piece. Pursuing and destroying the leftist "oppressors of freedom," Garza maintains, is not a matter of "personal feelings," even when his own unacknowledged feelings (greed, jealousy, bitterness) may be prompting his actions. Rather, "[i]t is politics. It is business" (86).

A pillar of the community, Garza is used to being addressed in terms that reaffirm his social superiority. "Yes, Señor Garza" is repeated, mantra-like, throughout much of the novel, almost always spoken by unseen lackeys whose very anonymity reinforces Garza's sense of power. In Garza the equation of economic interest and counterrevolutionary politics is most obvious; for him, doing "business" means thwarting the Communist threat, and withdrawing from the business (as, for instance, the ironically named "Señor Paz" tries to do) means allying oneself with subversives. Economic bustle and moral righteousness are inseparable in Garza's world; it just so happens that much of his economic strength stems from criminal activity. Thus the gangster world of Garza, Salas, Peter Rio, and company becomes a nexus for political counterinsurgency. In this world the suspicion of leftist ties is the deepest shame and greatest threat.

Here Hernandez taps into the history of Latin America in the Cold War era, for behind the novel's equation of organized crime, big business, and counterrevolution lies a host of U.S.-sponsored debacles in Latin American history, the muddy legacy of the Monroe and Truman doctrines. U.S.-engineered incursions, interventions, and coups (Cold War skirmishes, from a USAcentric viewpoint) have become part of the warp and woof of Latin American history: Guatemala, Cuba, Brazil, Chile, Nicaragua. In this milieu the influence of both the United States and the Soviet Union looms large, as shown early on when Ofelia, Gina, and Ruben attend a Communist meeting with little Luba in tow (32). Here "Eisenhower" is burned in effigy, and festive partygoers paint Luba's face with a hammer and sickle. As they return from the meeting, Ofelia and company are stopped and questioned by an anti-Communist group led by Gomez, a local man whom Ruben has known, it seems, all his life (32–33). Thus their community is fearfully split by Cold War politics.

"BOTH OUR PARENTS LEFT US WHEN WE WERE LITTLE"

To grasp such political issues and personalize them requires an overarching sense of history. It is Hernandez's deft manipulation of history, of time, that generates the bitter ironies of *Poison River*, as the novel's plot comprises a decades-long pattern of reflections, echoes, and repetitions. In fact this pattern can only be grasped by reading across the generations, as we witness the repeated corruption or poisoning of familial and sexual relationships (the very relationships that give the whole of *Heartbreak Soup* its raison d'être). In particular, the severing of parent-child bonds takes on central importance, as Maria's abandonment of Luba sparks not one but ultimately two searches for familial closure. First comes the quest for Luba herself, prompted by Peter's relationship with Maria and pursued by the enigmatic Señor Pito for some twelve years; second, Blas and Peter's "search" for Peter and Luba's lost son, Armando Jose. This second search will, as Blas says, take "the rest of our lives," as indeed Pito's quest for Luba lasts the rest of his (151).

Before book's end, the reader knows that Armando Jose has died of heart failure (an event confirmed twice over) and that Blas knows this too. Thus Blas and Peter's quest becomes an ironic, dead-end counterpart to Pito's successful quest for Luba. In each case, the whereabouts of an abandoned child are at issue, and in each case love motivates the quest. In Blas's case, it is his love for Peter that prompts him to carry on this charade, for, as the gangster Moises puts it, "Blas did what he did just to win Peter for himself" (154). As Peter's efforts to

find Luba were initially prompted by his love for Maria, so Blas's offer to spend the rest of his life "searching" for Armando Jose stems from his desire to be with Peter and take care of him.

These searches are but one aspect of the sundered family relations that shape the novel. When Blas asks Luba what she and Peter have in common, she quips, "Both our parents left us when we were little. We both like dancing. More?" (65). Beneath Luba's flippancy lies a shred of truth, though the facts are more complicated than this: As Luba soon discovers, Peter's father has *not* walked out of his life entirely; in fact Fermin Rio soon returns and takes up residence in his son's house, where he keeps an eye on Luba and secretly intercedes in Peter's affairs. Fermin did not actually abandon his son when he was "little" but twice has fallen out with Peter over women: first Maria, later the transsexual Isobel, both of whom the jealous Fermin beat savagely. Peter, to whom beating women is anathema, provokes his father by calling up the memory of his own mother, whom Fermin apparently abused in like fashion: "Only a punch or two . . . it's nothing, eh, Papa? Like it was nothing to Mama, either, was it Papa? Nothing" (126). (Peter's mother's fate remains unknown.)

This sore point between Peter and Fermin underlies Peter's tender yet paternalistic regard for women in general, and Luba in particular. His aversion to hurting women is so strong that at one point he viciously beats a club patron for throwing a glass at one of his dancers, all the while lecturing him thus: "You never ever ever strike a woman!" (74). This attitude also prompts Peter to protect Luba by threatening others with violence: "[I]f there is *one* tiny cut on my wife's body that wasn't there before; *one* bruise, just *one* tear from her eyes . . ." (88). Behind this ferocity are Peter's memories of his mother, memories that kindle a rage inspired by his father but now redirected.

The novel's father/son conflict deepens its critique of masculine power. Both Fermin and Peter represent aspects of patriarchy: Fermin, violent and controlling, is sharply unsentimental about women; Peter, affectionate and also controlling, is sentimental and protective. Fermin views male/female relations fatalistically, as he discloses to Peter late in the novel: "The constant battle between the left and right is the least of the world's worries, eh, son? It's the war of the sexes that's always been life's true headache. Heh heh—but what's life without a worthy struggle, eh? Without a strong woman to fight with from time to time. Your mother—she wasn't much of a fighter . . . You were luckier with your little fire brand Lubita" (149). Peter, now disabled by a stroke, can only sit by passively, muttering his lovers' names, as his father holds forth. Fermin goes on to reveal that it was he who killed the transsexual Isobel, whom he describes as "the biggest mistake of the lot" and "neither a man nor a woman." Indeed, Isobel's transgender identity threatens the male/female binary that props up *Poison River*'s entire world, and Peter's love for Isobel likewise threatens his position therein. Fermin recognizes this: Isobel was an anomaly, a "mistake" who could only be "a source of pain and confusion to normal men like us . . . " (149). She had to be removed. Peter feels differently: his love for Isobel represents a rebellion against his father's values and, more broadly, an unconscious resistance to the prevailing misogyny of the novel's world. This resistance climaxes in violence, as Peter, slurring out Isobel's name, finally rises from his stupor and rams the end of his cane down his father's throat, killing him (a gruesome but poetically apt climax).

In a sense, then, Luba's flippant remark is correct: Peter *has* been abandoned by his father, insofar as he has been both brutalized and alienated by Fermin's violence. And of course she herself has been abandoned by her mother, Maria, a loss she can never really come to grips with but that nonetheless shapes her character. The signs appear early on: as a little child Luba begins to think of her cousin Ofelia as "Mama Ofelia," for Ofelia takes the place of Luba's absent mother (29). Just so, Luba herself later assumes the place of Ofelia, and even her name, for her blind, bedridden aunt Hilda (43).

Luba's loss is ironically reinforced by her possession of Maria's only heirloom, a hollow book filled with keepsakes, which she cannot open. Given this book on the day of her wedding to Peter, Luba later seems to regard it as a nuisance, yet refuses to let anyone else handle it. Urged on by friends, Luba tries to have it opened but cannot. When the book *is* finally opened (by police officers during their questioning of Luba), it discloses photos of Maria and other memorabilia—such as the bloodied earrings worn by Gina on the night of her murder, placed there by Ofelia. "Junk," Luba declares, "All of it." Yet she playfully attempts to mimic the glamour poses assumed by Maria in the photographs (95). Dreaming of her mother, she sees her husband suckling at Maria's breast in an eerie, Frida Kahlo-like image: Peter's head is adult, but his body small and childlike. Then she wakes to find Peter poring through the keepsakes from the book. Luba, distraught, only wants to get rid of these reminders of the unknown past, and Peter, not disclosing his prior knowledge of Maria, accedes to Luba's wishes. He consigns the box and its contents to the fire, to be burned out of Luba's life, and his, forever (96). (A flashback later reveals that Peter has opened the box before, unbeknownst to Luba, just prior to their wedding.)

For Luba the question of her mother's identity and whereabouts is only painful: "No more talk about my mother—! She left me—! She's dead! Dead—!" (137). Yet Maria does not disappear so easily. Indeed, after Luba's so-called miscarriage a vision of Maria appears, dreamlike, over the hospital bed that Luba and Peter share. She tells Luba that her supposedly stillborn son, Armando Jose, is alive (information that is later to be contradicted). The image of Maria appears again, briefly, heirloom box in hand, as Luba is carried away from Peter's home (and the life of a gangster's wife) by Fermin and the mysterious Gorgo. The memory of her mother's absence lies deep within Luba, prompting her to distrust all such relationships. As she says to her infant daughter, Maricela, prophetically, at novel's end, "Ahh . . . You'll leave me one day, Maricela . . . just like *all* the others . . . " (187). For Luba loss is the way of life, and her past simply that: long gone, an inaccessible mystery.

Poison River, then, is a tale of relationships disrupted or denied, as well as relationships sought or resumed (for example, when the adult Luba rediscovers her cousin Ofelia after years apart). Hernandez's vast temporal canvas allows for the exploration of such relationships over a spread of many years, an exploration that generates telling echoes and ironies. Both Luba and Peter are wounded by life, and hardened; both are haunted by lost or sundered relationships with their own parents; and, finally, both are caught in a world in which "business" (the business of ownership, control, and use) short-circuits or corrupts intimate relationships.

Peter, for his part, treats Luba kindly, yet does business ruthlessly. His life is built around an exaggerated split between cozy domesticity and the harsh realities of business, which, by his own admission, is "an eventual dead end." In a sense, he is quite knowing about what the business entails: "Either you die or worse; somebody you love" (75). Still he insists, "The world just takes getting used to, baby . . . then you can use it" (61). Indeed his ambition *is* to use it: "Peter Rio is a name to remember, Luba. [. . .] A name with the potential to dry the Pacific, to flood the Sahara . . . " (53). His talent, he says, is "management" (60), yet his coolly entrepreneurial exterior is belied by the tenderness of his emotions: toward Maria, toward Isobel, toward Luba. The business "transaction" that finally breaks Peter—the surrender of his son to the black marketeers, which precipitates his stroke—stems from the uneasy overlap of his "business" and his private life, notwithstanding his vain attempts to keep the two entirely separate. The loss of Armando Jose, the climax of a series of events stemming from his tense relationship with his father and his love for Isobel, brings his reign as a gangster boss to a messy, protracted end. In a sense, then, *Poison River* is Peter Rio's tragedy: though often callous and condescending, and bristling with compensatory machismo, Peter emerges as a fully humanized character, more vulnerable than his status would seem to suggest.

Luba, for her part, becomes increasingly coarse, unfeeling, and alcohol-sotted after Peter's stroke, as the emotional pillars of her life come tumbling down. While she persists in drinking and nightclubbing, "Papa Fermin," as she calls him, seeks to control her. (Though already thrown out of the house by Peter, Fermin tries to bring Luba back to the nest.) Alienated from her father-in-law, Luba becomes more and more unfeeling toward her disabled husband, of whom she says, "I'm not sure he's got any brains left working in his head" (140). Deprived of both a lover (police captain *Joselito* Ortiz, strangled by Fermin) and a son (Armando *Joselito*, dead), she begins to shut herself up in drunkenness, and waltzes carelessly through the affairs of Peter's gangster associates with an increasingly sardonic air: "You boys get back to whatever bullshit you were up to . . ." (141).

Once cloistered by the paternalism of Peter (whom she calls "Daddy"), Luba survives after his stroke by cultivating her own ignorance and blocking out the "business" of the world. Yet she learns to get her way during her subsequent travels by invoking her husband's power and status (155). Unaware of the causes or extent of what's happening around her, Luba remains blinkered in her vision to the very end, focusing exclusively on herself, her family, and a series of short-term sexual partners. Thus she preserves the naiveté of her adolescent years with Peter. While her cousin Ofelia knows what is happening around her—the country is in a state of civil war by novel's end, though Ofelia shields Luba from knowing it—Luba's lens on the world remains microscopic. For example, she doesn't realize that the stench hovering over a certain spot comes from a pile of rotting corpses just out of her sight (164). Thus Peter's protectiveness leads to Luba's lifelong habit of willful myopia; like Peter, she fails to recognize that her affairs and the affairs of the world are intertwined (an intertwining already argued by Hernandez in *Human Diastrophism*, and powerfully reinforced here).

Despite Luba's willed ignorance, political violence brackets *Poison River*. The fate of Ofelia's Communist colleagues (at the beginning of the novel) and the looming war between "military" and "rebels" (at the end) suggest a microcosm of Latin American history during the Cold War. Luba remains oblivious to this history, living it but looking *through* it without ever understanding it—without understanding, that is, the political forces that have disrupted and complicated her life. Meanwhile, political ideology, criminal activity, and sexual desires overlap and reinforce each other. Repeatedly, characters like Garza and Salas argue political positions that mask their personal investments and motives; repeatedly, politics mixes haphazardly with personal vendettas, sexual amours, and familial conflict. Political principle gives a respectable face to personal animus and informs the various personal and "business" developments in Peter's circle. Political conflict shapes Luba's life from infancy (the Salas-sponsored attack on Gina, Ruben, and Ofelia) to adulthood (the war-prompted departure of her lover Antonino, father of Maricela). She, however, remains clueless. The ironies of Luba's life, and specifically how that life has been shaped by the abstract yet very real forces of ideology, are made plain by Hernandez's manipulation of history on a vast scale; yet Luba never confronts them.

TIME (AND AGAIN)

Again, it is Hernandez's fluid sense of time that gives *Poison River* such political and emotional heft. His graphic negotiation of Luba's history (sometimes back and forth across years in a single page) gives the novel a scope beyond the narrowly personal, because sifting through her life exposes meaningful social patterns: political and sexual ideology, commerce, crime, corruption. Yet *River* remains intimate; the novel observes these patterns as they shape individual lives. Hernandez understands that time, in comics, is a function of *space*, the visual space of the page, and this enables him to personalize ideological and social issues, through the twinned images of absentee mother (Maria) and lost daughter (Luba). Both women are comic epitomes of feminine pulchritude within a profoundly male and (not coincidentally for Hernandez) profoundly corrupt culture. Their relationships to men, and to each other, are matters of time.

This radical sense of time reaches its height during an extended flashback sequence, two-thirds into the novel, which quickly replays the history of

Maria's involvement with the gangster Garza and with the father-and-son musical team of Fermin and Peter Rio (the Rios become part of Garza's gangster circle). Maria, having abandoned Luba and Luba's father, Eduardo, has become Garza's mistress but soon enters into an affair with Fermin; while Peter, his affair with Garza's wife, Ramona, cooling, falls in love with Maria and begins making love to her too. Caught between these three men—Garza, Fermin, and Peter—Maria inspires each to a different extreme. The jealous Garza, who tends to express himself with guns, shoots his pistols off wildly and quarrels bitterly with his wife. The equally jealous Fermin, suspecting that there is yet another for Maria besides Garza, vents his unfocused rage by beating her. Fermin's son Peter, swept away by love for Maria, hires Senor Pito and his son Gorgo to track down Luba (a move that will lead to his own meeting with, and marriage to, Luba some twelve years hence). Maria herself, a vain, promiscuous moll who magnetizes men with her beauty, represents a vision of voluptuous feminine charm so ripe as to border on self-parody; indeed, the stereotypic extremity of her character brings out, and holds up for ridicule, the masculine possessiveness of the three lovers.

The end result is a tangled weave of dysfunctional relationships, a web that allows Hernandez a great deal of play with time as he leaps from one relationship to another. The pace is unrelenting: as the flashback unfolds, these affairs overlap and develop with startling speed, and the tension between single image and image-in-series is severe. On one page, for example, we see Maria's relationships with all three men, summarily evoked (fig. 34). Fermin admires her body and speaks nonchalantly about her affair with "that crook" Garza; Peter begins *his* affair with her, and even confesses love to her; and Garza dreams of Maria bearing him children to carry on his "war against the oppressors of freedom," that is, leftists (124). In fact all three relationships are quickly conveyed in the middle tier of this single page, as three successive panels show us, first, Peter's tense, sweaty reaction to Fermin and Maria's bantering; second, Maria and Peter in bed, Peter aflush with love and intemperately confessing it (in

Figure 34. *Poison River* 124. © 2004 Gilbert Hernandez. Used with permission.

contrast to his father's blasé attitude); and third, Maria and Garza, as the latter dreams of fathering children by her. The page is a marvel of compression; the narrative barrels ahead without pause. Maria's ambiguous whisper, "Children . . ?", leads us into the next tier of panels, and a new scene, as she runs from Peter, distraught over (presumably) her abandonment of Luba. In a crucial twist, Peter offers to locate Maria's daughter.

What is notable here is not Maria's character per se, but the way her seeming *absence* of character, her stereotypic perfection and consequent emptiness, make her the perfect magnet for the desires of the three men, each of whom longs for affirmation from Maria but of course cannot trust her. That Maria embodies a stereotype of feminine affectation and charm is precisely the point: though she remains inconstant, unpredictable, and thoroughly amoral, her continual costume changes and affected good looks make her a perfect vehicle for the men's desires. (The front cover of *Love & Rockets* No. 45 [July 1994] finds Maria competing in the "Miss Luminosa" contest for 1948, in which *every* contestant has an identical beauty mark on her right cheek!) Maria's story becomes the men's story, a story in which all of the relationships follow a predictably dysfunctional pattern. The men change, and her costume changes, but the overall pattern stays the same.

Nowhere is this more evident than in a one-page, nine-panel sequence (new to the collected edition) in which Maria attempts to end her relationships with the three men by running away (128). As she tries, repeatedly, to leave by bus, she is stopped by men who want to marry her, take care of her, and make her stay (fig. 35). The same scene repeats itself, with variations, several times. Maria wears different clothes in each of the first six panels, and in the odd-numbered panels (one, three, and five) talks to Peter, Fermin, and Garza respectively. Thus we know that this sequence covers a significant span of time, and a number of discrete incidents, in her life. Yet the movement between these panels is deceptively easy: the flow of dialogue and action implies continuous movement within a single scene.

A hand reaching for Maria in panel two leads easily to Fermin's dialogue in panel three, though the two panels depict two different incidents (as signaled by Maria's change of clothes). A similar confusion occurs between panels four and five: again, a hand reaches for Maria, leading to Garza's placatory speech in the next panel, but again Maria's appearance changes between the two images. By thus blurring our sense of time, Hernandez suggests a pattern of repeated behavior. The dialogue and actions suggest a seamless sequence, yet the shifting costumes and rotating male characters point out the passage of a great deal of time.

This page depicts separate incidents from Maria's life, yet verbal echoes suggest that these incidents all follow logically from a pattern of dysfunctional relations with men. In panel two, the ticket seller tells Maria that her bus will take her to Chilo to catch a train; in panel four Maria attempts to purchase a ticket to Chilo for the same purpose. In each case someone off-panel calls her name and reaches out for her. In panels three and five, lovers try to keep Maria by promising marriage, and in both she responds, "All right. . . ." On the bottom tier of the page (panels seven through nine), Fermin, Garza and Peter share the same fate, loss of Maria, and all three call out for her in vain. Each man appears different, yet each calls for her in a questioning tone, revealing his surprise and aloneness as she finally escapes from him. These last three panels suggest a gradual loss of hope, as Maria's lovers seem to lose the power to speak: we go from Fermin's "Maria . . ?" to Garza's "Mar . . ?" to, finally, Peter's hopeless, inarticulate "M . . ?" The interplay of word and image links these separate instances within a consistent behavioral pattern and provides a sense of direction to what would otherwise be a radically disjointed sequence. Though time leaps forward with dizzying speed, via uncued scenic transitions, repetitions in both dialogue and composition ease the image/series tension and allow us to see these drastic shifts as part of a predictable, indeed inevitable, process.

Such whiplash transitions occur throughout *Poison River* but most tellingly when Luba finally

Figure 35. *Poison River* 128. © 2004 Gilbert Hernandez. Used with permission.

Figure 36. *Poison River* 143 (excerpt). © 2004 Gilbert Hernandez. Used with permission.

escapes from the gangland life. Wandering drunkenly from a gangster meeting in Peter's home (Peter's stroke has rendered him helpless), Luba drifts through the hedges outside, where she encounters a young man from the meeting and begins to have sex with him. She is "rescued," however, by her homicidal father-in-law, Fermin, who strangles the man (fig. 36). Luba glimpses the murder, prompting a flashback to a key incident earlier in the novel: the terrorist attack in which her cousin Ofelia was raped, beaten, and left for dead by counterrevolutionary thugs (39–41). This traumatic memory harks back to Luba's early childhood, and Luba herself, as a small girl, is shown witnessing the rape. The adult Luba then collapses, muttering, as if overcome by the memory, and on the following page images from her past interrupt the flow of action: first Maria, holding the hollow book that has become Luba's inheritance; then a lucid Peter, who says, "I love you, Lubita" (144). These disjointed breakdowns not only reflect Luba's drink-induced stupor but also signal the dark passage from this part of her life to her subsequent life without Peter. From here

on, Luba's life will be spent on the run—until she discovers Palomar at novel's end.

"JUNK" AND INFORMATION: *POISON RIVER* AS METACOMIC

As *Poison River* leapfrogs through time, it insists on the overlap between personal and political history, examining, like *Human Diastrophism*, the interchange of private and public life. It also extends the implied self-criticism of *Diastrophism* by commenting acidly on mass culture and its impact (a concern seen early on in *Heartbreak Soup* with the introduction of Luba's movie theater).[5] Films figure prominently in *Poison River*, as cousin Ofelia brings young Luba to the movies and, later, as Fermin gets Luba a TV set, on which she watches movies against Peter's wishes. For Peter, movies are the stuff of cheap fantasy and beneath contempt: "the lowest and silliest form of telling stories" (91). For Luba, in contrast, movies are an education of sorts, offering heretofore-unseen visions of such stuff as, ironically, "Gangsters and murder and men cheating on their wives" (all topics appropriate for Peter and his circle). Fermin's gift of the TV puts Luba back in touch with the movies she experienced as a child, movies she apparently no longer consciously remembers.

Luba refuses to part with the television despite Peter's claim that it will "rot your brain" (91). Besides movies, the TV offers news, which offends Peter even more deeply—news that brings to Luba such controversial issues as birth control and abortion. Such stuff, he argues, consists merely of "[s]implistic and biased views on politics and any sensational aspects of human suffering that might titillate" (91). Of course, such news also directly challenges Peter's cloistral attitude toward home and hearth (note that Fermin, less idealistic and more cynical than his son, is the agent of this challenge). Luba's confrontation with the news of the world, filtered through TV, recalls the television-mediated climax of *Human Diastrophism*: human suffering indeed. Though Fermin's efforts to bring her "the information of the world" run counter to Peter's chivalric paternalism, Luba remains mesmerized by the TV and won't let it go.

But the most prevalent form of pop culture on display in *Poison River*, and the one for which Peter reserves his deepest contempt, is "funnybooks"—that is, ironically enough, comics (fig. 37). In the person of the blackface comic-book character "Pedro Pacotilla" (glimpsed back in *Diastrophism*), comics represent an affront to Peter's civilized self-image. This insult is so degrading that Peter takes pains to differentiate between his own name (the English *Peter*, or, as Luba learns it, *Pee-ter*) and "Pedro." "Everybody who's been degraded with the name *Pedro*," he argues, "ought to sue or something . . ." (53). Pedro, of course, is everywhere: a thick-lipped, black-skinned, Sambo-like icon beaming from not only comics but also advertisements, billboards, and lighted signs. In one telling moment, Peter criticizes his mistress Isobel for letting her daughter play with a Pedro doll (135).

Ironically, little Luba receives much of her early education from Pedro comics. Ofelia and Luba read *Pedro* together, Ofelia prompting Luba to *read*, not just "look at the pictures" (28). Luba heartily enjoys the Pedro comic books; indeed, she seems to love them, whereas she shrinks in fright from the "progressive art" (Frida Kahlo) to which Ofelia tries to introduce her. In fact Ofelia takes some heat from her leftist friends for feeding Luba's mind this way. As in the real-life anti-comics movements of the 1950s, so in Hernandez's tale: criticism of Pedro comics stems from the left as well as the right. Ofelia's Communist friend Gina, for instance, roundly criticizes Ofelia for teaching Luba to read with this "junk," which she condemns as racist: "Pedro's the good little black boy who's happy to be poor and uneducated; and they draw him like a monkey!" (30). Gina's remarks echo many real-life studies of comic books and children's literature, in which the ideological implications of familiar icons—Babar, Curious George, Barks/Disney's Uncle Scrooge, and so forth—have been laid bare (see, for example, Dorfman and Mattelart's seminal *How to Read Donald Duck*, and Dorfman's subsequent *The Empire's New Clothes*). Indeed, the character Ruben notes that there have been "attempts by educators and the like to have Pedro comics banned," a reminder of the realities of Hernandez's chosen field: comics have been attacked by not only conservative but also progressive political figures (notably, Wertham, whose condemnation of the comic book industry made him an inadvertent bedfellow of rightist censors).

Ruben also remarks that, thanks to the merchandising of Pedro, "the little shit will probably outlive us all" (30). Unnoticed by the adults, the child Luba replies, "Indubitably!", a comment on the durability of Hernandez's medium as well as subtle testimony to the vocabulary Luba has picked up through her comics reading. Of course, her remark also turns out to be true in a literal sense, for both Gina and Ruben are soon slain by counterrevolutionary thugs; yet Pedro lives on in sign and poster, neon and print. Indeed Pedro's smiling countenance recurs again and again, ever unresponsive to circumstance, as many of *Poison River*'s characters die off. Most notably, Pedro appears, without explanation, immediately after the gangland massacre that kills off

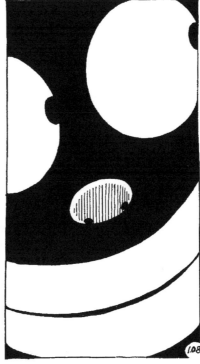

Figure 37. *Poison River* 108 (excerpt). © 2004 Gilbert Hernandez. Used with permission.

Garza, young Salas, and numerous henchmen (fig. 37). As they die in a welter of blood, bullets flying, Pedro Pacotilla outlives them all, his face a perfect icon of comic imperturbability (108).

In fact Pedro is something of an icon for the "business" in which Peter and his circle are so obsessively engaged. The image of Pedro shows up over and over in the city, in lights and on billboards, a signifier of blissed-out consumerism. First, when Luba's father, Eduardo, carries her through the city streets, begging for their survival, Pedro's smiling cartoon face mocks Eduardo's poverty and desperation (18). Later, Pedro turns up again, on billboards, when Peter and his fellow musicians are talking amongst themselves about business (52); later still, the image of Pedro serves as a backdrop for Peter's first face-to-face meeting with young Salas, as they discuss a drug deal (62). Representative for a soft drink ("Robo Cola"), Pedro appears in the background again and again, an ever-present reminder of commerce, indeed of "business" at its most aggressive.

Like many popular cartoon characters, Pedro is polysemic: he can mean many things. If he can be young Luba's passport to literacy, he can also be a mocking symbol of Peter Rio's economic ambitions. Indeed, by the time Garza and Salas go down in a hail of bullets, Pedro has become their silent spokesman. He is also an ironic emblem of hope, appearing one last time as Blas and the disabled Peter head north, toward the United States, supposedly to search for the lost child, Armando Jose. The smiling image of Pedro puts the lie to Blas's promise to look for the dead child. As the two ride off into the sunset (so to speak) in a taxicab, Blas sees a bright future ahead: "Aw, it's going to be good, Peter; I promise. It'll be so good . . ." (151). The cartoon image of Pedro, ever grinning, looks down from several billboards sans comment—but the image speaks volumes.

Thus *Poison River* tips its hand, drawing even comic art itself, as a fund of stereotypic, politically charged imagery, into Hernandez's larger political and cultural argument. Like *Human Diastrophism* before it—and indeed like Spiegelman's *Maus* and many other alternative comics—*River* becomes a metatext, an interrogation of its own medium; it too insists on the political implications of comics. Everything in *River* is up for grabs. Just as, in previous tales, Luba's movie theater and Howard Miller's self-interested photojournalism serve to comment on mass culture and mass media, so too Pedro, in *Poison River*, opens a self-reflexive dimension, a space for auto-critique.

The novel's final pages are self-reflexive in a different sense, for they strive to contain *River*'s alarming story by bringing us full circle, back to the sheltered village of Palomar, but now for the "first" time. Luba, Ofelia, and Maricela stand outside Palomar, looking down at it, while the young Palomarans Jesus, Satch, and Toco look on. In short, we are at the very threshold of the first *Heartbreak Soup* story, "Sopa de Gran Pena." For the seasoned reader, this recursion is reassuring, yet also a bit odd: after *Poison River*, how can Palomar ever be the same? To read these last pages is to experience both the shock of recognition and a bewildering sense of displacement. This is Palomar, yes, but how did all of that backstory get in here?

THE DEATH AND THE REBIRTH OF *LOVE & ROCKETS*

Indeed *Poison River* may have crammed in *too* much. The story was a daunting experiment, a graphic novel in the truest sense, serialized over some four years in twelve installments. What's more, it unfolded at the same time as *another* graphic novel by Hernandez, a teeming chronicle of life in multicultural Los Angeles titled simply "Love & Rockets" (later collected as *Love & Rockets X*). "Love and Rockets," conceived as a "break" from the density of *Poison River* (Knowles 54), nonetheless grew into a psychologically complex and bitingly topical story in its own right (though beyond our compass here). In short, Hernandez was then producing two different stories, each at a heady pace. Under this pressure, *Poison River*, which began as a series of carefully structured chapters, soon devolved into smaller, less shaped, and less cohesive installments, making no concessions to *Love & Rockets'* serial readership. The artist would later recall feeling thoroughly absorbed by *River* and "fit[ting] the chapters in L&R as space allowed"

(Gilbert Hernandez to the author, 22 Mar. 2000). Each issue of the magazine brought an allotment of pages, but unlike *Human Diastrophism*, *River* dispensed with even token attempts to acclimate those readers who entered in medias res.[6] As the graphic novel grew in breadth and complexity, the serial per se faltered. *Poison River* became the supreme test of readers' loyalty, during a period when both Gilbert and Jaime Hernandez (then working on his own eight-part novel, *Wig Wam Bam*) pushed their audience's endurance.

The experience, apparently, proved exhausting to both Gilbert and his readers. Looking at this period in hindsight, Hernandez would complain that he had "almost cut [his] head off doing *Poison River*," yet had received little response beyond, "Oh, that was hard to read" (Gaiman, Interview 95). As a serial, *River* alienated even some of *Love & Rockets'* core audience: the tide of enthusiasm that had greeted the magazine years before retreated, and, according to Hernandez, "our star began to dim" (Knowles 54). In other words, fan mail stopped coming and sales dropped (Hernandez to the author). Thus *Love & Rockets* risked losing its status as the standard-bearer for alternative comics. Later the artist would admit that he himself found *River* a trying experience: "I would sit at the board and bust my head open, trying to finish this stuff, and then I'd trash the page and start over" (Knowles 54). Post-*Poison River* issues would therefore be promoted with a promise to return to shorter, less involved stories. The collected graphic novel version of *Poison River*, released well after the story's serialization (1994), incorporated some forty-six pages of new material, including not only suggestive title pages (as noted above), but also many pages of interpolated narrative designed to deepen, explicate, and smooth over its tortuous story. (Changes in the collected *River* range from minor graphic refinements, such as lightening the color of Maria's eyes, to major structural revisions, such as expanding the crucial flashback of chapters 11–13 by two pages.)

After *Poison River*, and the structurally simpler but thematically challenging *Love & Rockets X*, Hernandez returns to Palomar in a new mood, downplaying politics so as to iron out and extend the *Heartbreak Soup* storyline. This period, still complicated but now more episodic, seems rather hermetic and self-involved; the stories bespeak consolidation if not retreat. Hernandez, by his own admission, "backed off from any profundity," and a door once opened now began to close (Huestis 68). The artist would later reflect: "I had two political stories in me, HD [that is, *Human Diastrophism*] and PR [*Poison River*], and that's it. Unless I came upon something political that I would've liked expressed, I preferred to keep away, as not to repeat myself or half-ass any truth about other people's misery" (Hernandez to the author). This candid self-assessment shows a brusque honesty, as well as a desire not to sit still creatively. It also shows an awareness of diminished scope.

After the trial by *River*, there was still the population of Palomar to deal with. The final stories in *Heartbreak Soup* (issues 41–50 of *Love & Rockets*) aim for complete closure, showing the aging of Palomar under Luba's mayorship. Many longtime characters, including Luba's daughters Maricela, Guadalupe, and Doralis, emigrate to Southern California. Other children come, and other relationships, including Luba's reuniting with the now-disfigured Khamo (terribly burned in his attempt to save Tonantzin at the end of *Diastrophism*). Humanly rich though they are, these last tales, such as "Farewell, My Palomar" and "Luba Conquers the World," move toward a foreordained conclusion: Luba's decision to leave Palomar behind forever. Plot-wise, this move is justified by the arrival of would-be killers connected to Luba's past, an intrusion presaged by the reappearance of her onetime protector Gorgo, from *Poison River* (now a very old man). With these reminders of Luba's past suddenly intruding on her life, the sanctuary of Palomar no longer seems inviolable, and, with the fiftieth and final issue of the original *Love & Rockets*, Luba departs Hernandez's fabled village for good.

This farewell to Palomar might seem to have been designed to open up Hernandez's work once again to broader sociopolitical issues; after all, from here Luba's story will shift to the Los Angeles first depicted in *Love & Rockets X*. However, other aspects in the arc of *Love & Rockets* 41–50 frustrate such a reading. Specifically, Hernandez introduced elements that suggest a narrowing of interest to his own private cosmos: he began to elaborate further, and inject new material into, the history of Luba's family and even absorbed prior non-*Heartbreak Soup* material into Luba's life. Ironically, this inward-spiraling approach came even as he considered shifting toward "completely different types of stories" (Huestis 68). In seeking to avoid the vast, by-now cumbersome workings of his own fictional history, Hernandez only tied it into a tighter, more intractable knot—in part because he was driven by the impending end of *Love & Rockets* and a need to bring out numerous story elements that he had "backed up" for years (Huestis 68). Depending on one's viewpoint, leaving Palomar was either about cutting the Gordian knot of continuity or carrying Hernandez's interest in Luba to its logical extreme. From the artist's perspective, it "was simply about not 'ruining' it," a remark that suggests Palomar could not easily accommodate the increasing complexity of Luba and her family tree (Hernandez to the author).

With hindsight, the result of all this seems to have been further complication, but without the vaulting thematic complexity seen in *Poison River*. Luba's family becomes increasingly connected to her hitherto unrevealed half-sisters, Petra and Fritzi, two characters imported from Hernandez's previously unconnected erotic humor series, *Birdland* (1990–92), a would-be lark published under Fantagraphics' "Eros" imprint (undertaken as yet another escape valve for the pressures of *Poison River*). As Luba's daughters migrate to California, Petra and Fritzi, two exaggerated icons of femininity much like their mother, Maria, travel to Palomar to be reunited with their half-sister. While the flight of Luba's daughters to California opened the possibility of pungent commentary about Latino/a life in the United States, Hernandez focused equally on the unexpected business of grafting the carefree *Birdland* to Luba's more complex history. (At the time this effort seemed quixotic, to say the least, but since then he has used these characters to create some of the most fully realized erotic fiction in comics.)

Gilbert's sketchbook work from this period testifies to his growing fascination with Maria, Luba, and their progeny (see *L&R Sketchbook 2* [1992]). Maria's own storied life, and sexual couplings, provide the backstory for an increasingly baroque world based on this single family. The result is a series of tales that continue to blend past and present, but without *Poison River*'s sociopolitical sweep. Some of these stories—notably, "A Trick of the Unconscious" and "The Gorgo Wheel"—also blend the naturalistic and the fantastic, as Hernandez unexpectedly reinjects elements of genre fantasy into his world. This turn to fantasy climaxes not with a Palomar story but with two curious experiments: "Satyricon" (*Love & Rockets* No. 46, 1994), a Gilbert story about *Jaime's* early science-fiction characters; and "My Love Book" (No. 49, 1995), a mocking interrogation of the autobiographical comics genre (to which we shall return in our next chapter). In these fascinating one-off tales (both reprinted in *Hernandez Satyricon*, 1997) Gilbert's self-referential gambits take on an increasingly sardonic, self-mocking, and pessimistic air.

With the final *Heartbreak Soup* tale, "Chelo's Burden" (*Love & Rockets* No. 50, 1996; *Palomar* 499–522), Hernandez attempts to bring the series full circle. In the process, he achieves several stunning narrative coups. For one, he blithely unites his own universe with elements of brother Jaime's *Locas* world (through the appearance of one of Jaime's signature characters). He also rekindles a number of issues previously established, yet long ignored, including Sheriff Chelo's infertility and the impact of photojournalist Howard Miller's visit on the town. (In a wonderfully ironic scene, Luba's daughter Maricela and her son *Jaime* discover Miller's book of Palomar photos in a California library.) Yet the most telling element of this final story, and the most troubling, is the reappearance of the artist Humberto, neglected since *Human Diastrophism*, who has found a way around his promise never to make art again. It is here that Hernandez's self-reflexive examination of his art comes to a head.

Ostracized for his failure to act in *Diastrophism*, Humberto is a figure virtually erased from the subsequent continuity, until this final chapter finds him, older but still obsessed, secretly making statues of Palomar's citizenry and sinking them in the nearby lake (a point hinted at issues before). Beneath the waters of the lake lies a fabulous recreation of Hernandez's cast, standing on the bottom, hidden from sight (fig. 38). "One day this stream will be gone and the statues will be exposed," says Humberto. "Reaching ever upward toward God—the sun—like eternal flowers and I will be forgiven my sins . . ." (517). The implications are bleak: from the possibility of a revolutionary art, questioned but still hinted at by Augustin's mural at the end of *Diastrophism*, Humberto has moved to a underwater (underground?) art, one he can do only as long as he remains hidden. Hernandez now envisions an art enabled by its very obscurity. Like Hernandez, Humberto himself has created a composite portrait of Palomar—but has sent it to the bottom of the pool, a standing relic reminiscent of the famed Terra Cotta army of Qin Shihuangdi or the mummified victims of Vesuvius.

It is hard not to see a despairing trend here, a fictionalized response to the pressures and disappointment caused by the tentative reception of *Poison River*. In the wake of that immensely complicated and ambitious novel, *Heartbreak Soup* seems to swallow its own tail, leading to the dissolution of *Love & Rockets* itself at Gilbert's suggestion, and the abandonment of his trademark series (Huestis 68). The sendoff in "Chelo's Burden" is grand, full with remembrances and resonances for the seasoned reader, but the dénouement nonetheless seems fated.

"Chelo's Burden," though, does succeed in imposing an overall shape on *Heartbreak Soup*, a logic that is not merely cumulative but symmetrical. The rounding off of the series, including Humberto's sudden, heavily freighted reappearance, allowed Hernandez to leave *Love & Rockets* on a high note and to move on. It cleared the way for an attempted renegotiation of his position within the comics field. This was no easy task: to turn one's back on a successful brand like *Love & Rockets* is to take an enormous professional risk, though one that, potentially, opens spaces for new, innovative work. Indeed, from 1996 onward Hernandez was extraordinarily disciplined

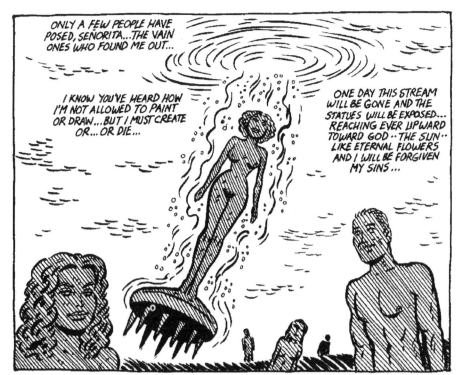

Figure 38. Humberto's fugitive art, from "Chelo's Burden." *Palomar* 517 (excerpt). © 2004 Gilbert Hernandez. Used with permission.

and prolific, offering up a dizzying variety of projects (until the much-hyped return of *L&R* in 2001).

Immediately after *Love & Rockets*, Hernandez launched into a six-issue series of disconnected and surreal stories, *New Love* (1996–97), which included one explicitly Palomar-related serial, "Letters from Venus." (Venus is Luba's niece, and lives in California.) Much of *New Love* eventually found its way into a book, suggestively titled *Fear of Comics* (2000), which short-circuits expectations and defies easy summary. Mockingly playing on comic book formulas, and occasionally spilling over into free-wheeling graphic experiments, this work is fitful, sometimes disturbing, but always playful and energetic. At the same time, Hernandez created the "good girl" (a fan euphemism for sex- and pinup-oriented) adventure series *Girl Crazy* for another publisher, Dark Horse Comics, known chiefly for heroic fantasy. Frivolous and well-crafted, *Girl Crazy* (1997) represents another funky genre outing, another seeming escape from the pressure of Hernandez's ambitions. Its quaint science fiction landscape, female superheroes, and weird critters recall the fractured SF

of his early, pre-Palomar stories, such as "BEM" and "Music for Monsters" (1979–83). Yet *Girl Crazy* lacks the provocative ironies of its predecessors; despite the artist's irrepressible sense of play, the series comes off as a frothy indulgence of comic book clichés. Like *Birdland*, Hernandez's droll foray into erotica, *Girl Crazy* has a whiz-bang, insouciant quality.

These cathartic ventures behind him, Hernandez then returned to his best-known creation, in a new series titled simply *Luba* (1998–2005). This post-Palomar series was set in the United States and promoted with a promise to make the material accessible to new readers. The marketing of this series, with nominal focus on a single character, and its packaging as a comic book in standard format, as opposed to *Love & Rockets'* magazine size, marked a seeming surrender to the reigning logic of comic book collectordom. In contrast, numerous alternative cartoonists have recently abandoned the comic book per se in favor of different packages (the comic book being by no means the only vehicle for an artist of Hernandez's reputation). Yet his embrace of the comic book was inspired not only by pragmatic considerations but also by a growing skepticism toward avant-garde or (in his phrase) "art school" comics, which he has criticized for over-assertive packaging and a "cold, abstract" approach (Hernandez to the author, 22 Mar. 2000). By contrast, *Luba* and subsequent projects ally Hernandez with a more traditional comic book aesthetic and, notwithstanding the formal rigors of his work, an approach to storytelling that privileges economy and accessibility.

Hernandez has also achieved the kind of breakneck prolificacy associated with mainstream comic book artists. In the late nineties he went through an invigorating burst of productivity, for, alongside *Luba*, he produced several other comic books: *Measles* (1998–2001), an eight-issue anthology for younger readers, edited by Hernandez with contributions from others; *Luba's Comics and Stories* (five issues to date, 2000–), an omnibus spinoff of *Luba* focusing on secondary characters; *Goody Good Comics* (2000), a one-shot potpourri à la *New Love*; and, as illustrator, nine issues of cartoonist/writer Peter Bagge's humor comic, *Yeah!*, published by mainstream giant DC (1999–2000). More recently, Hernandez has sortied into mainstream genre work, doing a blasé SF/crime thriller for DC titled *Grip* (five issues, 2001–2002) and even a run as scriptwriter on the *Batman* spinoff *Birds of Prey*, another take on female superheroes (2002–2003). (This mainstream work strikes me as detached and juiceless, as if his ironic distancing from genre makes it hard for him to take the work straight.)

Coming after Hernandez's struggles to write novels in serial form, this emphasis on periodical comic books is unexpected, and the sheer size of his output almost daunting. Yet this change was, perhaps, a grab at freedom. If Hernandez wanted to be sprung from the tight contours of *Love & Rockets*, he made his bid for independence through sheer, driving effort, using the traditional comic book as his ticket out. Notwithstanding the crisis of the latter-day *L&R*, this recent explosion of work testifies to a renewed faith in "the infinite artistic possibilities of the comic book medium" (*New Love* No. 6). Those telling words belong to Luba's niece, Venus, star of *New Love* and *Measles*, a fan whose unselfconscious engagement with comic books, like the young Luba's in *Poison River*, harks back to the medium's heyday as mass entertainment, before the funneling in of fan culture. Hernandez's recent projects find him engaging the comic-book-as-social-object as never before, exploiting it with a wary nostalgia.

This is so despite the artist's suspicion that comic book serials may never qualify as Art: "I feel art comics, as in novels, shouldn't have characters that continue after the piece" (Hernandez to the author, 22 Mar. 2000). Here he sells himself short: while this suspicion reflects long-lived aesthetic norms in literary criticism (note the invocation of the novel as point of comparison), it diminishes the achievement of *Heartbreak Soup*, in which the use of continuing characters, and the tension between serial and novelistic aims, yielded some of Hernandez's strongest, most provocative work. The economic and creative tension between series and novel arguably accounts not only for *Love & Rockets'* depth of setting and character but also for its aggressive formal innovation: In order to build sustained, novel-length stories from within a comics magazine, Los Bros Hernandez pushed the tension between single image and image-in-series to the extreme, so as to leap through time, interpolate new material in the "past," and tell and retell stories recursively. As confusing as this method could be to the uninitiated or occasional reader, it developed out of the periodical mode, and the meaningful gaps in reading offered by that mode.

Yet Hernandez's response to periodical form and the commodity nature of comics remains ambivalent. While his recent comments on the comic book "mainstream" have targeted the narrowness of the industry and the exclusivity of collectors (see, for example, "Destroy All Fanboys"), his own work after *Love & Rockets* has been acutely aware of the comic book as such and has craftily capitalized on the format. The six issues of *New Love*, for example, balanced an ongoing serial with experimental short features, the former anchoring the comic book and the latter exploiting it. While the serial aimed for a larger coherence, the individual comic book issues reveled in their particularity. This artistic tug-of-war, endemic to periodical fiction, is central to Hernandez's work, and indeed to alternative comics.

Gilbert Hernandez's work continues to waver between upkeep of his established characters and more radical experiments. Once again he is linked to *Love & Rockets*, for early in 2001 Gilbert and his brothers Jaime and Mario Hernandez revived *L&R* as a triannual comic-book-sized series. This highly promoted relaunch, apparently driven partly by financial need, enjoyed heavy media coverage and recaptured many fans, despite the fact that Gilbert and Jaime had been prolifically writing and drawing their own respective comic books from 1996 onward. The *Love & Rockets* title, Gilbert conceded, was "the perfect showcase" for their efforts (Elder 4), and he declared that "Volume II" would be their "second wind" (Arnold 64). Outside of *L&R*, though, Gilbert remains prolific and unpredictable; he continues to work on his own *Luba* series (and its spinoffs), and also does occasional mainstream work for hire. Perhaps as a result, his contributions to *Love & Rockets* Vol. 2 have thus far been all over the map. While Jaime has continued focusing on his signature character Maggie, Gilbert has skipped around, re-exploring beloved secondary characters, detailing the life of Luba's half-sister Fritz, illustrating his brother Mario's meandering thriller "Me for the Unknown," and offering brief installments of *Julio's Day*, a series in a rural, Palomar-like setting yet unconnected to any previous work. *Julio*, which has been billed as the life story of one man from birth to death, promises to be what *Heartbreak Soup* is not: a single tale, with "characters that [do not] continue after the piece"; as such it may be Gilbert's bid to create an artistically autonomous novel. Gilbert has described it as a way of "get[ting] rid of the excess" of Palomar, focusing on a single tale, and "restraining himself" (Adams, "Return Flight" 26). Thus far, however, relatively little of *Julio* has appeared in print. In the meantime, Gilbert's most impressive

work since 1996 continues to involve Luba and her family, and a good chunk of this has been collected in his recent book, *Luba in America* (2001).

Luba in America, with its startling riffs on Latino/a culture, media celebrity and (as ever) polymorphous sexuality, picks up where Gilbert's "Letters from Venus" left off. Yet in a sense it is the grandchild of *Poison River* and *Love and Rockets X*, raveling out Luba's (Maria's) family line from the former and exploring the Los Angeles set up in the latter. Again Luba is only the nominal focus: the story covers many characters and spins out in short, giddy flights, tighter and punchier than Gilbert's novels of yore. Luba's character is continually enriched by the unfolding story, but she is only one among the many. The work, scrappily American, is in love with diversity and brims with decadent pleasures.

Hernandez's latest projects warrant their own considered treatment, beyond our scope here. Suffice to say that he remains restless and prolific and that he has reinvented himself more than once since the end of the first *Love & Rockets* in 1996. Behind his current work stands the monumental *Palomar*, or, in its original form, *Heartbreak Soup*, an extravagantly rich series that represents a benchmark for long-form comics—as well as a sobering example of the limits posed by serial publication. The reshaping and tightening of its core stories, *Human Diastrophism* and *Poison River*, as revised for their book editions, suggest the enormity of the challenge Hernandez faced when turning this series into a genuine saga. Moreover, the fitful growth of that saga shows how developments in narrative form (for example, the treatment of time) may be urged on by the needs of the commercial medium. Finally and above all, what makes these questions worth pondering is the excellence and urgency of the work itself: a wayward masterwork, thirteen years in the making, that exploits the inherent tensions of comic art in the service of a brilliant literary imagination and probing social vision.

CHAPTER FOUR

"I MADE THAT WHOLE THING UP!"

THE PROBLEM OF AUTHENTICITY IN AUTOBIOGRAPHICAL COMICS

About four-fifths into the comics memoir *Our Cancer Year*, lymphoma victim Harvey Pekar hauls himself out of bed, slowly, groggily—his mind addled by a psychoactive painkiller, his body numbed to near-paralytic heaviness as a result, apparently, of chemotherapy. Narcotized and reduced to merely "rocking through patterns," Harvey continues to slip in and out of consciousness even after he stands. In fact he slips in and out of *self*-consciousness as well, for his mind keeps turning over that most basic of questions, "Who am I?"

At the bottom of the page in question (fig. 39), Harvey rises with a wordless groan, head sagging. His image is dark, formed of heavy contour lines and brusque, energetic cross-hatching; his surroundings are white and detailless, the panel that holds him borderless, exploded. The page itself, its surface broken into six panels, is organized and dominated by large patches of empty white space. In this open space, Harvey appears free, adrift, and very much in danger of losing himself.

Turning the page, recto to verso, we face a much different surface (fig. 40), more fragmented yet also more claustrophobic. Images of varying size crowd together, some bordered, some not; some are defined by thin hatching, others by blobs of inky black. Across the top, two panels of dense brushwork show Harvey's face in extreme close-up, a shadow against a shadowy background. Dry brushstrokes pick out his features—half-conscious in the first image, then alert in the second, as a title suddenly pops into his mind: *American Splendor*.

Harvey's eyes widen, staring directly at us as the distinctive logotype *American Splendor* appears in a thought balloon over his head. *American*

Figure 39. Joyce Brabner, Harvey Pekar, and Frank Stack, *Our Cancer Year* (n. pag.). © Joyce Brabner and Harvey Pekar. Used with permission.

Splendor seems to be part of the answer to his question, "Who am I?"—but only that, a part. In the next tier of panels, he in effect reiterates the question: seeing himself in a bathroom mirror, he turns to his wife Joyce (that is, Joyce Brabner) and asks, "Am I some guy who writes about himself in a comic book called American Splendor? . . . Or I am just a character in that book?" Uncertain of who he is, Harvey stands naked, bereft and puzzled, isolated within a round frame that focuses everything on the question of his identity. Is he author *and* character, or just character?

Harvey, obviously, is far gone. His body has betrayed his mind, and his mind, reduced to zero, now has to struggle to recover the fundamentals of his identity, in both personal and vocational terms. In short, Harvey must recover his sense of who he is. Even as this alarming sequence (co-written by Brabner and Pekar, and drawn by Frank Stack) reveals the psychological and neuropathic fallout of cancer therapy, it turns on a broader, more abstract issue: how we fashion our very selves through the stories we tell. Who is Harvey—creator, creation, or both?

This is a question that readers of Pekar's autobiographical comics have faced for the better part of thirty years, for Pekar, more than any other comics author, has demonstrated the interpenetration of life and art that autobiography can achieve. Harvey is the main character in the magazine/comic book series *American Splendor*, and Pekar its scripter and guiding hand; though not interchangeable, the two are one. Through its sporadic serialization (since 1976), *American Splendor* has offered readers a chance to grow with both Harvey-the-persona and Pekar-the-author, always with the tantalizing possibility that one might be collapsed into the other—or perhaps not. Pekar has succeeded in mythologizing himself, transforming "Harvey" into a property that belongs to him (or he to it?) but which nonetheless exceeds him. By turns gregarious and recessive, openhearted and suspicious, sensitive and coarse, the working-class hero of *American Splendor* emerges as a complex, provoking character who just happens to bear an unmistakable likeness to his creator.[1]

Pekar's achievement is to have established a new mode in comics: the quotidian autobiographical series, focused on the events and textures of everyday existence. Joseph Witek's groundbreaking study *Comic Books as History* (1989) aptly describes this mode as one of consciously literary yet "aggressively humdrum" realism (128). For Pekar, such realism is a matter of paying attention: his distinctive approach depends on keen-eyed (and -eared) observation of anything and everything around him. His gift for

109

Figure 40. *Our Cancer Year* (n. pag.). © Joyce Brabner and Harvey Pekar. Used with permission.

such observation is consistent with his voracious appetite for knowledge; indeed, for Pekar autobiography is a means of autodidacticism, as his comics represent a struggle for an understanding both emotional and intellectual. *American Splendor* is a sustained inquiry into the underpinnings of daily life, including the vicissitudes of economic competition; the social obstacles posed by class, occupation, gender, and ethnicity; and the cultural nuances of everyday speech. The series observes all of these phenomena from a defiantly personal, working-class perspective, offering an accretive autobiography that is at once diverse, unpredictable, and organically unified. This autobiography is impressive in scope, comprised, as

of this writing, of more than thirty magazine and comic book issues and some six book-length compilations of stories from same (discounting the collaborative *Our Cancer Year*).

In the course of assembling this body of work, Pekar has inspired a school of serialized comics autobiography, including a slew of alternative comic book titles released between the latter 1980s and the mid-1990s: Colin Upton's *Big Thing*, Ed Brubaker's *Lowlife*, Dennis Eichhorn's *Real Stuff*, the latter issues of Chester Brown's *Yummy Fur*, the early issues of Seth's *Palookaville*, Joe Matt's *Peepshow*, Mary Fleener's *Slutburger*, Julie Doucet's *Dirty Plotte*, Joe Chiapetta's *Silly Daddy*, and others. These titles have yielded a number of notable book collections, such as Brown's *The Playboy* (1992) and *I Never Liked You* (1994), Doucet's *My Most Secret Desire* (1995), Fleener's *Life of the Party* (1996), Brubaker's *A Complete Lowlife* (1997), and Matt's *The Poor Bastard* (1997). As these titles suggest—note how so many of them are more confrontational than the quietly ironic *American Splendor*—this new school of autobiographical comics has tended to stress the abject, the seedy, the anti-heroic, and the just plain nasty. If the method of this school has been documentary, the dominant narrative modes have been tragedy, farce, and picaresque. In the wake of Pekar, these scarifying confessional comics have in fact reinvented the comic book hero.

Now, heroism in comic books has never been simple. The heroic fantasies of early American comic books were often shot through with inoculative doses of irony—grace notes of self-mockery that compromised their assertive bluster. Indeed, such saving irony defines the founding examples of that arch-genre of comic books, the superhero, in which power must be closeted or checked for the sake of preserving the status quo. Yet it took the scabrous revelations of underground comix to radicalize this sense of irony, transforming amused suggestiveness into full-out polemic. Savage irony typified the undergrounds: as we have already seen, comix took the shopworn industrial icons of yesteryear and invested them with a new, anarchic, almost self-denunciatory energy. This new mode demanded new "heroes."

Underground comix admitted a new psychological realism and, concomitantly, a potential for radical cultural intervention. Whereas comic books before had but nibbled, the undergrounds sunk their teeth into the very hands that fed them, venting a long pent-up energy that exploded the narrowly conceived boundaries of the medium. The newly coined comix (as described in chapter 1) offered not only new economic terms and a new, more individualistic model of production but also the necessary inspiration for these in a new level of adult and achingly personal content, both fantastic and, as time went on, naturalistic. From this brief, fecund period came the impetus for an exclusively adult species of graphic narrative, to which Pekar, arriving at the end of the

underground period, brought a radical appreciation for the mundane.

What has become of the comic book hero since then? As noted in chapter 1, current descriptions of the comic book industry assume a split between, on the one hand, a dominant fannish emphasis on superpowered heroes, and, on the other, an alternative, post-underground outlook, from which larger-than-life heroism has been evacuated in favor of heady satire or in-your-face realism. This characterization is of course overdetermined and somewhat reductive, reflecting decades of conflict within the industry itself (an industry still cramped by its reputation for self-censorship and cupidity). Today's alternative comic books frequently attack this industry, reveling in their disavowal or cynical reappraisal of the medium's troubled history. Indeed, rejection of the corporatist "mainstream" gives the post-underground, alternative scene everything: its raison d'être, its core readership, and its problematic, marginal, and self-marginalizing identity. It is here, on the activist end of comic book culture, that autobiographical comics have flourished, overturning the corporate comics hero in favor of the particularized and unglamorous common man or woman.

If alternative cartoonists acknowledge any sort of heroism, it consists in a collective effort to assert the versatility of comics as a means of expression, apart from the diversionary trappings of the escapist genres so entrenched in the American industry and fandom. As Witek remarks, this effort represents "an implicit rejection of the death grip that fantasy has long held" on the art form (*History* 153). Part of this project, Witek reminds us, is the promotion of comics that refuse fiction altogether, favoring history, reportage, the essay, and the memoir. Thus "nonfiction" comics have come into their own, and, in Pekar's wake, autobiography has emerged as the nonfiction comic's most familiar and accessible guise (rivaled only recently by graphic journalism à la Joe Sacco).

In short, underground comix and their alternative descendants have established a new type of graphic confessional, a defiantly working-class strain of autobiography. Confronted by these new, highly personal comics, the venerable cartoonist and teacher Burne

Hogarth (whose own work embodies a fervid Romanticism) once called them "a remarkable fulmination of the inner light of people who have never had a voice" (Young, "Comic Art" 52). Even as he chided autobiographical cartoonists for the bleakness of their work, Hogarth recognized that work as an historic novelty—and an extraordinary achievement. The example of such cartoonists, coupled with increasing access among part-timers and amateurs to affordable means of reproduction (for example, photocopying, in the diffuse but vital field of minicomics), has turned autobiography into a mode of central importance for alternative comics in North America, and, increasingly, around the world (see, for example, Groensteen, "Les petites cases"). Indeed, this "problem child" of the undergrounds, as the *Comics Journal*'s Frank Young once called it, has become *the* defining mode of comics' self-styled counterculture ("Peeping Joe" 37).

Yet, paradoxically, such first-person comics can also appeal to the confirmed habits of "mainstream" comic book fans and the industry that woos them. While autobiographical comics represent, in Ray Zone's phrase, a "necessary byroad" on the way to maturity (Fleener 9), they also accommodate fandom's preset habits of consumption, insofar as autobiographical comic book series are well adapted to the market's emphasis on continuing characters, ongoing stories, and periodical publication. In this case, the autobiographer's cartoon persona supplies continuity, while the use of "real life" as inspiration insures a bottomless fund of raw material. Indeed, a number of creators have sustained fairly long autobiographical series (such as those listed above), series containing both novel-length stories in piecemeal form and shorter stories well suited to comic book or magazine format. Telling tales about yourself is a gig that can go on forever, or at least for a very long time. No wonder, then, that during the eighties such comics became, in the words of a bemused Art Spiegelman, "a real growth industry" ("Symptoms" 4). This "industry" has since downsized—as we'll see, autobiographical comics soon came under attack as the latest cliché, and few of the above-named projects are still ongoing—but by now the genre has established a set of narrative conventions that continue to shape alternative comics.

In sum, this post-Pekar school of autobiography, like the current comic book field as a whole, is a paradox: a collision of mainstream commercial habits and countercultural sensibility. Even as serial autobiography accommodates fandom's emphasis on characters and creators as heroes, it challenges the presumptive hold of fantasy on that market (the kernel of such fantasy being the superhero). To a field fed on the adventures of glamorous *übermenschen*, autobiography provides a salutary alternative with its schlemiels and sufferers, hangdogs and gadflies. Yet its episodic, often picaresque (Pekaresque?) nature still caters to the outworn tradition of periodical comic book publishing (notwithstanding the success of Pekar's book-length compilations in the mainstream press). Thus autobiography has become a distinct, indeed crucial, genre in today's comic books—despite the troublesome fact that comics, with their hybrid, visual-verbal nature, pose an immediate and obvious challenge to the idea of "nonfiction."

They can hardly be said to be "true" in any straightforward sense. There's the rub. But therein lies much of their fascination.

IDEOLOGY, ACCURACY, INTIMACY

As a genre, autobiography is of course difficult to define and well nigh impossible to delimit. Protean in form, it applies the narrative techniques of fiction to stories implicitly certified as "true," insofar as they defer to a level of experience "outside" the bounds of text. The tacit rules of the genre demand fidelity to such experience, yet storytelling demands license; narrative needs shaping. Thus autobiography inevitably mingles the factual and the fictive (even among the most scrupulous of practitioners). This blurring of boundaries presents a conundrum that criticism has been able only to turn over and over, never to resolve: what has storytelling to do with the facts? In the words of Timothy Dow Adams, autobiography is a paradox, "a therapeutic fiction-making, rooted in what really happened; and judged both by the standards of truth and falsity and by the standards of success as an artistic creation" (*Telling Lies* 3).

If academic criticism has fretted over this paradox, autobiographers in comics have often barreled ahead without confronting it as such. Though some have recognized that the genre isn't about literal but rather about *emotional* truths, many have taken as gospel Pekar's dictum that persuasiveness resides in literal accuracy, in minute fidelity to "mundane events" as they happen. "The more accurate," according to Pekar, "the more readers can identify with them" ("Potential" 84). The goal is absolute "honesty," and in particular the disclosure of, to paraphrase the cartoonist Seth, things that "the regular media" ignore (Seth, Brown, and Matt 52).[2]

If autobiographical comics can be considered a movement, then its manifesto would seem to be Pekar's vision of "a literature that pushes people into their lives rather than helping people escape from them" (Groth and Fiore 215). Since 1976 Pekar has realized this vision in *American Splendor* as well as *Our Cancer Year* (1994), his collaborative memoir with his wife Joyce Brabner and illustrator Frank Stack. The former examines Harvey's social and occupational world in painstaking detail, highlighting the quiet, epiphanous moments that give life flavor and resonance (and, increasingly, offering Harvey's biographical studies of other people). The latter conflates the personal and the political, detailing both Harvey's battle against lymphoma and Joyce and Harvey's anxious engagement with global politics during the Persian Gulf War. *American Splendor* mixes dour naturalism with Pekar's self-conscious, first-person narration, which betrays the rhythmic influence of standup comedy and his own experience as a street-corner performer (Groth and Fiore 216, 223). *Our Cancer Year*, on the other hand, abandons Pekar's narrational shtick, combining documentary accuracy with Stack's expressionistic rendering to capture the rigors of cancer treatment. Both projects show a keen eye for the minutiae of day-to-day existence.

Such projects have an ideological subtext—specifically, a democratic one—since they celebrate the endurance and everyday heroism of "the so-called average person" in the face of corporatist culture

(Groth and Fiore 215). As Witek has suggested, Pekar's work resists this culture through "the assertion of individuality" (*History* 149). In this light, the personal is indeed political; as cartoonist Justin Green implies in his seminal *Binky Brown Meets the Holy Virgin Mary* (1972), "social issues" and individual "neuroses" are irrevocably linked (Green 10). (We will return to *Binky* in our next chapter.) Ray Zone cements this connection between personal and political in his introduction to the work of Mary Fleener: the "explicit foreground 'subject'" of autobiography (that is, the autobiographer him or herself) stands in a dialectic tension with the "implicit background 'object'" of culture (Zone 11). Thus autobiography in comics, as in prose, often zeroes in on the contact surface between cultural environment and individual identity. Indeed, therein lies much of its impetus, and value, as Witek observes of Pekar's work (*History* 149–52 passim).

What makes such implicitly political content possible is Pekar's ideal of conformity to the facts of one's experience. Of course, as soon as we say this we are in trouble, for Pekar's ethic of accuracy runs counter to the epistemological skepticism of our age. How can one be faithful to objective "truth" when such truth seems inaccessible or even impossible? How in fact can we speak (as above) of "a level of experience 'outside' the bounds of text," when contemporary theory teaches us that to apprehend reality is to textualize it from the get-go? Therein lies the impetus for a current of skepticism in both autobiography theory and, increasingly, autobiographical comics. The balance of this chapter will examine the ways in which comics struggle to absorb and capitalize on this skeptical or self-critical tendency.

Paul Jay sums up the skeptical position thusly: "the attempt to differentiate between autobiography and fictional autobiography is finally pointless" (*Being in the Text* 16). This view is widely shared among literary critics; many have argued that autobiography is no more privileged or "truthful" than fiction-making (regarding this argument, see, for example, Adams, *Telling Lies*; Eakin; and Zinsser). Indeed by now it would seem that, as Adams puts it, "the presence of fiction within autobiography is [regarded as] no more problematic than the presence of nonfiction within the novel" (*Light Writing* xi). The issue remains a live one for the as-yet little-studied genre of autobiographical comics, in which ideologically fraught claims to truth collide with an anxious distrust of referentiality (a distrust aggravated by the inevitable backlash against autobiography as a market genre). Yet, ironically, the disavowal of objective truth may serve to shore up the genre's claims to veracity; indeed, grappling with such skepticism would seem prerequisite to recognizing and fully exploiting the genre's potential for truth-telling. Only by exploring such doubts can the emotional "honesty" of autobiography be recovered.

Salvaging the genre's claims to truth means rescuing its potential for radical cultural argument—and there *is* something radical about the intimacy of graphic self-representation. Autobiographical comics since the late seventies, inspired by Pekar's mundane observations as well as the grotesque confessions of cartoonists such as Dori Seda and Justin Green, have decisively stressed what Pekar himself calls "unpleasant facts" (Groth and Fiore 216). These facts include the kinds of psychosexual and scatological details that tend to escape even the most adventurous mainstream fiction. Cartoonists such as Aline Kominsky-Crumb (*Love that Bunch!*) and Joe Matt (*Peepshow*), to take two well-known examples, have staked out the very frontiers of self-exposure, spotlighting their own manias and fears with a frankness and insistence that amount to a compulsive howl of despair. Whereas Pekar himself (as Witek has observed) has retreated from such harrowing intimacy, in favor of focusing more intently on his intellectual and social milieu (*History* 127), many autobiographical comics of the eighties and nineties privilege the most minute and shocking details of their authors' lives. It is this intimacy that authenticates their social observations and arguments.

Still the question persists, how "true" can these self-centered reflections be? How accurate? At some point the appearance of bracing "honesty" runs the risk of hardening into a self-serving, repetitive shtick. Despite the implied claim to truth that anchors the genre, the autobiographer's craft necessarily includes exaggeration, distortion, and omission. Such tendencies become doubly obvious in the cartoon world of comics, in which the intimacy of an articulated first-person narrative may mix with the alienating graphic excess of caricature. One may fairly ask how a cartoonist can use these disparate tools without seeming to falsify his or her experience. If autobiography promiscuously blends fact and fiction, memory and artifice, how can comics creators uphold Pekar's ethic of authenticity? How can they achieve the *effect* of "truthfulness?"

THE CARTOON SELF

In comics, such questions inevitably have to do with appearances, in particular the graphic likeness of the autobiographical protagonist and its relation to the artist's own sense of self. If autobiography has much to do with the way one's self-image rubs up against the coarse facts of the outer world, then comics make this contact immediate, and graphic. We *see* how the cartoonist envisions him or herself; the inward vision takes on an outward form. This graphic self-representation literalizes a process already implicit in prose autobiography, for, as Stephen Shapiro has argued, the genre consists less in faithfulness to outward appearances, more in the encounter between "successive self-images" and the world, a world that repeatedly distorts or misrecognizes those self-images (Shapiro 426). If autobiography is a kind of rhetorical performance in which one, as Shapiro says, tries to "persuade the world to view one's self through one's own eyes," then autobiographical comics make this seeing happen on a quite literal level, by envisioning the cartoonist as a cartoon. This is the autobiographical comic's most potent means of persuasion: the self-caricature.

Prerequisite to such caricature, it would seem, is a form of alienation or estrangement, through which the cartoonist–autobiographer regards himself as *other*, as a distinct character to be seen as well as heard. Yet, as Paul Jay has suggested, such a process of becoming an object, indeed a parody of oneself, may enable a subject "to choose, and thus control, identity" ("Posing" 210). Objectification of the self, through visual representation, may actually enable the autobiographer to articulate and uphold his or her own sense of identity.

Jay arrives at this conclusion through the study of photography. Writing on the relationship between photos, visual memory and self-representation, he asserts that a photographic portrait, while seeming to force its subject into a posed and thus inauthentic guise, may actually open up opportunities for commentary and resistance, insofar as the objective image may be reappropriated, internalized, and subjectified (209–10). Knowledge of how one looks, or can look, may be enabling for the individual subject, inasmuch as such knowledge allows him or her to grapple with and transform that "look." Indeed, as Linda Haverty Rugg observes of writer Christa Wolf, "it becomes necessary to imagine the self as photo-object [fr. German *Fotoobjekt*] in order to begin the process of self-knowledge" (*Picturing Ourselves* 214–15).

Such self-objectification necessarily precedes or informs autobiography, for the genre represents nothing less than (in Rugg's phrase) "an exertion of control over self-image" (4). Like the subversive self-mockery of those subalterns who reappropriate hateful epithets for their own ends, a cartoonist may actually find him or herself through a broad, cartoony, in some sense stereotypic self-depiction. Such visualization can play a vital role in the understanding and affirmation of individual identity; paradoxically, playing with one's image can be a way of asserting the irreducibility of the self as agent.

The cartoon self-image, then, seems to offer a unique way for the artist to recognize and externalize his or her subjectivity. In this light, comics autobiography may not be alienating so much as radically enabling. As Susan Stanford Friedman has argued of women's autobiography, the form may allow the artist to break free from "historically imposed image[s]" and to fashion "an alternative self" (Benstock 83). Yet, at the same time, the placement of this self-image among other figures within a visual narrative confers an illusion of objectivity. *Seeing* the protagonist or narrator, in the context of other characters and objects evoked in the drawings, objectifies him

or her. Thus the cartoonist projects and objectifies his or her inward sense of self, achieving at once a sense of intimacy and a critical distance.

It is the graphic exploitation of this duality that distinguishes autobiography in comics from most autobiography in prose. Unlike first-person narration, which works from the inside out, describing events as experienced by the teller, cartooning ostensibly works *from the outside in*, presenting events from an (imagined) position of objectivity, or at least distance.[3] William Lowell Randall, in *The Stories We Are*, makes just such a distinction between *events* (things that happen) and our *experience* of events (the way we regard things that happen). By his argument, events are "outside" us, while experience is "inside." Going further—into territory oddly apropos of comics—Randall distinguishes between the stories we may tell about ourselves, *expression*, and the stories others may construct about us, based on outward *impression* (54–57). In brief, expression works from the inside out, while impression works from the outside in. Yet, complicating Randall, we might say that to tell a story of yourself in comics is *to seek expression through outward impressions*, because comics tend to present rather than narrate—or, at times, alternately present *and* narrate. Comic art's presentational (as opposed to discursive) mode appears to problematize, or at least add a new wrinkle to, the ex/impression dichotomy.

Cartooning does work from the outside in, using culturally significant stereotypes (for example, in style, facial features, and posture) to convey impressions of people that are seemingly spontaneous yet deeply coded (that is, ideologically motivated). As many cartoonists and critics have observed, stereotypes are the raw material of cartooning, hence of comics; even relatively realistic comic art draws on representational and cultural codes that depend on typing (see Töpffer 15–17; Eisner, *Comics* 101 and *Storytelling* 17; Ware in Juno 39–40). Yet, as Art Spiegelman has argued, sustained comics narrative has the power to individualize the stereotype, dismantling it in whole or in part ("Drawing" 17–18). Thus characterization is not limited to blunt types, even though it may exploit them. Our own sense of identity may develop through a similar process, as we choose, explore, and discard successive stereotypic "selves" that act as rough approximations of the hoped-for "inner" self we but vaguely apprehend.[4]

To be sure, the use of such images may impose limitations on the autobiographer. Elizabeth Bruss has argued, regarding autobiography in film, that visual self-portrayal drives a wedge between the "expressive" and "descriptive" functions of autobiography, whereas language conflates the two. First-person narrative, says Bruss, allows the "I" as subject of expression and "I" as object of description to blur together: "In speaking 'I' merges easily, almost inextricably, with another 'I' whose character and adventures I can claim as my own" (306–7). In contrast, visual representation divides expression from description, posing "an impassable barrier" between observer and observed. In film, then, the autobiographical subject cannot help but break down into a "person seeing" and a "person seen." Cinema, she concludes, "dismantles" self-consciousness, which she regards as an effect of language (317). Yet it seems clear that visual self-depiction is not wholly void of expressive potential, even in the supposedly neutral and pitiless medium of photography, for, as photographer Dana Asbury has said of photographic self-portraits, the manipulated likeness includes not just information but "emotional interpretation" as well ("Photographing the Interior"). The photographer *can* work introspectively, though in an external, seemingly unself-conscious medium.

This applies even more obviously to drawn self-portraits, in which emotional interpretation often exceeds and even sabotages literal description. The huge expressive potential of self-portraiture is argued by, for example, Joan Kinneir in *The Artist by Himself*, an anthology of self-portrait drawings: "[Self-portraiture] gives us access to an intimate situation in which we see the artist at close quarters from a privileged position in the place of the artist himself and through his own eyes" (15). The impossibility (barring mirrors) of this happening in a literal sense—both observing and being observed—adds to the fascination of self-portraiture as a genre. Cartooning, shorn of the referential literalness expected in photography, freely partakes of this paradox with a variety

of expressionistic effects. Again, "outside-in" and "inside-out" blur together.

Comics, then, despite their speciously "outside-in" approach, can evoke an author's internal self-concept, insofar as the act of self-portraiture encourages a simplified, exaggerated depiction of known or desired attributes. In brief, the outward guise reflects inward attitudes: objectification enables self-understanding and self-transformation. Indeed, it may be that all self-recognition depends on such a dialectic between inward recognition and outward semblance. McCloud's *Understanding Comics* lends popular support to this view, arguing that we continually intuit our sense of our own appearance in broadly "iconic" (McCloud means cartoony) terms. By his argument, the face we envision, the face we *put on*, is a mental cartoon of a face, an abstract construct that *guides* our sense of what we "say" with our looks (34).

This claim is of course debatable (*are* our facial expressions guided mainly by internalized cartoons?). More troublingly, McCloud overextends the argument into a naïve model of reader response: because self-recognition involves a degree of simplification, he claims that highly simplified, cartoony images invite reader "involvement." In other words, cartoons become loci for "identification" through their very simplicity (42). In this McCloud follows the notion of the "beholder's share" as put forth by E. H. Gombrich: "We tend to project life and expression onto the arrested image and supplement from our own experience what is not actually present" (17). Like McCloud, Gombrich describes the face as a "mask," one built out of "crude distinctions" that we generally take in "before we notice the face" as such (13). Yet McCloud errs in, one, assuming the universality of these culturally coded distinctions or attributes (36); and two, arguing that the reader identifies with or is "sucked into" the cartoon image in some absolute sense (42). The claim for universality is undone by McCloud's own observations about the differences between the graphic symbols used in different cultures, specifically differences between expressive conventions in western comics and Japanese *manga* (131). More to the point, the argument for identification runs afoul of the visual nature of comics, for, as Bruss reminds us, visual narrative tends to dismantle the first-person point of view, dividing the person seeing from the person seen (307). The logical principles or signifying practices of comics, no less than film, militate against a thoroughgoing identification of observer and observed. While a limited claim might be made for reader empathy, positing complete identification stretches the case beyond credulity (regarding the vexed issue of "identification," see Barker, *Comics*; Frome).

Yet, though the connection between reader and cartoon may not be as absolute as McCloud claims, there does seem to be an intimate connection between *cartoonist* and cartoon—a claim that depends neither on universality nor on absolute psychological identification. The crux of the matter is the way the cartoonist chooses among expressive conventions to create a cartoon "likeness" (more accurately, sign) that conforms to his/her inward sense of self. As Perry Nodelman observes (apropos of picture book illustration), such a highly simplified portrait constitutes not a literal likeness so much as an inventory of abstract attributes: a horizontal line can stand in for a mouth, a vertical for a nose, two dots for eyes, and so on (28). These attributes are understood, not as resemblances, but as symbols, rather like words; verbal recognition of features precedes the cartoon encoding of same. Visual self-portrayal thus enacts a self-understanding that is at least partly verbal in nature. Though seemingly "objective," the outward image in fact mirrors an internalized, abstract self-concept—a self-consciousness prerequisite to personal narrative.

If this is so, then Harvey Pekar's creative process precisely mirrors this transition from verbal understanding to visual expression. Pekar scripts his comics through rough, stick-figure breakdowns and verbal notes, which he then passes on to various illustrators to complete. As Witek points out, the artists must translate these verbal and symbolic inventories into complete pictures, adding in the process new visual information that complicates Pekar's persona (*History* 137). Perhaps it is no accident that Pekar, a writer rather than artist, pioneered the autobiographical comics series, for as a writer he had to know how to abstract his own character, in the form of simplified diagrams and nuanced dialogue. Such self-knowledge is primarily verbal. (Note, though, that the dominant examples of comics autobiography after Pekar have been by cartoonists working alone, achieving a degree of control, and at times a solipsistic self-regard, which would seem to be denied to Pekar's collaborative approach.)

In sum the cartoon self enacts a dialectic tension between impression and expression, outer and inner, extrinsic and intrinsic approaches to self-portrayal. While the written text in a comic may confide in the reader much like unaccompanied, first-person prose, the graphic presence of the image at once distances and inflects the autobiographer's voice. Whereas first-person prose invites complicity, cartooning invites scrutiny. Hence the curious detachment, the semblance of objectivity, which critic Frank Young observes in such post-Pekar cartoonists as Chester Brown and Joe Matt ("Peeping Joe" 38). It's a fiction of "honesty." Yet what happens when this external self-image, this visual persona, becomes unfixed? What if it warps or mutates, and thus betrays the artist's shaping hand?

THE SELF AS SUCCESSIVE SELVES

Cartoonist Dan Clowes dives into this very possibility in his four-page rant, "Just Another Day" (from his *Eightball* No. 5, 1993, reprinted in *Twentieth Century Eightball*), a *reductio ad absurdum* of quotidian autobiographical comics. In this satire, Clowes, then known for caustic, cynical essays in comics form, manipulates his own persona to expose the impossibility of telling the truth in comics, while ridiculing the excesses of disclosure seen in Pekar, Kominsky-Crumb, and others. Reinventing his visual image from panel to panel, Clowes reveals "Dan Clowes" himself to be as plastic and imaginary as any other comics character. As the story nears its end (fig. 41), Clowes leaps from one stereotypic self-image to another, while torn, discarded pages representing the other versions of himself pile up on the floor, ultimately obscuring his features in a morass of crumpled

Figure 41. Dan Clowes, "Just Another Day." *Twentieth Century Eightball* 47 (excerpt). © Daniel Clowes. Used with permission.

paper. The point, finally, is obvious: what passes for frankness in comics must be a matter of both subjective vision and graphic artifice, a shotgun wedding of the untrustworthy and the unreal.

From the outset, Clowes trades on known facts about himself and his work. Since so many of his comics rely on thinly fictionalized personae, Clowes starts "Just Another Day" with a panel, a title card so to speak, that explicitly identifies *him*, the genuine "Daniel G. Clowes," as both creator and protagonist (fig. 42). Yet right away something seems oddly *off* about this credit line, for the name "Daniel G. Clowes" bears the symbol for a registered trademark, as if Clowes himself is but a marketable property, a character to be variously drawn and exploited, ad infinitum. Throughout the story arrows point to "the Real Clowes," or "the Real *Real* Clowes," even as the possibility of a "real" Clowes recedes infinitely, vanishing behind a succession of disparate caricatures: the average joe, the "big-shot wheeler-dealer," the "sensitive artiste," and so on. The story's closing caption, which reads "etc., etc.," suggests both that these permutations could go on forever and that Clowes finds the very prospect of confessional comics absurd.

"Just Another Day" warrants a closer look because of the brilliant way in which it peels back layers of falsehood, one by one. On the first page, we find a bleary-eyed Clowes doing his morning wake-up routine before a bathroom mirror. Graphic license is at a minimum here, so that the "Clowes" character appears evenly proportioned and realistic (that is, true to the conventions of comic book realism). The second page, however, reveals the scam, as Clowes' stand-in is abruptly recontextualized within a very different milieu—that of a Hollywood movie set, in which Clowes, the so-called "real" Clowes this time, acts as director as well as cartoonist (fig. 43). Clowes-the-director pauses in his drawing to "talk to the readers," offering an explicit version of the rationale that, tacitly, lies behind autobiographical comics: "If I show the minutae [sic] of my daily life truthfully, no matter how embarrassing or painful, maybe you'll respond to that truth and realize that we perhaps share the same unspoken human traits and you and I will have a beautiful artist/reader experience. Dig?" (45). Thus Clowes distills and mocks Pekar's ethic of fidelity to mundane truths. This smug explanation reduces the implicit aims of autobiography to a numbing banality. By making the intent explicit, Clowes short-circuits it.

As his story shifts into cool satire, Clowes begins to reshape, graphically, his very self, resorting to blunt

Figure 42. Clowes, "Just Another Day." 44 (excerpt). © Daniel Clowes. Used with permission.

caricature. For instance, the head of the so-called "real" Clowes, unlike his stand-in's, seems grotesquely out of proportion to the rest of his body, while his toothy smile and slitted eyes advertise his insincerity. The sequence that follows (in which the stand-in "Clowes" sniffs his dirty socks, echoing the grotty intimacy of such cartoonists as Kominsky-Crumb and Joe Matt) restores the graphic "realism" of the first page, but now in brackets, for we know that the entire sequence is a put-on. Broad caricature returns as the director "Clowes" unpacks this scene, debunking the always implied claim that such embarrassing details are representative rather than just plain weird: *I made that whole thing up!"* he gloats. "I've never done anything like that in my *life!!"* The reader who identifies with such scenes, he sneers, must be a "fucking sicko!!" (46). By this time the so-called "real Clowes" has become a familiar Clowesian type: the swollen epitome of smarmy self-satisfaction.

What follows is a strangled mea culpa for the story's overlapping falsehoods, as Clowes shifts from cell-phone-wielding "big shot" to hand-wringing "artiste," and thence to diverse other stereotypes. Staring into the mirror at one point, in an echo of the story's opening, the "Clowes" character drives home the crucial point that "it's weird trying to do comics

about yourself. . . . It's almost impossible to be objective." The difficulty lies, he suggests, in the artist's own ever-changing self-image, and the possibility that even full disclosure will be received as mere rhetorical posturing: "[I]f you are willing to embarrass yourself you have to make sure it's not just to show what a cool, honest guy you are . . ." (47). Even complete "honesty," Clowes implies, serves some self-inflating purpose.

"Just Another Day," though extraordinarily smart, is not unprecedented; in fact it seizes on an idea put forth rather offhandedly some twenty-one years before, by comix pioneer R. Crumb, in his two-page strip "The Many Faces of R. Crumb" (*XYZ Comics*, 1972, reprinted in *Complete Crumb*, vol. 9). "Many Faces" (fig. 44) presents almost twenty distinct personae within its twenty panels. Crumb's strip boasts no narrative or discursive continuity like Clowes's but instead rattles off a list of discrete and seemingly incompatible personalities: "the long-suffering patient artist-saint," for instance, or the "sentimental slob," or "the youth culture member in good standing." Billed simply as "an inside look at the complex personality" of the artist, "Many Faces" offers no rationale apart from its central question, implied until the very end, "Who is this Crumb?" Yet, anticipating

Figure 43. Clowes, "Just Another Day." 45 (excerpt). © Daniel Clowes. Used with permission.

Clowes, Crumb places the very act of creation at the heart of the strip; the strip asserts its own constructedness. As throughout *XYZ Comics*, and indeed much of Crumb's work from this period, the primacy of *drawing* as a subject serves to connect what would otherwise be a freewheeling series of non sequiturs.

Indeed, drawing is foremost in Crumb's mind. The first panel shows Crumb masturbating to one of his own so-called "sick cartoons," while a caption tells us that he is "'hard' at work in [his] studio." Thus an intimacy between artist and art is established: Crumb takes sexual pleasure in his own handiwork. From the outset, then, the real and the drawn are purposefully confused. Crumb asserts both the almost palpable reality of his drawings and their artificiality.

This giddy image of masturbation leads logically into the next panel, which reveals that the cartoonist gets what he wants by "drawing a picture of the desired object." Here the drawing equates a woman with a Lincoln Continental and a stack of old 78 rpm records, while the cartoon Crumb leers in anticipation—a moment of crassness bracing in its candor yet typical of Crumb's work. The vision of Crumb himself has changed from one panel to the next; more important, the second panel acknowledges Crumb's solipsism, both through its candid dehumanization of the woman and through the text's recognition

that the drawings serve Crumb's desires for acquisition and mastery. As so often in Crumb, confession tips over immediately into lampoon, palliating the bitter truth, but the point has been made: both Crumb's elastic sense of self and his treatment of others are shaped by his feelings and desires. Thus these two apparently anomalous panels at the top of the story prepare for the parade of images to follow. The real subject of what follows, after all, is not so much the "truth" about Crumb himself as his ability, through drawing, to impose an arbitrary vision on the world *and* on himself. The drawings may be confused with the real, but Crumb reminds us that they are neither true nor sufficient in themselves.

Throughout the remaining eighteen panels Crumb assumes various guises, many of which, such as *artist-saint*, *booshwah businessman*, and *media superstar*, testify to his ambivalence about passing from private self to public personality. (This ambivalence saturates *XYZ Comics* as well as the contemporaneous *People's Comix*.) The very random, non-narrative quality of this series also testifies to the plasticity of the artist's self-image, in a way that Clowes's more argumentative approach cannot: if none of these images is adequate to unlock the "real" Crumb, then all are nonetheless part of the way he sees himself. As Crumb says in the end, again prefiguring Clowes, "It all

Figure 44. R. Crumb, "The Many Faces of R. Crumb," first page. *The Complete Crumb Comics*, Vol. 9, page 21. © 2004 R. Crumb. Used with permission.

Figure 45. Gilbert Hernandez, "My Love Book." *Hernandez Satyricon* (selected panels). © 2004 Gilbert Hernandez. Used with permission.

depends on the mood I'm in!!" It is the drawing that gives these momentary, untrustworthy impressions the weight of truth.

This aggressive unpacking of the cartoonist's persona anticipates the problems of authenticity later encountered by the post-Pekar generation. In response to that generation, a similar antagonism marks Gilbert Hernandez's bizarre parody of the genre, titled "My Love Book" (from the achingly self-conscious penultimate issue of the original *Love & Rockets*, 1995, reprinted in *Hernandez Satyricon*). If Crumb revels in the plasticity of his persona, and Clowes uses multiple selves to attack autobiography's claims to truth, then "Love Book" goes further still. Prompted by a confessed impatience with the autobiographical comics genre (Young, "Comic Art" 55), Hernandez teases the reader with a disjointed series of confessional vignettes, between which his visual personae shift so radically that we can confirm their common identity only through the repetition of certain motifs in dialogue and action. Over its fourteen pages, "Love Book" offers not only a bewildering array of formats (three-page stories, single-pagers, and brief strips) but also a string of bizarre Gilbert-inspired protagonists: a young superhero-as-bedwetter; an Edward Munch-esque critter; even an anthropomorphic pig (fig. 45). As the artist's own image metamorphoses, generic conventions are yanked out of joint: seeming

revelations about Hernandez's adolescence and family life are wrapped in the clichés of superheroics, science fiction, and funny animals.

Throughout this scattershot collection, certain ideas repeat themselves. Maternal discipline, for instance, is a recurrent theme: harshly punished by mother, both the cute li'l pig of the strip "Pig" and the superhero of the story "Bully" talk to God in prayer. (God, of course, takes the mother's side.) Hernandez's Hispanic background and the racism he presumably endured because of it come up in "Bully" as well as the gag strip "The Artist." Bedwetting is a motif in both "Bully" and the cruel "And So It Was," which suggests guilty memories of his father's death. Adolescent sexual desire informs both "Loser in Love" and "Valentine," the latter a remembrance of Gilbert's courtship with his wife, Carol, mockingly certified by "the Carol Seal of Veracity." Such thematic repetition lends a sense of unity to an otherwise random assortment of tales.

Like our Crumb and Clowes examples, "My Love Book" is arch and self-reflexive. Among other things, the story serves as a sidelong commentary on the impending end of *Love & Rockets*, which had served Gilbert and his brother Jaime as a personal anthology for some thirteen years (see chapter 3). As a departure from Gilbert's usual work, "Love Book" flirts with the reader's prior knowledge, beginning with a two-page teaser in which Gilbert and Jaime

Figure 46. Hernandez, "My Love Book." 57 (excerpt). © 2004 Gilbert Hernandez. Used with permission.

assume the role of heroes in a ham-fisted commentary on their own careers (fig. 46). Facing "the moment of truth"—implicitly, the end of *Love & Rockets*—the two artists declare that this will be, not an end, but a "grand new beginning," from which there can be "no turning back!" (57). Thus "Love Book" points to itself in a manner similar to Crumb and Clowes; the primacy of the artist is ironically asserted at the outset.

On the following page (fig. 47) Gilbert prepares what he calls an "effigy" to act in the story of his life. In an echo of James Whale's film *Frankenstein* (Universal, 1931), Gilbert's roly-poly assistant "Nixon" replaces the effigy's "normal penis" with an *abnormal* one. Thus the effigy, wound in a false skin and sporting a shriveled member, is already a Frankensteinian mishap, a patchwork man of dubious authenticity. Leaning over his drawing board, the artist orders his assistant, "Get me—I mean *it* into position," a moment of confusion that suggests the impossibility of an authentic autobiographical comic. This effigy prepares us for the various personae that inhabit the following pages.

"My Love Book" ends with brutal pessimism, with what at first seems the most straightforward, or least

embroidered, of Hernandez's personae: a flaccid, pudgy self-portrait in sharp contrast to the heroic ideal at the story's start (fig. 48). (This antiheroic self-image, incidentally, has reappeared in Gilbert's subsequent work.) Haunted by his principal characters, as well as the then-recent death of the much-loved cartoonist Jack Kirby, *this* Gilbert looks back at his career in comics, musing, "It wasn't such a bad gig, was it?" (67). Gazing at several slogans, taped to his studio wall like so many Post-It notes, Gilbert says with bitter humor, "*Heh* . . . Can't believe I ever wrote this shit . . . Wonder if I ever *really* believed it?" These bumper sticker-like messages again destabilize the artist's persona, since they seem at odds with the portrait of Hernandez that emerges through other stories and even in "Love Book" itself. Thus even this final, low-key persona is awash in ambiguity. Its fictionality is finally underscored by the impossible, suicidal climax, as, in a self-conscious echo of Nirvana's Kurt Cobain, Gilbert shoots himself in the mouth.[5]

The story's last panel manages to be at once risible and disturbing, the bloody suicide commenting acidly on the pending conclusion of *Love & Rockets*. The fatal image also adverts to, again, the limits of autobiography. With this bitter irony, "Love Book"

Figure 47. Hernandez, "My Love Book." 58 (excerpt). © 2004 Gilbert Hernandez. Used with permission.

muddies its own implicit assertion of truth. Who *is* this Gilbert? The assertive hero of the opening, sure of a grand destiny? Or the pathetic, crapped-out caricature of wasted talent shown at the end? Perhaps, as Crumb asserts, it all depends on the artist's mood.

In the last analysis, what are the above stories after? What do they reveal? If autobiographical comix take as their starting point a polemical assertion of truth over fantasy, then these comics serve to reassert the fantastic, distorting power of the artist's craft and vision. They carry us to the vanishing point where imagination and claims to truth collide. Yet these pieces still demand and play on the reader's trust; *they still purport to tell truths.* Crumb, Clowes, and Hernandez, finally, do not disallow autobiography as such, but ironically reaffirm its power by demanding recognition of its implicit assumptions. Ultimately, the implied compact between author and reader—what Philippe Lejeune famously called the autobiographical pact—is upheld even as it is abused (see Lejeune 3–30 for discussion of autobiography as a "contractual" genre).

FICTIVE BUT NOT FICTITIOUS

In a sense, the above stories assert truthfulness through falsity. Comics, like any form of narrative, can falsify circumstances by subjecting the vagaries of experience to the hindsight of exposition, the rigors and temptations of storytelling—what George Gusdorf calls "the original sin . . . of logical coherence and rationalization" (Gusdorf 41).[6] Yet by flaunting the falseness of their personae, Crumb, Clowes, and Hernandez reconfirm the power of comics to convey something like the truth. Artifice and candor go hand in hand. This fundamental irony comes into sharper focus if, following Timothy Dow Adams, we invoke Merle Brown's distinction between the *fictive* and the *fictitious*: a story may be fictive yet truthful, insofar as it "implies as part of itself the art of its making"; in contrast, a story (autobiographical or otherwise) that does *not* acknowledge its own making is merely fictitious (Brown 62; Adams, *Telling Lies* 11). The fictive, then, problematizes itself, while the merely fictitious strives for transparency.

By Brown's criterion, these three stories are fictive but not fictitious, for they acknowledge their own construction too frankly. While these tales revel in artifice, in the end they present the artist's own techniques to us with such self-critical candor that implied claims to truth, though now bracketed, still inform our reading. These tales bear out Paul John Eakin's observation that "[a]utobiographers themselves constitute a principal source of doubt about the validity of [their] art" (276); yet this doubt, this radical self-questioning, reinforces rather than corrodes the seeming veracity of autobiography, for the texts' admissions

Figure 48. Hernandez, "My Love Book." 67 (excerpt). © 2004 Gilbert Hernandez. Used with permission.

of artifice defer the question of trustworthiness to a new level, that of the very act of creation. Here is where the truth of the autobiography resides, for this truth, as Janet Varner Gunn has said, lies "not in the 'facts' of the story itself, but in the relational space *between* the story and its reader" (143). These cartoonists exploit that metaphoric space, inviting readers into complicity.

If autobiographical comics offer a specious objectivity, then Crumb, Clowes, and Hernandez take pains to subvert it. Yet paradoxically this subversion cements the pact, the generic understanding, between readers and author, for these comics attempt to avoid falsification by acknowledging the reader's presence

and making demands on his/her sophistication. Through deconstructive playfulness, these pieces effectively underscore Gunn's observation that "the authorship of autobiography is tacitly plural" (143). After all, autobiography, as Gunn notes, is a performance, a game—a social act that calls for a "plural, not singular, reflexivity" (140). Clowes, Crumb, and Hernandez invite us to play this game: our input is solicited, and our skepticism flattered, by their refusal to be simply "honest"—that is, fictitious.

We might call this strategy, then, authentication through artifice, or more simply *ironic authentication*: the implicit reinforcement of truth claims through their explicit rejection. In brief, ironic authentication makes a show of honesty by denying the very possibility of being honest. The strategy reaches its zenith of playful aggression in the above three tales, which, paradoxically, glorify the self through a form of self-abnegation—that is, through the very denial of an irreducible, unified identity, one that cannot be falsified through artistic representation. In each case the self-assertion of the author rests on the plasticity of his self-image, on his awareness of the slipperiness of individual identity. The core identity of each is precisely what *cannot* be represented, and it is this very lack that, ironically, prompts the project of self-representation.

If this constitutive absence underlies autobiography in general, it becomes especially clear in the form of comics, where a series of discrete images, each one substituting for the one before it, represents sequence and continuity. The syntax of comics—specifically, its reliance on visual substitution to suggest continuity—puts the lie to the notion of an unchanging, undivided self, for in the breakdowns of comics we see the self (in action over a span of time) represented by *multiple* selves. The tension between single image and image-in-series disrupts (in the words of Linda Haverty Rugg) "the singularity of the autobiographical pact by pointing to a plurality of selves" (13). The representation of time through space, and the fragmentation of space into contiguous images, argue for the changeability of the individual self—the possibility that our identities may be more changeable, or less stable, than we care to imagine. The three stories above flirt with this unsettling possibility, and testify to anxiety about it, yet each attempts to celebrate, through ironic refraction, the "auteur" behind the curtain, the cartoonist whose craft makes these multiple representations possible.

Once established, the idea of ironic authentication sheds light on the representational strategies behind autobiographical comics in general. Indeed this self-reflexive dimension can be seen even in comics by Harvey Pekar. For instance, "The Harvey Pekar Name Story," as shown in chapter 2, puts paid to the notion of a singular self, through its ironic use of a grid filled with near-identical "Pekars" (refer back to fig. 11). The frustration of the narrator has everything to do

with his failed attempts to assert his individuality in the face of multiple selves. "A Marriage Album," a collaborative tale in which Pekar and his wife, Joyce Brabner (with illustrator Val Mayerick) recall the circumstances of their marriage, takes an opposite tack: it shows different and conflicting pictures of Harvey, culled from past *American Splendor* stories, to suggest how Joyce's image of him was influenced by his comics prior to their first face-to-face meeting (fig. 49). This highly fraught moment, as Witek suggests in *Comic Books as History*, calls attention not only to the diverse styles of Pekar's collaborators but also to "the various fictionalizing personae Pekar [has] adopt[ed]," hence to the inherently fictive nature of his autobiographical work (139). As in *Our Cancer Year*, so here: art filters into life, alerting us to our own participation in the author's self-construction.

In conclusion, despite the seeming naïveté of autobiographical comics in general, such ironic authentication informs many of the keystone works in the genre. Moments of self-referential play can be found, for instance, in such seminal examples as Green's *Binky Brown* (to which we turn in our next chapter) and Kominsky-Crumb's early "Bunch" stories. Though Crumb, Clowes, and Hernandez take this strategy to a skeptical and disorienting extreme, such self-reflexive gestures are to some degree essential to the genre. Granted, some cartoonists gleefully blur the distinction between auteur and cartoon persona: take for example Crumb and Kominsky-Crumb in *Dirty Laundry* and *Self-Loathing Comics* (husband-and-wife collaborations in which each cartoonist draws him/herself), or the remarkably indiscreet Joe Matt (whose *Peepshow* often serves as a passive-aggressive intervention in his own real-life relationships). Ironic authentication, however, calls attention to this very distinction, life vs. art, and thus answers the justified skepticism of readers. In short, this strategy continually renegotiates the compact between author and audience, certifying the genre's truth claims through unabashed falseness.

It may be that ironic authentication simply exaggerates the irony inherent in trying to tell one's own story through the hybrid visual-verbal means of comics. Comic art, after all, is a potentially complex

Figure 49. Harvey Pekar, Joyce Brabner, and Val Mayerick, "A Marriage Album." *More American Splendor* (n. pag.). © Harvey Pekar. Used with permission.

narrative instrument, offering forms of visual-verbal synergy in which confused and even conflicting points of view can be entertained all at once. The interaction of word and picture—that basic tension between codes—allows for ongoing intertextual or metatextual commentary, a possibility that threatens the very idea of a unified self. Complex, multivalent meanings, irreducible to a single message, are possible in comics precisely because of this visual-verbal tension, which enables the author to represent simultaneously various aspects or readings of him or herself. Ironic authentication points up this complexity, both challenging and yet affirming autobiography's regard for truth. The above examples represent a salutary loss of innocence—the recognition that, for autobiographers, "truth" must be a matter of craft as well as honesty.

CHAPTER FIVE

IRONY AND SELF-REFLEXIVITY IN AUTOBIOGRAPHICAL COMICS

TWO CASE STUDIES

Regarding autobiographical comics, hindsight reveals an ironic, self-reflexive impulse at work in many of the genre's urtexts. The ironies may not always be as bald, or as cynical, as in the key instances from our previous chapter, but nonetheless they are crucial, often contributing to a sense of distance between the "naïve" self depicted in the autobiography and the older, more sophisticated self responsible for the depiction. This distancing is *critical* in two senses, that is, both analytical and all-important. As Louis Renza long ago observed, the autobiographer experiences his "signified past self as at once the same as his present self . . . and yet strangely, uniquely, as *other* to it" (317). The worldview of the autobiographical subject, often a confused young naïf, contrasts with the more mature and comprehensive, or simply more jaded, view of the author. In comics, this sense of *other*ness may be enacted by the tension between representational codes: the abstract or discursive (the Word) versus the concrete or visual (the Picture). Such verbal-visual tension opens up a space of opportunity, one in which pictorial metaphors can multiply promiscuously, offering a surreal or wildly subjective vision to counterbalance the truth claims that certify the text as autobiographical. Thus bizarre, "unrealistic," and expressionistic images may coexist with a scrupulously factual account of one's life. The resultant ironies confer an authenticity that is emotional rather than literal: that of the present talking to the past.

But why does the "authenticity" of autobiographical comics matter, anyway? To be frank, the very idea of authenticity (or its pejorative flipside, *in*authenticity) carries a moralistic and metaphysical charge that should rouse our skepticism. As our previous chapter reveals, talking about "authenticity" in nonfiction comics is dicey at best—the sort of thing that invites anxious throat-clearing and the fretful overuse of quotation marks. Yet, as before noted, the ethic of "authenticity" (there I go again) stands in polemical contrast to the fantasy genres that have for so long dominated the comics mainstream. Invoking "authenticity" means taking a stand—this is one of the fundamental appeals of alternative comics—and autobiographical comics that strive after authenticity have the potential for radical cultural argument. Again, there is a democratic subtext to the genre and at its best an awareness of the linking, indeed inextricable knotting, of the personal and the political. Simply put, the idea of authenticity offers an escape from escapism (in the narrowest, most retrograde sense).

Some will argue, indeed some *have* argued, otherwise. For instance, cultural historian Ian Gordon, reviewing Joseph Witek's *Comic Books as History*, balks at Witek's appraisal of Harvey Pekar. Gordon suggests that Pekar's work, far from linking the personal and the political, remains "banal [and] narcissistic," and charges Pekar with an "inability to conceive of human relations except as they apply to himself" ("'But Seriously, Folks . . .'" 345). For Gordon, Pekar's self-regarding comics, and the reception of same, are symptoms of "a culture of narcissism." This accusation alludes, of course, to Christopher Lasch's famed *The Culture of Narcissism* (1978), an Olympian analysis undergirded by Freud and distinguished by a broad and penetrating critique of various media and cultural forms. By now Lasch's indictment has a familiar ring to it: the post-sixties retreat into privatism, as opposed to political action; the rise of a "therapeutic sensibility" that centers everything on the self; the relentless trumpeting of personal gratification, at the expense of enduring social relations; the neglect of historical continuity—indeed the whole depressing parade of the so-called "Me Generation," of which Lasch provided the most magisterial and perhaps most radical critique. By positioning his reading of Pekar within the horizons of Lasch's larger critique, Gordon would seem to score a palpable hit (the historical near-coincidence of Lasch's book and Pekar's *American Splendor* perhaps helps).

Indeed Lasch, in his attack on New Journalism and the self-help and confessional literature of the seventies, seems to anticipate some commonplace criticisms of autobiographical comics. He criticizes "the confessional mode" for presenting personal experience without reflection, in "undigested" form, and also for appealing to "salacious curiosity" rather than the search for deep understanding. Perhaps most damning, Lasch faults such writing for failing to achieve "the detachment indispensable to art" (17). His criticism extends to specific elements, or tics, of style, such as "self-parody"—more specifically, that "perfunctory [and] self-deprecatory" strain of humor that disarms criticism by offering writers a convenient way out, a means of "disclaiming responsibility" and "ingratiating themselves" to the skeptical reader (18–19). This charge seems born out by, for example, the aforementioned "Many Faces of R. Crumb," in which disquieting self-revelation eases immediately into self-deprecating overstatement (see chapter 4). As Lasch sees it, this type of work, far from being honest, is fundamentally "evasive," as it "waives the right to be taken seriously" and seems determined merely to attract undeserved attention or sympathy (20–21).

Such charges are hard to answer, not least because they blur together aesthetic and moralistic judgments under the warrant of psychoanalysis, with its authoritative, clinical vocabulary. Lasch's study is sweeping; his argument extends from the clinical literature regarding narcissism (Freud, Kernberg, Klein et al.) to an omnivorous critique of various cultural forms and institutions, and, ultimately, to an attack on post-industrial capitalism, which, he argues, "elicits and reinforces narcissistic traits in everyone" (232). In this light, the upwelling of new forms of personal narrative (in comics and in literature more generally) appears merely a symptom of collapse, or retreat, into a pathological me-first-ism that logically fulfills rather than resists the cultural crisis of late capitalism.

This far-ranging analysis has implications for what we now habitually call postmodern culture, especially as Lasch touches on such topics as historical amnesia, the ubiquity of advertising, and the idea of "consumption as an alternative to protest or rebellion" (73). In the latter we should include the marketing and consumption of "rebellion" itself, as an idea, a stance, even a "style." Indeed advertising now routinely exhorts us to "think differently" and offers, as incentive, images of culture heroes who became such by virtue of their supposed individualism. From this viewpoint, autobiography's "assertion of individuality" (established in our last chapter) could be construed not as a principled resistance to corporate culture but rather as a form of surrender. Individualists, rebels, and "hipsters," in particular the heroes of the sixties' "anticommercial" counterculture, are the pillars of today's commercial hype. Indeed, as Thomas Frank points out in *The Conquest of Cool* (1997), the counterculture has become "an enduring commercial myth," and "hip" a ubiquitous commercial style, indeed "the vernacular of the [1990s'] much-hyped economic revolution" (32). By this light, resisting a too-obvious commercialization, as indeed Pekar's *American Splendor* and many other autobiographical comics do, is but another form of commercial come-on. Everybody wants to be an individual, everybody wants to "fight the power." What makes autobiographical comics so special in this regard?

Such a view apparently underlies Gordon's indictment of Pekar, a writer for whom, he says, "other people's experiences only achieve importance as they relate to [himself]" (345). Lost in this criticism, however, are two considerations. First, autobiography, with its focus on the everyday, has the potential to shed light on issues of real political and cultural heft; as Lasch says, "social questions inevitably present themselves also as personal ones" (26). Second, autobiography is not always and inevitably a genre for the self-absorbed, or the strutting "individualist." On the contrary, much autobiography derives its interest from its enactment of dialogical and inter-subjective relationships—in short, from its social acuity. Autobiographical comics in particular often treat the author's visible persona as an interlocutor and

storytelling device, a means for getting at, and shaping, the stories of *other people's* lives.

Joseph Witek long ago observed this tendency in Pekar's work (*Comic Books* 142–43, 149–53). In the years since Witek's study, Pekar (perhaps partly because of the influence of his wife, writer Joyce Brabner) has become even more interested in using his life experience as a way of bringing others' to light. The intersubjective, indeed collaborative, potential of Pekar comes to the fore in many of his projects. Take, for instance, the shared memoir *Our Cancer Year*, with Brabner and illustrator Frank Stack, in which the interplay between Pekar's and Brabner's viewpoints parallels the interweaving of personal and political crises (as described in the previous chapter); the one-shot comic book *American Splendour* [sic]: *Transatlantic Comics* (1998), based on British artist Colin Warneford's personal account of living with Asperger's Syndrome, and illustrated mostly by Warneford himself from Pekar's script; and the recent *Unsung Hero* (2003), a retelling of the Vietnam experiences of African-American war veteran Robert McNeill, drawn by David Collier from Pekar's script, and evidently based on McNeill's own oral testimony.

These long-form projects only enlarge on a tendency apparent in Pekar's work from early on, for, as often as Pekar has made himself and his struggles the center of attention, he has also turned his observing eye on others and solicited *their* stories. The near-constant presence of Pekar himself, as interlocutor and recorder, serves not as a mere salve to the author's ego but rather as an authenticating device (rather like the foregrounding of the writer's experience in the New Journalism). At times this interchange results in a complex tracing of connections between the author's personal activity and his gathering of other people's tales. This technique, modeled by Pekar, has since shaped many autobiographical and journalistic comics, such as, for example, the eccentric historical comics of David Collier (*Just the Facts, Portraits from Life*) and the emotionally wrenching reportage of Joe Sacco (*Palestine, Safe Area Goražde*)—both sometime Pekar collaborators. In the best of such comics, autobiographical self-reflexivity serves to pry open larger political and cultural issues; *ironic authentication*, as defined in our last chapter, enables the careful and complex handling of a larger social/historical focus.

In chapter 4 we established ironic authentication as a tempting strategy in nonfiction comics, a means of graphically asserting truthfulness through the admission of artifice. Thus defined, ironic authentication gives authors a way of anticipating, answering, and taking advantage of their own (and their readers') skepticism. By way of conclusion I suggested that this kind of irony only exaggerates the ironies always potentially present in comics, due to the form's fundamental tension between verbal and visual codes. This tension enables the graphic enactment, on the picture plane, of the critical estrangement or *distancing* between the autobiographer and his/her "past self" (as depicted in the work). Such irony may confer emotional truths while confounding any literal sense of authenticity. Broadly speaking, ironic authentication makes the autobiographical comic reenact or "speak to" its own making.

This kind of irony, then, allows for not only various playful metacomics—comics about making comics about making comics, ad infinitum, as in our previous examples from Crumb, Clowes, and Hernandez—but also comics about subjects that are almost impossibly hard to handle, where questions of truth and artifice are fraught with special urgency, both psychologically and politically. The balance of this chapter will examine two autobiographical comics of the utmost urgency, to show how self-reflexivity can enable both psychological intimacy and bold social argument. I hope what follows will also suggest why autobiography, of all things, became central to alternative comics—and indeed became comic art's most traveled route to growth, enrichment, and recognition as a form of literature.

JUSTIN GREEN: HONESTY THROUGH METAPHORICAL OVERKILL

The first of our examples, perhaps the *ur*-example of confessional literature in comics, is Justin Green's one-shot comic book *Binky Brown Meets the Holy Virgin Mary* (1972). *Binky*, published by the pioneering underground comix company Last Gasp Eco-Funnies (of Berkeley, California), is recognized as a precursor to Pekar; indeed it is often cited as the wellspring of autobiographical comics. Estren's *History of Underground Comics*, for example, argues for *Binky*'s wide influence and praises its unparalleled mix of "social commentary, social satire, and social realism" (289–91). Rosenkranz's *Rebel Visions* (quoting Green) alludes to the passionate reader response the book engendered (189); more concretely, *The Comics Journal*'s Bob Levin observes that *Binky* sold some 50,000 copies, an extraordinary figure for comix (101). Most famously, *Binky* inspired the seminal first-person comics of Crumb, Kominsky-Crumb, and many others (Spiegelman, "Symptoms" 4).

Green's groundbreaking work warrants a close look because it at once anticipates, and stands in sharp contrast to, the insistently mundane and more or less "realistically" rendered comics of the Pekar school. (*Binky* foreshadows, for example, Gilbert Hernandez's protean, wildly shifting approach to autobiography, seen in our previous chapter.) More important, *Binky* is an extraordinary achievement in its own right: a fantastic, bleakly humorous mix of informed anti-Catholic polemic and self-scourging confessional. Over its forty pages, Green uncorks his psyche, examining in harrowing detail the collision of Catholic doctrine and his own neurotic, guilt-driven personality (since diagnosed as a case of Obsessive-Compulsive Disorder, though no such explanation was available to Green at the time of *Binky*'s creation [Green 8]). The book depicts the mutual reinforcement of religious dogma and psychological obsession, a cruel synergy that all but consumes its titular hero. Binky, a profoundly restless character, is tormented by self-doubt, thus devoted to constant checking, double-checking, and triple-checking to make sure no sins are committed (or at least none left unatoned). The book, in keeping with this psychological profile, is a work of obsessive genius.

Green's particular obsession, as detailed in *Binky*, involves imaginary rays of carnal lust emanating from his penis, his limbs, and even material objects, rays that he must prevent from striking representations,

Figure 50. Justin Green, "Binky Brown Meets the Holy Virgin Mary." *Binky Brown Sampler* 42 (excerpt). © Justin Green. Used with permission.

whether visual or verbal, of the Holy Virgin Mary (and the Catholic Church more generally). These rays threaten to converge on the Virgin in much the same way that, in classical perspective, invisible lines connect parallel objects to a common vanishing point—a resemblance that Green, an almost neurotically meticulous craftsman, duly acknowledges. Indeed, the exact form of Green's compulsion seems to match perfectly his vocation as artist: his cartoon alter ego, Binky Brown, visualizes a world of gridlike precision, in which invisible vectors of sin crisscross the landscape. This, obviously, is an artist's conceit.

Binky's obsession requires positioning himself within the discipline of classical perspective—a curiously rectilinear worldview for one consumed by guilt and fear. Green at once underscores and resists this linearity, for graphically his artwork enacts a struggle between geometric severity and organic fluidity. For instance, as he describes his Catholic school's insistence on "order, uniformity, rigidity, and obedience," Green draws a precise square-tiled

pattern on the classroom floor, and shows one of Binky's teachers, a severe nun, ordering her charges to "line up [their] desks with the tiles!" The panel before this shows a nun beating Binky with a "metal architect's ruler" (18). Later, as the comic explains Binky's obsession for "straightening" things, the drawings parody his obsession, turning the character and his environment into flat, angular shapes in contrast to the freehand energy of Green's usual figures (fig. 50). Binky himself, walking past a chair that offends his sense of order, becomes a parody of *Superman*'s once-popular character "Bizarro" (a square-headed, crystalline version of Superman who lived on a cube-shaped world and spoke in a fractured, childlike dialect). In Bizarro-speak, Binky says, "Uh-oh—chair make trouble!" He then straightens the offending furniture so that "all is well" (42).

On the facing page, an assortment of penile objects (weathercock, badminton racket, soda bottle, and so on) appears in a baffling, non-perspectival splash panel that takes up two-thirds of the page,

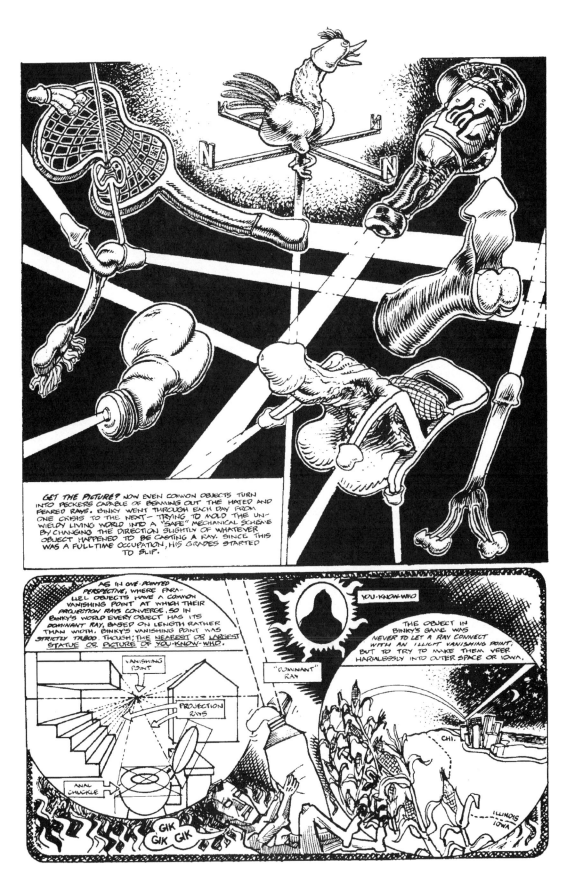

Figure 51. Green, "Binky Brown." 43. © Justin Green. Used with permission.

each object projecting its "pecker ray" (fig. 51). These tumescent shapes, veined and fleshy, recall the curvy, LSD-influenced abstractions of such underground comix artists as Victor Moscoso, and their resistance to conventional perspective belies Binky's efforts (and the Church's) to "mold the unwieldy living world into a 'safe' mechanical scheme" (43). Just beneath, a round or "bull's-eye" panel contains an explanation of Binky's perspectival obsession, replete with a diagram of "projection rays" and "vanishing point." At the bottom of the page, Binky, shown struggling with a giant toothpaste tube to prevent its ray from striking "you-know-who," again appears in an oddly angular rendering, as if his body was made of sheared quartz.

Such self-reflexive playfulness characterizes *Binky* right up to the end, as Green nods repeatedly to the very act of drawing. The creation of *Binky* itself is drawn into the story, as a sign of Green's desperation, a purging of his guilt, and a way of humorously underscoring his critique of Catholicism. For example, the penultimate panel finds Binky, having spurned Catholicism and recognized his obsession as such, eyeing a stack of overdue library books: *First Catechism*, *Perspective*, and *Fun with a Pencil* (fig. 52). The titles of these three books testify to the overlap in Brown/Green's psyche between artistic vision and religious neurosis, as they recall the hero's indoctrination into the Church, his grasp of classical art, and his dedication to drawing. In the background, a cartoon by R. Crumb hints at a different source of inspiration: metonymically, Crumb (also a lapsed Catholic) stands in for the underground comix movement, then in its heyday, which liberated Green artistically, inspiring him to set forth his personal story in comics form.

Obviously, the "pencil" in the third book's title, *Fun with a Pencil*, can substitute metaphorically for the feared *penis*, the original source of the rays that have so monopolized Binky's imagination. Green knowingly employs this metaphoric likeness between artist's tool and penis, beginning with the frontispiece (inside front cover) to the comic book (fig. 53). Here, in a full-page drawing, a caricature of Green appears: naked, hands and ankles bound, he

hangs upside down with a pen in his mouth, drawing a comics page (10). His ink bottle is labeled "Dad's blood"; a phonograph beside him plays a warped record of "Ave Maria." He draws by candlelight, while cherubim hover overhead, with plunger, toilet paper, and toilet bowl brush in their hands. Positioned between the artist's legs is a long, sickle-like blade, perched dangerously close to his groin.

Here Green, in a "confession to [his] readers," admits that *Binky* represents an effort to, as he says, "purge myself of the compulsive neurosis which I have served since I officially left Catholicism on Halloween, 1958." Begging indulgence for focusing on "the petty conflict in [his] crotch," the cartoonist suggests that portraying his neurosis in "easy-to-understand comic-book format" may help others similarly afflicted, and thus constitutes an act of intervention in a "social" issue: "If we neurotics were tied together we would entwine the globe many times over in a *vast chain of common suffering*" (10, emphasis in original). The very balloon that contains his words appears bloated and venous, wrapped in thorns and held to the wall by an enormous nail, a Christological allusion that suggests both the depth of Green's impiety and the desperation of his cause. From the outset, then, the pen becomes both an affront to Catholicism and an active substitute for or sublimation of an endangered sexuality, the mobile alternative to a penis held motionless, hostage, by a symbolic threat of castration. A reference in the indicia below to the Catholic Guild's comic book series *Treasure Chest* (1946–72) cements the link between Green and the Catholic tradition, even as it announces the "adults-only" nature of this comic ("Youngsters Prohibited," as the front cover proclaims).

This illustration is the first of many extravagant visual metaphors employed by Green to illustrate and intensify his autobiographical polemic. These metaphors, as Joseph Witek suggests, give *Binky* a surreal, wildly comic quality that sets it apart from Pekar's later, more naturalistic efforts (*Comic Books* 128). Most notably, Green himself becomes a recurrent metaphor: the image of the artist with pen in mouth reappears three times in the tale itself. First,

Figure 52. Green, "Binky Brown." 50 (excerpt). © Justin Green. Used with permission.

Green uses this image to smooth over a transition between his years in parochial school and his arrival at "a 90% Jewish public school" (29). More specifically, he deploys this self-caricature to redirect the reader from a polemic on Catholic doctrine back to his life story per se. Second, the bound cartoonist's likeness pops up as Green explains the impossibility of keeping pace with his "daily prayer quota," that is, his laundry list of penances (44). As "snowballing guilt" transforms Binky into a literal snowball (or Sisyphean boulder?), rolling downhill from Purgatory to Hell, the image from the frontispiece appears in a tiny inset panel, as if the cartoonist were speaking directly to us.

Finally, the story's last page recalls the frontispiece again (50). Here the second panel abruptly pulls us out of the story itself, recontextualizing Binky (triumphant in his rejection of guilt) as a mere drawing on paper (fig. 54). We see the pen, gripped between the artist's teeth, blotting and scratching on the page

within the page, the ink defacing the drawing even as Binky, in the comic within the comic, struggles to overcome his guilt complex. Barely comprehensible, the cartoonist blurts between clenched teeth, "Shek-ik! Almesh fineshk!"

This weird interpolation (almost finished?) suggests that, for the cartoonist, the creation of *Binky* itself has become an elaborate act of penance. It seems that, despite Binky's climactic self-transformation, Green remains entangled in the guilty compulsions of former days, and the crafting of *Binky* itself represents yet another ritual "purging" of these feelings (as the frontispiece suggests). Indeed, the final panel undercuts Binky's victory over Catholic guilt, as it reimagines the cartoonist as a (phallic) fish, lurching down the sidewalk, pen in his mouth. As a cop wearing the sign of the Cross follows, waving a fishnet, the captioned text parodies accounts of evolution, with references to Binky creeping out of "the primeval morass of superstition," taking a "desperate" leap such as those taken by "our brave ancestors, the fish." This ambivalent, comically reductive ending testifies to the tenacity of his neurosis and the impossibility of simply purging it through a violent catharsis (as Binky attempts to do at the climax, by literal iconoclasm, that is, by smashing massproduced Virgins with a hammer). The very process of creating *Binky*, then, becomes a crucial part of Green's tale of obsession: and this is the vanishing point where Green becomes Binky Brown, Binky becomes Justin Green.

Thus *Binky Brown Meets the Holy Virgin Mary* is itself a purgative ritual (comparable to Binky's final confrontation with the mass-produced 39-cent Madonnas). The pen, one phallic item *not* explicitly identified with the penis (though *Fun with a Pencil* hints at this possibility), becomes a more potent symbol than the hammer seen at story's end or the various other shaftlike instruments invoked throughout (baseball bat, fire hose, and so on, all associated with the feared "pecker rays"). The comic, which begins with young Binky's accidental shattering of a Madonna statue, becomes in the end the supreme gesture of iconoclasm, hinted at by the back cover, which shows a lion, wearing a "B" for

Figure 53. Frontispiece to "Binky Brown." *Binky Brown Sampler* 10. © Justin Green. Used with permission.

Figure 54. Green, "Binky Brown." 50 (excerpt).
© Justin Green. Used with permission.

"Binky," attacking the Virgin and revealing her to be a devil in saint's clothing (52).

Years later, Green would admit that, at the time of *Binky*, he styled himself "a warrior against the Church" (8). Notwithstanding his subsequent retreat from this uncompromising position, *Binky* shows the ferocity of his rejection quite clearly, as Binky decries "that mean ol' nasty, whining Catholic God who demands all our love, all the time . . . an unattainable ideal!" (48). Yet Green's polemic admits of ambiguity: for instance, one priest, "Father Innocenzi," appears liberal, lenient and understanding, and tells Binky that "God is merciful" (34); likewise, "Sister Virginia," one of the nuns at Binky's parochial school, is shown favorably—even though Binky himself rejects her when she leaves the convent, calling her an excommunicant and "weakling" (18–19). The story, then, focuses less on the abuse of temporal power by the clergy and more on the inner world of the child, Binky; less on the bare facts of Green's upbringing, more on the development of his tortured self-image vis-à-vis the Church and especially the Virgin.

To this end—and here is what makes *Binky Brown* such a bold and effective piece of work—Green deploys an array of extravagant visual metaphors. Though he lovingly captures the cultural landscape of his formative years in the fifties (for example, clothing, comics, and Cadillacs; furniture, TV, and rock 'n' roll), Green also takes flight graphically through a series of disorienting conceits that capture young Binky's *psychic* landscape with equal precision. At first such conceits are confined to young Binky's dreams and fantasies, but then they gradually assert themselves into his daily life through passages of Green's anti-Catholic argument (for example, parochial school students are brainwashed and turned into marionettes, replete with strings). Eventually, elements of fantasy begin to intrude everywhere: Binky's Jewish father, for instance, appears as a horned devil, and a girl he idolizes literally stands on a pedestal. At one point, rejected by this girl, Binky literally falls down in "th' dumps," then extricates himself with pious reminders of Christ's suffering (fig. 55). In this sequence, the weight of Church dogma appears as a monkey on Binky's back,

Figure 55. Green, "Binky Brown." 27 (excerpt). © Justin Green. Used with permission.

bearing a Cross of its own, while a "Sinstopper's Guidebook" (cribbed from the "Crimestopper's Text-book" in Chester Gould's *Dick Tracy*) counsels against the sin of despair (26–27).

These visual metaphors come more often as Binky's psychic world becomes more and more dominated by his guilty obsessions. Finally, this movement toward metaphor climaxes in the discovery of the "pecker rays," which turn every extremity of Binky's body into a penile projector (42). Over and over, hands and feet appear as huge penises. Consensus reality vanishes for whole sequences as, for example, Binky tries to plug the holes in his "psychic dam" (made literal in the drawings) or assumes the angular, Bizarro-like countenance described above. Most important are the changes in Binky himself, some subtle, some not: he ages; his nose grows; his physique alternates between anemic stringiness and well-muscled beef-cake (50). In addition, Green employs a huge arsenal of layout strategies, graphic devices, and delineative variations: panels and panel borders change shape; diagrammatic arrows, thought balloons, signs and mock-scholarly documentation run rampant; wide-open, white panels contrast with zipatone grays and densely crosshatched backgrounds, some approach-ing an engraving-like texture. Throughout, voluptuous curves battle with rigid, carefully ruled edges, as if enacting the artist's own struggle between icono-clasm and guilt. Those expecting a documentary realism, to authenticate Green's polemic, will be per-plexed by his anarchic visual imagination and over-flowing technique.

While Green does not worry the problem of authenticity per se, he uses myriad devices that put paid to the idea of an unproblematic objectivity: visual symbolism, verbal and ideographic commen-tary, parody and ever-changing graphic design. Thus *Binky*, inspiration for the autobiographical comix movement to follow, demonstrates how the persona of the cartoonist is always inevitably in doubt—how a mocking visual self-reflexivity informs even the foundations of this genre. Indeed, radical subjectivity is the focus of *Binky*, and Green's cartoon world is as aggressively imaginative as Binky's own inner world is obsessive and guilt-wracked.

Green's blending of scarifying psychological con-tent and profuse visual metaphor has been an important reference point for several generations of cartoonists. In particular, he anticipated a school of visionary autobiography that has recently reappeared on the alternative comics scene with terrific force: Take for example French artist David B.'s six-volume family memoir *L'Ascension du Haut Mal* (1996–2003, translated into English as *Epileptic*, 2005), with its long historical reach and beautiful, fierce, dreamlike imagery; or, for a strikingly different example, Madison Clell's *Cuckoo* (2002), a rough-hewn, graphically fragmented yet wholly persuasive account of living with Dissociative Identity Disorder. Such work has helped widen the prevailing sense of what comics can do, and it is the possibility of such work that makes the autobiographical comics genre so urgent.

MAUS AND WHAT CANNOT BE REPRESENTED

Yet arguably the most urgent and complex of auto-biographical comics, and certainly the best known among American readers, is Art Spiegelman's cele-brated *Maus* (two volumes: 1 in 1986, 2 in 1991). In *Maus*, ironic authentication appears at its knottiest and most politically fraught, as Spiegelman puts claims to truth under the greatest pressure. Admit-tedly inspired by the urgency of *Binky Brown*, *Maus* nonetheless avoids Green's relentlessly allegorical and parodic iconolatry; it also skirts the corrosive cynicism we have seen in Crumb, Clowes, and Hernandez. Despite this, *Maus* represents the ne plus ultra of self-reflexive irony in comics. Spiegelman's intergenerational memoir of the Jewish Holocaust and its psychological fallout serves not only as a his-tory, a biography of the author's father (Vladek Spiegelman), and an autobiography but also as an extended essay on the pitfalls of trying to represent the unrepresentable.

This self-critical aspect comes into focus through the story's notorious gimmick, the representation of human beings through anthropomorphic animals: Jews as mice, German gentiles as cats, Polish gentiles as pigs, and so on. This gimmick, as others have remarked, toys with biological determinism by metaphorically turning ethnic and nationalistic con-flicts into natural predator/prey relationships (for

example, cats against mice). Thus Spiegelman runs the risk of mystifying the historical bases of European anti-Semitism and German imperialism. Robert C. Harvey presses this point in *The Art of the Comic Book*: Spiegelman's animal metaphor, he argues, "plays directly into [Nazism's] racist vision" (244). The device, he maintains, "threatens to erode [the story's] moral underpinnings" (243). Harvey's criti-cism underscores the risk inherent in the book's strategy: the predatory cats of Spiegelman's vision may perhaps be seen as simply fulfilling their natural roles as predators; worse yet, the persecution and extermination of the Jews may be written off as a simple consequence of their own "natural," mouse-like timidity.

Yet, paradoxically, Spiegelman's visual metaphor succeeds by self-destructing and thus undercutting such essentialist readings. The text takes pains to call attention to the inadequacy of the metaphor, over and over, as if to expose Spiegelman's artifice for what it is. The fallacy of representing cultural differ-ences by outward traits (for example, Jewishness through mouseness) is repeatedly thrust in the reader's face as a problem. For instance, Polish Jews repeatedly pass themselves off as gentiles by wear-ing pig *masks* in the drawings, though in fact they are not so much pretending to be something as pre-tending *not* to be something. Spiegelman himself appears as a mouse, as a man, and as a man in a mouse mask. Meanwhile "real" animals, such as horses, police dogs, and cellar-dwelling rats, exist side by side with the artist's metaphorical ones. Photos of human beings appear as well, further dis-mantling the metaphor. Moreover, the words never once refer to Spiegelman's cast of characters as any-thing but human; thus the animal metaphor impacts the visual but not the written text, an inconsistency Spiegelman knowingly courted when creating the book (Groth and Fiore 191).

In this light, one could be forgiven for asking, "Why bother to use the animal metaphor at all?" Indeed, some have roundly criticized Spiegelman's use of the device as glib and irresponsible. Hillel Halkin, reviewing *Maus* for *Commentary* in 1992, argues, "The Holocaust was a crime committed by humans against humans, not—as Nazi theory held—by one biological species against another. . . . To draw people as animals . . . is doubly dehumanizing, once by virtue of the symbolism and once by virtue of graphic limitations" (56). Halkin's objections assume a literal reading of the character's animal faces, but in fact the animal metaphor is just that: a metaphor, a sign rather than a literal representation. The animal-like depictions of people are not representational in any conventional sense. As Adam Gopnik puts it, "*Maus* is in no way an animal fable. . . . The Jews are Jews who just happen to be depicted as mice" (31).

In fact Spiegelman deliberately exploits the "graphic limitations" of his style to force us to look beyond the device. His mouse-characters boast only the most rudimentary vocabulary of facial expressions; their emotions are cartooned with a broad, brusquely rendered but telling simplicity (for example, eyeballs empty white or solid black; brows straight or arched). One doesn't so much look *at* the characters' faces as *through* them. Indeed, this is one of Harvey's objections to the device: the characters' "mouseness," he argues, does not contribute to the story (*Comic Book* 245). It appears, then, that Harvey's critique of *Maus* rests on a paradox: Spiegelman flirts with a dangerous essentialism, yet, in the end, his use of metaphor is not essentialist enough, literal enough, to exploit the qualities of the animals invoked. What Harvey neglects is the very *anti*-essentialist nature of Spiegelman's project.

Maus's drawings succeed by indirection. By defamiliarizing the already familiar details of the Holocaust, Spiegelman's "funny animal" drawings reacquaint us with the horrors of genocide in the most offhand and intimate of ways. As Witek points out, this technique enables *Maus* to avoid the "overdetermination of meaning"—the "already told," prepackaged and numbing pieties—associated with the subject (*Comic Books* 102–3). If the metaphor works, it works by unraveling itself in sheer horror. The value of Spiegelman's method lies in our recognition of its inadequacy.

In *Maus,* moments of formalist play (characteristic of Spiegelman's early work, but here subordinated to the story's understated drama)[1] often revolve around the failure of the animal metaphor. For instance, at one point Vladek worries about his wife, Anja (Art's mother), whose more obviously "Jewish" appearance may handicap their efforts to escape the Nazis. The drawings show both husband and wife in pig masks but only Anja sports a long, ropy, mouse-like tail (1:136). Later, in volume 2, the guilt-ridden Spiegelman appears at his drawing board, his mouselike face a mask held on by string, as he discusses the critical reception of volume 1. Thus Spiegelman seeks immediacy through tortuous complexity. *Maus*'s animal metaphor authenticates Spiegelman's account of the Holocaust by calling attention to its own artificiality. The effect is of innocence lost, yet reinvoked through the archest of ironies.

Spiegelman practices ironic authentication not only by short-circuiting the animal metaphor but also by continually juxtaposing past and present. As many critics (for example, Witek, Joshua Brown, Michael Staub) have observed, *Maus* points to the circumstances of its own making, calling attention to the way Spiegelman's relationships with his father and mother urged on and influenced his work. Revealing ironies emerge as the book tries to bridge the generations: *Maus* shows the inescapable fallout of Nazi genocide as a long shadow cast over survivors, survivors' children, and the generations to come. The Spiegelman-protagonist, Art, relives aspects of the Holocaust through his recollections, withholdings, and nightmares, in particular through interviews with his father Vladek, whose story *Maus* becomes. Thus Art recreates the Holocaust in the present, not as the vague, implicit understanding he once had, but as a specific, vividly imagined series of events. These events, conjured from Art's collaboration with Vladek, help to rationalize the cultural displacement of his parents as survivors, as well as his own personal anomie as a survivor's son. To justify this therapeutic work, Spiegelman grounds the story in the particulars of family life, repeatedly reminding the reader that this is but one partial, inevitably distorted account of the Holocaust, contingent on his tangled relationships and colored especially by his ambivalence toward his father.

This narrative strategy is dangerously self-involved, and some readers have balked at it. For example, Harvey has faulted *Maus* for being primarily about the blinding self-regard of a young artist, that is, Spiegelman himself: "[W]hat Spiegelman ultimately shows us . . . is not the relationship between son and father but the relationship between artist and subject. . . . [*Maus*] is not so much about the experience of the Auschwitz survivor as it is about the obsessions of the artistic temperament" (*Comic Book* 243). Such critiques of *Maus* threaten to devolve into ad hominem attacks on the author, thusly: Spiegelman is a callow, ungrateful son who uses the bare-naked "honesty" of *Maus* both to denigrate his father and to aggrandize his own efforts as an artist. (Such an argument runs through Harvey Pekar's critique of *Maus*, source of prolonged debate in *The Comics Journal* beginning in 1986.)

To be sure, Spiegelman walks a fine line, daring to expose both his occasional callousness as a son and his almost paralyzing self-consciousness as an artist. Yet this self-referentiality is not simply a matter of a self-involved artist kvetching about the difficulty of his work. As Joshua Brown suggests, this framing of the Holocaust by Art's own troubles serves to authenticate *Maus* as an act of historiography, for it interrogates the very limits of memory and storytelling (96). Though *Maus* may not be "about" any one thing, it concerns, among other things, history both as lived experience *and* as a conscious undertaking.

Maus's historical account, as James E. Young argues, must include the circumstances of its own transmission, "the present circumstances under which [it is] being remembered" (678). Art's self-contemplation and *Maus*'s self-reflexiveness stem from the impossibility of knowing the past thoroughly and objectively, and the resultant need to ground historiography in a sense of personal context. The fundamental unknowability of the Holocaust requires a history that, as Young puts it, "makes events coherent" but "gestures toward the incoherence" of experience (668). Thus Harvey misrepresents *Maus* when he claims that the work is a "portrait of the artist" above all else, for the self-involved, *kunstlerroman*

aspect of *Maus* works to ratify the text as a historical account. The story's focus on its own making goes hand in hand with Spiegelman's scrupulousness as historian, reminding us that, in Joshua Brown's terms, remembering and setting down such a story is not a matter of recovering bald facts but "a constitutive process, . . . a construction of the past" (95). If the past—a reality "worse than my darkest dreams," as Art puts it—can never be quite recovered, but only evoked, Spiegelman wants to make sure that we do not miss this distinction. *Maus* is an evocation, not a full recovery, and its insistence on this very fact implicitly reinforces its trustworthiness *as* an evocation. This is why past and present continually collide, *must* collide, with each other in the text.

Throughout *Maus*, Spiegelman uses self-reflexive devices to achieve a historian's authority. The text's self-referentiality, besides justifying *Maus* as auto/biography, also undergirds Spiegelman's sense of history in an immediate, practical way. Art's desire for a historian's intimate knowledge of particulars—his grasping after details in his interviews with Vladek—explains not only the book's diagrammatic emphasis on objects, settings, and processes, but also the insistently ironic self-awareness of the interview scenes. The book is self-referential because it has to be, to explain and thus justify itself as a constitutive process. Rhetorically, *Maus*'s emphasis on what Art does *not* know (such as scenic details, Jewish liturgical tradition, or how to choose among conflicting accounts) reinforces the image of Spiegelman as a painstaking researcher. By showing himself finding out about these things, he authenticates his history all the more.

Even doubts about Vladek's account become evidence of Spiegelman's scrupulousness. In one memorable instance, Art's research and Vladek's own story disagree: was there, or was there not, a camp orchestra playing as prisoners were marched through the gates of Auschwitz? Vladek remembers none, but Art insists that "it's very well documented" (2:54). Oddly, the text does not show Art seeking corroboration of this ironic detail until *after* the first of two panels depicting the orchestra in question. In the second of these panels, after Vladek has disputed

Art's version, the composition remains the same, except for a longer procession of prisoners, whose marching rows obscure the orchestra almost entirely. Thus, while Spiegelman upholds his own version of events, his use of visual detail implies an explanation for Vladek's divergent view: there were simply too many bodies between Vladek and the orchestra for that detail to register.

Such collisions of past and present are a constant in *Maus*, but take varied forms. For instance, early on—just two pages into Vladek's reminiscence—Art interrupts his father, asking for clarification of a key point: Why is Vladek telling the story of his relationship with a lover, Lucia, when Art had asked him to "start with Mom," that is, with Vladek's courtship of Art's mother, Anja? This interruption, the first of many in *Maus*, inspires a testy comeback from Vladek: "All this was *before* I met Anja—just listen, yes?" (1:14). As *Maus* progresses, these interruptions in the flow of Vladek's story increasingly affect the page layouts, as elements from the present literally *overlap* elements from the past.

Such overlapping is a habit of Spiegelman's: Vladek's tale is repeatedly interrupted, punctuated, and glossed in the process of its telling. Typically, these overlaps show the "present" commenting on the "past": an inset panel may reveal Vladek's narrating presence in a particular scene (for example, 1:74), or, often, Vladek and/or Art may stand "in front of" a panel, partially obscuring it (for example, 1:105, 1:115, or 2:26). In many cases Vladek and Art's exchanges are unbound by panel borders and seem to crowd Vladek's narrative. Less often, an element from the "past" obtrudes on the "present," violating panel borders and overlapping the image of Vladek and/or Art. These moments, at which the relationship between *then* and *now* is graphically reversed, typically signify crucial events in Vladek's tale. For example, during Vladek and Anja's courtship, she sends him a photograph of herself (fig. 56). This photo overlaps Vladek's image in both the "present" (sitting on an exercise bike, c. 1980) and the past (Vladek framing the photo, c. 1936).

This graphic intrusion of the past on the present takes its most disturbing form in volume 2's chapter,

"Auschwitz (Time Flies)," in which the fine points of mass execution and burial are finally diagrammed in horrific detail. Late in the chapter the recurrent image of the crematorium chimney, which serves as a nerve-wracking leitmotif throughout (2:51, 2:55, 2:58), thrusts upward through a panel border, impinging on Vladek and Art's conversation in the present (2:69). The chimney, the last image on the page in question, serves as a visual reinforcement of Vladek's climactic utterance, "For this I was an *eye-witness*"; in fact the whole page has been leading to this. Yet the chimney also reads non-linearly, for, as Gene Kannenberg Jr. has pointed out, it penetrates the panel above ("Form" 155). The smoke from Art's own cigarette seems to waft upward from the "cremo" smokestack in an obscenely droll visual joke.

Indeed, throughout "Time Flies," past and present interpenetrate in an obscenely literal way, as Spiegelman's anxiety about his own limitations as historian reaches fever pitch. In this sequence, as *Maus* delves into the details of life in Auschwitz, Spiegelman suffers a profoundly debilitating case of writer's block, as if the thought of the Nazi camps has finally disabled him. Corpses pile at the foot of his drawing table; corpses line the streets. Flies buzz around the rot of the bodies, and a Nazi guard tower looms outside the artist's studio (2:41–43). Art the character becomes "Mr. Spiegelman" here, for at this point in the narrative we pull away from the remembrance of Vladek and Art, to a nearer "present," circa 1987, in which Spiegelman struggles to put his material in comics form. This "Spiegelman" is a man in a mouse mask, tied on with string. As in Clowes, Crumb, and Hernandez, so in Spiegelman: his sense of identity is revealed as plastic, strategic, and merely local. His masklike "mouse" face has become just that, a mask.

In this chapter, during an interview with his analyst Pavel (also a survivor), Spiegelman's mouse-ness (or masked-ness) becomes radically ambiguous. The close shot/reverse shot exchanges between Spiegelman and Pavel sometimes betray the strings tied around their heads, sometimes not (2:44–46). Are they men, or mouse-men? Furthermore, Spiegelman's stature changes throughout this sequence, as

Figure 56. *Maus* 1:17 (detail). From *Maus I: My Father Bleeds History* by Art Spiegelman, copyright © 1986 by Art Spiegelman. Used by permission of Pantheon Books, a division of Random House, Inc.

he goes from adult to child to adult once again. By now his self-image is in jeopardy, his sense of purpose and identity confused by his intimate awareness of history, which bears down on him like a terrible weight. Yet by focusing his anxiety on the crafting of *Maus*, Spiegelman seems to find a way out: the production of the text itself offers both a challenge and a comfort, a way of narrowing if not overcoming his radical sense of doubt. In short, Spiegelman's struggle for historical accuracy is part and parcel of his emotional struggle, as the work both stokes and contains his anxiety. Thus the conversation between Spiegelman and Pavel inevitably shifts from discussing his sense of emotional desolation ("mostly I feel like crying") to getting scenic details straight: how do you depict a tin shop in Auschwitz (2:46)? Spiegelman's tortured present is shaped not only by history but also by historiography.

In this chapter "past" and "present" dissolve into each other. Faced with the enormity of what Auschwitz means, Spiegelman cannot adequately separate the two. At the outset, a monologue piles up details about his own life and the lives of his parents and the atrocities of Auschwitz, all thrown together without differentiation or understanding:

Vladek started working as a tinman in Auschwitz in the spring of 1944 . . . I started working on this page at the very end of February 1987.

In May 1987 Françoise and I are expecting a baby . . . Between May 16, 1944, and May 24, 1944 over 100,000 Hungarian Jews were gassed in Auschwitz . . . (2:41)[2]

Though graphic juxtapositions of past and present occur throughout *Maus*, this scene relies on a purely *verbal* parataxis (literally, a placing side by side), unaided by visual transitions. Spiegelman's monologue here seems arbitrary, indiscriminate, and strange, perhaps because it forces us to share, momentarily, the perspective of the working artist, who constantly has to reconcile all of these happenings in his head. The success of volume 1 of *Maus* (published some five years prior) only cripples Spiegelman further, compounding his sense of guilt, as shown in a darkly comic sequence in which reporters and hucksters vie for the cartoonist's attention, offering to turn *Maus* into either a cause célèbre or a cross-media merchandising bonanza (2:42).

The frantic self-referentiality of this chapter, as Gene Kannenberg has persuasively argued, reflects Spiegelman's confused, even distraught, response to the critical and commercial reception of *Maus* volume 1 in 1986 ("Form" 151–54). "Auschwitz (Time Flies)" shows just how painful Spiegelman's "success" became and betrays a desire to clear up (or attack) misconceptions about *Maus*'s use of the animal metaphor. The chapter testifies to a crisis born of fame, a reading reinforced by Spiegelman's later comments about getting drawn into *Maus*'s "undertow" and resenting the resultant "objectification" of his self (Juno 13–14). The dominant feeling here is not unlike the anxious self-mockery of Crumb's "Many Faces," which is likewise a response to the alienation of self through celebrity (see our previous chapter).

Yet the self-reflexive nature of *Maus* goes well beyond such obvious moments of crisis, for, as the story progresses, Spiegelman increasingly alludes to decisions he made while actually crafting certain moments in the text. Scenes previously recounted by Vladek end up being revisited in the process of textualization by Art; ironic authentication reminds us of the particular choices involved in the construction of passages we have already read. For instance, one scene finds Art, Vladek, and Vladek's second wife, Mala, looking over a rough version of one of the earlier episodes in *Maus*, recently "sketch[ed] out" by Art:

> ART. *And here's you, saying: "Ach. When I think of them, it still makes me cry!"*
> VLADEK. *Yes. Still it makes me cry! (1:133)*

The scene in question (in which some of Vladek's friends are executed for black marketeering) appears just two chapters before (1:84).

Such scenes throw into question the seeming verisimilitude of *Maus*, while at the same time affirming its drive for truthfulness. Crucial to this strategy is the way Spiegelman calls attention to his various tools and sources of historical reference. For example, Art's use of a tape recorder becomes fraught with meaning in the last chapter of *Maus*, which begins with him listening to a recording of his father and musing, "Y'know, I've got over 20 hours of Vladek's story on tape now" (2:120). Ironically, what Vladek is telling on the tape at this moment is another scene previously recounted in the text: how his and Anja's first son, Richieu, died. Richieu and his cousins, we know, were poisoned by Anja's sister Tosha to keep them out of the hands of the Nazis, as shown in volume 1 of *Maus* (1:109). Here Vladek (on tape) assumes Tosha's part, and explains her decision: "No! I will not go in the gas chambers. And my children will not go in the gas chambers." He then continues in his own voice, saying, "So, Tosha took the poison not only to herself, but to *our* little . . .," a telling shift in emphasis that is cut off in mid-sentence by a phone call (2:121). This version of the event differs subtly but significantly from the version shown in volume 1, which stresses Tosha's desperation through a series of panels that zoom in on her face as she resolves herself to her plan (1:109). The earlier version, in contrast to Vladek's tape-recorded testimony, puts us squarely in *Tosha's* position, and thus further rationalizes her decision.

This sequence uses the tape recorder—ironically, a documentarian's tool—as a prop to underline the activity of Spiegelman as artificer, for the subtle disconnect between the two versions of Richieu's death shows how deliberately Spiegelman has shaped Vladek's story. The tape recorder thus performs a kind of ironic authentication, destabilizing *Maus*'s claims to literal truth. At the same time, the scene with the tape recorder reestablishes, beyond question, Spiegelman's debt to his father and his concern for documentary evidence. Thus *Maus*'s fidelity to "truth" is reaffirmed, even as our sense of Spiegelman's creative process is complicated.

This scene takes on added resonance because of its crucially timed reminder of Richieu, the unseen, unknown brother with whom Art confesses to feeling a kind of "sibling rivalry" (2:15) and to whom Spiegelman partly dedicates *Maus* volume 2 (it is also dedicated to his own daughter Nadja). Ironically, "Richieu" is what Vladek, having grown weak and delirious, calls Art in the book's final scene. Spiegelman highlights this irony by positioning the retelling of Richieu's death at the beginning of this final chapter—the chapter that brings *Maus* to a moving end with the image of Vladek and Anja's shared tombstone. This revealing use of the tape recorder enables Spiegelman to reunite symbolically the four members of his sundered family (Vladek, Anja, Richieu, and himself) within a single chapter.

Besides the tape recorder, photographs also perform ironic authentication in *Maus*. Specifically, they challenge Spiegelman's use of the animal metaphor by offering precisely analogical images of "real" human beings. Indeed, the presence of photographs in *Maus* goes against the grain of Spiegelman's narrative technique, for photos, despite their constructed nature, are generally assumed to offer a value-neutral, purely denotative vision of persons and places.[3] As such, they conflict with Spiegelman's cartoonal renditions of character, which are cryptographic rather than strictly representational. In fact *Maus* constitutes a visual argument between these two approaches: documentary photo-realism (privileged in Spiegelman's approach to setting and significant objects) and cartoonal symbolism (privileged in his treatment of character). The former, "realism," leans heavily on photographic and diagrammatic references to authenticate its claims, while the latter, symbolism, avoids photographic individuation, making Spiegelman's cartoon characters into generic counters *through* which we infer the actual people involved. Though Spiegelman makes expert use of verbal cues to distinguish one character from another, his *graphic* treatment of characters stresses their collective rather than individual identities. In contrast, photo-realism seeks to ground representation in the specifics of person and place.

This visual argument helps explain Spiegelman's complex protocols of authentication. Behind these protocols lie two contradictory imperatives. The first

is Spiegelman's professed preference for cartooning as "diagramming," as opposed to illustration (see his introduction to *Breakdowns*; "Commix" 69); this serves his desire to avoid a too-literal, sentimentalizing treatment of the Holocaust. Such a treatment, Thomas Doherty suggests, would threaten to play into Nazism's reactionary aesthetic, with its emphasis on the hypnotic qualities of the literal, the specular, and the speciously "realistic." Cartooning, Doherty points out, defines itself "against the aesthetics of photographic reproduction or realist representation" (74). A desire to avoid such literal-minded representation seems to underlie much Holocaust narrative, particularly visual narratives that favor indirection over "realistic" depiction. Recall in this regard Alain Resnais's documentary *Night and Fog* (1955), which combines horrific archival images with suggestive original footage of the now-abandoned camps, accompanied by voice-over commentary that problematizes the very idea of a Holocaust film. Alternately, Claude Lanzmann's *Shoah* (1985) avoids archival footage of the Nazi camps altogether, in favor of interviews with surviving captives and captors. Even Steven Spielberg's *Schindler's List* (1993), the best-known Hollywoodization of Holocaust narrative, employs stark black-and-white cinematography as a distancing and contextualizing device (Doherty 76). Spiegelman, suspicious of "realistic" graphics in comics, quite consciously deployed cartoonal simplification to avoid making the material banal.

Yet the Holocaust narrator also has an ethical imperative to represent details as accurately as possible. Fidelity to truth is essential to writing the Holocaust; anything less trivializes the matter. (Regarding fictionality versus "authenticity" in Holocaust narrative, see, for example, Horowitz's *Voicing the Void*, which makes particular reference to *Maus*.) Reliance on photographic reference is part of the drive for historiographic authority that inevitably underlies any serious depiction of the Nazi genocide. In *Maus*, Spiegelman takes pains to show himself digging for corroborative references, including not only diaristic but also photo-reference. When he cannot find such references, the absence of documentation makes it harder to "visualize" his story—as when, for instance, he cannot find visual evidence of what a tin shop in Auschwitz looked like (2:46). (The *Maus* CD-ROM, released in 1994, gives ample evidence of Spiegelman's efforts to shore up his research photographically.)

THE FINAL PHOTOGRAPH: HISTORY MEETS FANTASY

Besides much documentary material based at least in part on photographs, *Maus* incorporates numerous drawings of photos, as well as three actual photographs that directly challenge its animal metaphors. The presence of these photos in the text deserves further discussion, because Spiegelman's invocation of photography represents ironic authentication at its most complex. By including both photos and simulated photos, Spiegelman plays the contradictory drives for cartoonal symbolism and for photorealism against each other.

The first of the "real" photos, one of young Art and his mother, Anja, creeps in as part of Spiegelman's interpolated underground comix short story, "Prisoner on the Hell Planet" (from 1972), which comes back to haunt Art in volume 1 (100–103). Though small, and presented without explicit comment, this photograph concretely testifies to a mother-son relationship that otherwise exists only in the book's past tense. Like the claustrophobic scratchboard expressionism of "Hell Planet" itself, this photo undermines Spiegelman's predominant animal metaphor. The second actual photo appears in the dedication to volume 2: Spiegelman's unknown brother, Richieu, poisoned at age five or six. Richieu's portrait prepares for Art's discussion of him some ten pages later: "I didn't think about him much when I was growing up. . . . He was mainly a large, blurry photograph hanging in my parents' bedroom. . . . The photo never threw tantrums or got in any kind of trouble. . . . It was an ideal kid, and *I* was a pain in the ass. I couldn't compete" (2:15). The positioning of this photo, again, underscores the presence of the past in the lives of Spiegelman's parents, both his mother, Anja, and his father, Vladek. Indeed, the

latter seems to slip into the past completely at the end of volume II, as 2 calls Art "Richieu." This photo also points up the absurdity of Art's sibling rivalry with his "ghost-brother": though Art imagines that Richieu would have become a wealthy and successful "creep," as if to upbraid Art for his own failures (2:15), in reality Art knows nothing about him. Richieu has been reduced to nothing more than the static, unknowable figure ("It") in an old photograph.

The third and final real photograph, a postwar souvenir snapshot of Vladek in a "new and clean" concentration camp uniform, comes but two pages before the end of *Maus* (2:134). Here we finally see Vladek in human guise, and he appears shockingly real, in contrast to his minimalist "mouse" form throughout the text (fig. 57). This neat and handsome photo supports his earlier claim to have been "a nice, handsome boy" (1:13). The image is large, and tipped at a cockeyed angle on the page (a protocol of Spiegelman's: tipped panels are a formal intensifier used throughout to stress key moments). It comes as the climax of a sequence in postwar Poland, in which Anja waits anxiously for news of her husband. When she sees this souvenir, enclosed in a letter from Vladek, Anja cries out, "My God—Vladek is really alive!" (2:134). This photo presages their final reunion and is evidently an object of great symbolic heft in the Spiegelman household. "Anja kept this picture always," says Vladek. "I have it still now in my desk!"

On hearing this, Art immediately goes to find this image, saying, " I need that photo in my book!" The next panel shows him gazing at the snapshot. "Incredible!" he says, while his bedridden father continues his tale (2:135). Indeed, the intrusion of the photo into Spiegelman's tale comes as an incredible formal and emotional shock. Larger than previous photos, this snapshot makes unprecedented claims on the reader. Unlike the photo of Anja and Art in "Prisoner on the Hell Planet," it is not bracketed by prior contextualization as part of a comic-within-a-comic. Unlike the dedicatory photo of Richieu at the beginning of volume 2, Vladek's portrait is incorporated into the narrative structure of the main text. This photo brings a non-metaphorical Vladek into the context of metaphor, finally overturning

Figure 57. Spiegelman, *Maus* 2:134 (detail). From *Maus II: And Here My Troubles Began* by Art Spiegelman, copyright © 1991 by Art Spiegelman. Used by permission of Pantheon Books, a division of Random House, Inc.

Spiegelman's substitution of animal faces for human ones. Beyond functioning as privileged testimony to Vladek's "real" existence—a sign that someone, somewhere, really posed for this photo, and may have really lived this story—the photo works ironically on a number of levels, and actually destabilizes rather than affirms *Maus*'s documentary realism.

For one thing, we are told that this photo represents a *carefully constructed* evocation of the Nazi camps. It's a souvenir, after all, paid for and posed by Vladek. It presents a handsome, idealized image of the camp prisoner, posed in front of a curtain whose vertical folds evoke studio portraiture at its most conventional (2:134). The mere fact that the uniform is new, clean, and well-fitted belies the seeming documentary value of the image, for Vladek's own narrative, earlier, shows just how difficult it was to get a clean, fitting uniform in the camps: In Auschwitz, he has told us, prisoners suffered from ill-fitting clothes and shoes, though he himself was at last able to secure clothes that fit him "like tailored"

by agreeing to tutor a Polish *kapo* (supervisor). When telling of this accomplishment, Vladek takes obvious pride in the way he was able to maintain a clean appearance even in the camps: "Always I was handsome . . . but with everything fitted, I looked like a million!" (2:33). The climactic photo of Vladek, two pages from the book's end, repeats this proud self-assertion, yet overshadows the harsh realities of life in the camps. The posed photo re-creates the Vladek of the camps who supposedly looked "like a million," but within the more civilized—thus incredible—context of a studio portrait. This is not a documentary photo, then, but a message intended for his beloved Anja, whom he wants to reassure. It is less a depiction of the reality of the camps than a gift, to remind his wife that Vladek has survived and remains the sturdy, handsome man she has known.

For another thing, this photograph purports to corroborate what is surely one of the most fanciful episodes in *Maus*: Vladek's version of what Anja's life was like in postwar Sosnowiec, Poland, during

147

their enforced separation. In this sequence, Anja consults not only the local Jewish organization but also a Gypsy fortune-teller, for some news of her husband (2:133). A six-panel scene in the Gypsy's wagon represents, presumably, *Spiegelman's extrapolation from his father's extrapolation* from a story Anja once told. It purports to give Anja's point of view, but we already know that Anja's point of view is inadmissible, because her story has been lost.

In effect, this imaginative scene denies that loss, a loss around which, as Michael Rothberg points out, Spiegelman has structured the entire narrative. Indeed, Art desires no less than to occupy (in Rothberg's phrase) "the impossible position" of Anja, who is not so much a presence in *Maus* as an absence, a lost trace (676). Said loss spurs the conflict between Vladek and Art in volume 1, when father reveals to son that he burnt Anja's records and personal effects in a fit of grief after her suicide. This confession angers Art, who feels the loss of his mother's story as a kind of artistic privation, at one point confessing, "I wish I got *Mom's* story while she was alive. She was more sensitive. . . . It would give the book some balance" (1:132). Anja's voice has been forever silenced, so that *Maus* becomes Vladek's tale perforce.

Anja is usually represented from Vladek's point of view. Her life, as Sara Horowitz notes, cannot be told "except through the prisms of her husband's and her son's memories" (3). Yet even Vladek doesn't know the minute details of Anja's experience; by his own admission, he does not know where Anja went while he was in Dachau, late in the war. He only knows that she made it back to Sosnowiec before him (2:103–4). So when Vladek purports to tell Anja's story, just a few pages before the end of the book, the impossibility of accuracy should be obvious. Anja's life in postwar Sosnowiec can only be a matter of conjecture.

In spite of Anja's essential muteness, the father-son collaboration here produces an imaginative episode involving her consultation with the Gypsy. Anja is shown as desolate, eyes downcast, shoulders slumped in misery. The Gypsy herself is (of course) a moth, with antennae, wings, and a kerchief tied around her head; she gazes into (of course) a crystal

ball, reliving Anja's past and foreseeing her future. The crystal first shows the image of "a child . . . a *dead* child" (Richieu's likeness appears in the globe, dressed in his trademark overalls), then reveals Vladek, in concentration camp uniform: "Now I see a man . . . illness . . . It's your husband! He's been very very ill . . . He's coming—he's coming home! You'll get a *sign* that he's alive by the time the moon is full!" (2:133). The Gypsy goes on to foretell Anja's life in "a faraway place," a new life including "another little boy," while Anja looks on, rapt. On the following page, the letter arrives with Vladek's photo—the *sign*—and Anja declares, "It's just like the Gypsy said" (2:134). The photograph of Vladek dominates the bottom half of the page, as if to lend authority to this fanciful episode.

Accuracy is not the point here; in fact fantasy plays a big part in these last few pages. The clichéd characterization of the Gypsy moth, for instance, fits into a larger pattern of comically indulgent animal metaphors shown in the last chapter. We see, for instance, Swedish reindeer in a Stockholm department store (2:125), as well as tiger-striped "mouse" children born of a Gentile woman and Jewish man (2:131). Such literal-minded metaphors play with the deterministic and stereotypic connotations of Spiegelman's technique, pushing it toward self-parody. Before this, we have occasionally seen animals representing other ethnicities or nationalities besides Jews, Germans, and Poles, yet such scenes are only vaguely suggestive, rather than specific, about the connection between animal metaphor and cultural identity. The last chapter, in contrast, depicts incidental characters in guises that specifically reflect cultural clichés or jokes: Swedish reindeer, Gypsy moths. These comical metaphors extend Spiegelman's cat-and-mouse logic into the postwar period, but also parody it: for the first time, *Maus's* animal figures become jokey. Such overkill forces us, once again, to recognize Spiegelman's gimmick for what it is. The real photo of Vladek that follows is the author's coup de grace, his ultimate exit strategy, for it explodes the metaphors on which the entire text is built.

This ultimate chapter revels in the collision of history and imagination: ironic authentication turns back on itself, in dizzying involutions. As *Maus* nears its end, Vladek increasingly lives in the past, and his photographic self-portrait is but one way that he idealizes his postwar activities. Through fantasy he directs his story toward his emotional reunion with Anja in Sosnowiec—the book's last page (2:136). Spiegelman directs the story this way as well, ordering his father's reminiscences non-chronologically, so as to focus everything at book's end on Vladek and Anja's joyful reunion. When we finally see the couple embrace, Vladek, now bedridden and apparently delirious, tells Art: "More I don't need to tell you. We were both very happy, and lived happy, happy ever after." Drifting off to sleep—in an ironic reversal of the conventional "bedtime story" scene, in which child sleeps and parent tiptoes away—Vladek says, "I'm tired from talking, Richieu, and it's enough stories for now. . . ." His unself-conscious drifting into the past reinforces our sense, slowly built throughout *Maus*, that nothing can be as real for Vladek as his formative experiences in the Holocaust. The photographic portrait drives this home, as does the tombstone at the foot of the last page, which names both Vladek and Anja: the two are again reunited, this time in death.

For Art, this moment must come as a bittersweet recognition, for he himself came after Vladek's wartime experiences. Indeed his father's final remarks effectively transform him into a living ghost of his brother, Richieu. In some sense Art disappears from the final moments of the narrative, while Vladek rewrites history as he would have it: "We were both very happy, and lived happy, happy ever after." Vladek's photograph, two pages prior, presages this move as it both ratifies and falsifies his experience as a survivor of Nazi genocide. In short, *Maus* moves away from verisimilitude even as Spiegelman brings the photograph forward to finally "show" his father. In the process, he achieves a kind of symbolic rapprochement with Vladek, in effect collaborating with him to bring Anja's story to life.

This final photograph must be read in context, for it subverts, and is subverted by, Spiegelman's use of drawn "photographs" throughout *Maus*. Photos are among the many paper objects that Spiegelman invokes and indeed "attaches" to his pages: for example, train tickets, diagrams, and maps. As noted in chapter 2, the presence of these drawn objects, mimicking found objects, reinforces the diaristic immediacy of *Maus* as an artifact: the pages resemble a scrapbook or album, in which heirlooms and personal narratives are interleaved. The most telling of these heirlooms are the photographs, which are usually charged with great emotional significance—as in, for instance, the aforementioned scene during Vladek and Anja's courtship, when Vladek frames a portrait photo sent by Anja (fig. 56). The emotional impact of that simulated "photo" is such that it seldom occurs to readers to question the very oddness of Spiegelman's technique (1:17). It *is* odd: the rendering of the "photo" carefully mimics the appearance of an old-fashioned photographic print, right down to its scalloped border, yet what we see of Anja, as ever, is her "mouseness." The photo as object, rendered with documentary realism, clashes with the object of the photo: a person as a mouse. For Spiegelman's characters, as in real life, photographs testify—they serve as documents, mementos, and declarations of feeling—yet the inescapable animal metaphor belies their seeming authenticity. Even more, the reproductions of actual photographs, and in particular the crucially positioned photo of Vladek, unravel Spiegelman's artifice.

The effect of the photo in *Maus*'s last chapter depends partly on the prominence of drawn photographs in the previous chapter, which climaxes with the opening of a box of family snapshots (2:114–15). This box, which Vladek has recovered from his closet, includes photos saved long ago by Richieu's Polish governess, as well as more recent snapshots that show the few surviving family members in the postwar period. Taken together, these photos testify to the losses that both sides of Art's family have suffered, for almost everyone seen in these snapshots has died. As Vladek and Art discuss family history, the photos overlap the panels of their conversation, crowding Vladek's dialogue balloons; finally, the snapshots seem to spill from the box, down the page, piling one on top of the other and bleeding off the bottom margin. They surround and hem in

Vladek and Art, who sit on a sofa talking about the past (2:115). Here again Spiegelman shows extraordinary care with the rendering of these pictures as objects. Varied borders (note that prewar photographs look distinctly different from postwar ones), dated inscriptions, even a face cropped from one of the photos—these graphic elements reinforce the power of these snapshots as testimonials. Yet the animal metaphor is constant, the book's cartoon shorthand dutifully preserved.

This scene in the penultimate chapter reminds us of the crucial importance of photos to Spiegelman's history but cannot prepare us for the shock of Vladek's "real," human countenance two pages from the end. The momentary defeat of metaphor in the last chapter boldly asserts the falseness of Spiegelman's drawn "photos" throughout the text. *Maus*'s visual argument between documentary realism and cartooning, underscored by Spiegelman's reliance on drawn photos, at last comes to a head in this singular image, this naked violation of Spiegelman's artistic decorum (2:134). Yet, again, this photo in no way represents a simple "reality." Rather, it is a simulacrum of Vladek's own devising, a deliberate reappropriation of his experience as the Nazis' prisoner. Moreover, Spiegelman has positioned it to corroborate a sequence that, as noted, shades from documentary scrupulousness to fanciful supposition. The photo represents the triumphant reassertion of a father's self-image into his son's text, an image that breaks through the self-imposed discipline of Spiegelman's metaphor. If the collaboration of Art and Vladek is, as Rick Iadonisi remarks, "a struggle for control" (53), then at this moment Vladek seems ascendant, and Art awed into silence.

Again, this climactic movement in *Maus* demonstrates ironic authentication at its most complex. Rather than trumpet the fictiveness of his creation—like Clowes, Crumb, and Hernandez in our previous chapter—Spiegelman appears to defer to the photograph as verifier, as an immediate, incontrovertible testimony of the life recorded in his book. He does not insist on the ironies of his work here, but rather seems to assert the truth, daring to break through his self-imposed limits. Yet the effect is all the more

complex, and more ironic, because Spiegelman acknowledges the deliberate, posed quality of the image, and positions it to comment subtly on his father's version of events, as Vladek slowly slips into an idealized past. The photo speaks not to the documentary truth but to what we *want* to believe. It affirms Vladek as a hero, in spite of all we know. As *Maus* moves toward the predetermined reunion of Vladek and Anja, we already know that their life after the war will not be a "happy ever after" but rather a confused and haunted one that leads to Anja's suicide; we already know that the story cannot "end" anywhere but will continue to haunt Art's life. We know these things, but still Spiegelman privileges Vladek's carefully groomed likeness, as if to support his father's turn toward a triumphantly happy ending.

In sum, this break with the book's reigning metaphor represents not an uncomplicated assertion of truth but an ironic tribute to his father's powers of imagination. The photo is no more "real" than Spiegelman's cartoons but seems to represent Vladek as Vladek would have himself represented. Beyond either naïve photo-realism or ironic symbolism, Spiegelman's placement of this final snapshot both affirms and subverts Vladek's role as a storyteller, allowing Vladek's ego-image (as knowing *Fotoobjekt*) to assert itself within his son's text. The photograph does not simply claim to speak the truth in the face of skepticism but rather cements the father-son collaboration, underscoring its profoundly intersubjective nature. Through Vladek and Art's collaboration, different versions of the truth have been negotiated and different interpretations of reality reconciled.

CONCLUSION

Maus demonstrates the potential, both artistic and sociopolitical, of autobiographical comics, and in effect has placed autobiography at the center of recent comics criticism. *Maus* also demonstrates, decisively, that "truth" in autobiography has to be earned, not just taken for granted. This truth is a matter not of verifiability but of trustworthiness, not so much a constant quality as the result of a continual renegotiation between the artist, his materials, and his audience (and in this case, his father, as both informant and collaborator). It is, in sum, a rhetorical matter. Ironic authentication, then, need not boil down to self-regarding playfulness or mere navel-gazing equivocation. On the contrary, it may represent a passage through skepticism and anxiety— anxiety at times strong enough to threaten the singularity of the self-image, as also seen in Clowes, Crumb, and Hernandez—toward a commitment to self-under-standing and honest communication.

In *Maus*, as in *Binky Brown*, the passage is dire. The claims of autobiographical comics are here put to the severest test, under the greatest pressure, due to the ethical demands of both familial biography and Holocaust narrative. Like Justin Green's critique of Catholicism, *Maus* dares to treat larger sociopolit-ical issues through the lens of personal trauma, and so demands the acutest sort of self-awareness. Indeed, self-referentiality proves essential to ratify-ing Spiegelman's comic as an act of cultural inter-vention. By continually questioning the naïve notion of autobiography as truth-telling, Spiegelman can recuperate the emotional claims of the genre and powerfully demonstrate that the personal is indeed political, and vice versa. Self-reflexivity becomes his means of achieving complicity with the audience, authenticating his vision of self and history, and speaking about an unspeakable reality "worse than my darkest dreams." To place himself within that history, Spiegelman has to unravel *Maus* and force us to take part in its making.

Clearly, *Maus* sprang from internal necessity. The same can be said of Green's *Binky Brown*, R. Crumb's "Many Faces," and the best of autobiographical comics in general. Green's work, for instance, cri-tiques what he viewed as an oppressive institution and explores how that institution fueled his anxi-eties, while Crumb's, on the other hand, offers the cartoonist a way of exerting control over his public self, as celebrity threatens to alienate him from his own likeness. Such autobiographical work, born of underground and alternative comics, reveals the art form's potential for both frightful intimacy and provocative cultural argument. This is why the auto-biographical genre matters, and why the anxious tension between artifice and authenticity remains a vital area for study.

CHAPTER SIX

WHITHER THE GRAPHIC NOVEL?

This book has bid for the recognition of comics as a literary form, and in particular for the understanding of alternative comics as an innovative and important field of comics production. We have sounded the origins of that field, charting its development through the comix counterculture of the 1960s and the subsequent rise of a specialized comics market, one that encouraged the newly recognized form of the graphic novel. We have considered the potential of comics as a medium—that comic art is not a form necessarily defined by simplicity or transparency but rather a potentially complex narrative instrument, and potentially challenging reading experience. We have seen that complexity play out in a major body of work, that of Gilbert Hernandez, in the process discovering how that work testifies to a tense negotiation between artist and marketplace—a tug-of-war between artistic ambition and commercial demand that ultimately affects both form and content. Finally, we have seen how alternative comics introduced an explicitly autobiographical mode that raised issues of self-representation and authenticity, complicating the always complex matter of autobiographical writing and suggesting the power of comics to imbricate the personal and the political. Major works such as Green's *Binky Brown* and Spiegelman's *Maus* reveal this power and constitute a significant departure, both from comics tradition and from the canons of traditional literary autobiography. At every level, alternative comics both appeal to and productively challenge our preconceptions about literature.

As of this writing, times are good for such alternative comics. In particular, the graphic novel has become a lively, burgeoning genre. Though mainstream publishers' interest in the genre has been fitful at best,[1] it is now definitely on the rise: graphic novels are surging into bookstores and libraries, and the book industry has put out the welcome mat, making room for comics in the trade press and at industry shows (for example, the Book Expo America 2003 included a "Graphic Novel Pavilion" and much programming focused on the genre). Since 2000 the genre has received a terrific boost from translated Japanese *manga*, most notably lines published by TOKYOPOP and VIZ; at the same time, Pantheon's graphic novel line (building on the success of Spiegelman's *Maus*) has put alternative comics on the front burner. Another encouraging sign has been the movement of comic book companies toward the general book trade, in particular the signing of distribution deals between alternative comics publishers and major book publisher/distributors (Fantagraphics with W. W. Norton in fall 2001, Drawn and Quarterly with Chronicle Books in fall 2002, then with Farrar, Straus & Giroux in summer 2004). The outlook for long-form comics is considerably healthier than in the past.

Indeed, as noted in chapter 1, the "graphic novel" has become a kind of totem, enjoying strong presence among publishers, booksellers, librarians, critics, fans—and scholars. Its time has come. Graphic novels have sparked salutary changes, both creative and critical, in the comics field; without these changes, one doubts that scholarly texts about comics would enjoy the kind of attention they are now receiving. Yet there is much about comics, historically and aesthetically, that may be lost in the drive to confer legitimacy on the graphic novel—and there remain economic complications, obstacles frankly, that may hinder the form's further development. Again we have to ask the sobering question of just how comics get to market and what packages or formats they are forced to adopt, or are likely to adopt—a question broached in earlier chapters but demanding fuller treatment. In short, we need to interrogate the idea of the "graphic novel" and carefully place it in its economic and generic context.

In the preceding, we have noted the difficulties that attend serial publication and the reformatting of comic book stories as "novels." We have also suggested, indirectly, that too exclusive an emphasis on the "graphic novel" can impoverish or obstruct appreciation of the art form. Since I once toyed with the idea of titling this study *The Rise of the Graphic Novel*—a wave of the hand at Ian Watt—I think I should finish it by explaining why I felt I had to discard

that title and why, until recently, I have found myself nervously bracketing the term "graphic novel" within quotation marks (as above).[2] As I do, I will return, one last time, to some of the economic/industrial issues that have bedeviled previous chapters and will try to suggest something like an economics of the art form. I think this is an important note to end on, as it has implications for future study.

THE DEVIL OF SERIALIZATION

By and large, graphic novels are created serially. The longer works studied in the above cleave to this rule: the graphic novel usually appears as successive installments, published periodically in anticipation of the completed work. As chapter 1 observes, this was the case for the graphic novels that catapulted the genre to at least a tentative respectability in the late 1980s: volume 1 of Spiegelman's *Maus*, originally serialized in *Raw* starting in 1980; Miller's *The Dark Knight Returns*, first published as four successive booklets in 1986; and Moore and Gibbons's *Watchmen*, published as twelve comic book episodes in 1986–87. This was also the case for many other acclaimed graphic novels between 1987 and 2000, whether distributed to the mainstream book trade or confined to the direct market: volumes by Los Bros Hernandez, Harvey Pekar, Chester Brown, Dave Sim, Dan Clowes, Chris Ware, Debbie Drechsler, Neil Gaiman, and many others. These projects sprang in whole or in part from periodicals. Some, like Drechsler's *Daddy's Girl*, work through thematic repetition and variation, compiling short, distinct pieces to achieve a greater cumulative effect. Others, like Sim's *Cerebus*, consist of hundreds of pages of unbroken continuity, collated from ongoing comic book series. Though there are exceptions to this general rule (to which we will return momentarily), serialization remains the standard.

The serialization of graphic novels parallels the practice of serializing long-form comics, or *bandes dessinées*, or *manga*, or what-have-you, in other cultures. The practice varies in popularity and importance from country to country. On the European scene, the serial has become less important in recent years: the history of francophone "BD" publishing, for instance, has been one of gradual shifting away from a primary emphasis on periodicals to an emphasis on the self-contained album format (Europe's nearest analogue to the "graphic novel"). In this connection, witness the discontinuation in 1998 of the respected French anthology (*A Suivre*), after twenty years of publication, and the absence of other such anthologies—*Pilote*, for example—which once provided a steady supply of serialized work in anticipation of albums. There are exceptions, of course (particularly in the small press, where avant-garde anthologies have performed an important role), but for the most part the francophone market has retreated from periodicals. (Given France's status as a magnet culture for continental comics, this shift has implications for all of western Europe.)

In the Japanese *manga* market, by contrast, serialization in huge, cheaply printed weeklies and monthlies continues to be the favored route for long-form narratives. Short installments in disposable magazines, which contain dozens of comics and scads of other editorial matter, pave the way for more durable volumes of collected work, with popular series spawning thousands of pages of continuity in book form. With *manga* accounting for a huge percentage (one typically hears estimates of a fourth to a third) of all publishing in Japan, the staple anthologies would seem in little danger of disappearing, and the material they support is increasingly finding its way into the United States and other countries (indeed *manga* are now flooding the U.S. market). In contrast to the BD tradition, in which the slender, hardcover album has become the standard, Japan's *manga* market privileges either frequent serial chapters or the much longer, often hundreds of pages long, book form—an economic arrangement facilitated by a rigid studio system of production.

There is ample precedent for such thriving serial publication in the history of literature. The practice of serializing long-form comics echoes the well-established (though now unusual) practice of selling novels through part-issue: by library subscription, within magazines, or in successive pamphlets. In fact the history of the English novel throughout the eighteenth and nineteenth centuries is predominantly one

of parts: novels were typically divided up into volumes through the institution of the circulating library, spread out over months in literary magazines (for example, Dickens in *Bentley's Miscellany* or *Household Words*, Thackeray in *Fraser's Magazine*), or issued as monthly pamphlets à la *Pickwick Papers* (see Erickson 158–62). Yet the fact of part-issue is often bracketed off or ignored in histories of this once disreputable, now central, literary genre. Granted, scholars have begun to ask about the effects of serialization on, say, Dickens's and Thackeray's works, but criticism still favors the monumental, collected novel over the relatively tentative and fragmented experience offered by part-issue. The widespread adoption of the term *graphic novel* would seem to reflect a similar preference among authors and critics of comics, but, as noted before, unfortunately tends to hide the complexity and precariousness of comics publishing, obscuring the long form's dependence on the serial.

Just as scholars have begun to study the effects of serialization on the form and content of the English novel, so we should give attention to the ways serialization inevitably shapes the long-form comic book or graphic novel. Besides the obvious advantages of financial support for the author—a matter to which I will return below—I would tentatively suggest three kinds of effects that serialization can exert on the graphic novel when viewed as a complete text:

(1) Serialization may influence the very structure of a graphic novel, as it encourages authors to build discrete episodes, linked by thematic and motific repetition, rather than tightly structured, overarching plotlines. For example, *Daddy's Girl* (1996), by the aforementioned Debbie Drechsler, approaches its harrowing subject, the tangled emotional and social consequences of sexual abuse, through a series of roughly chronological episodes, all centering on the isolation of the young protagonist, Lilly. Most of these episodes were previously printed in magazines or newspapers, but they have been sequenced in book form by Drechsler for a devastating cumulative effect. A prose analogue for this might be Sandra Cisneros's celebrated novel *The House on Mango Street* (1984), which consists of carefully sequenced stories, vignettes, and prose poems that, taken together, convey a young

Latina's struggle to understand a life of poverty and alienation. In closing her book, Drechsler uses the miniature form of the comic strip—a single-page vignette—much as Cisneros uses lyrical prose poems throughout her text, to reinforce theme and mood. A single page, punctuating the book, serves to sum up the awful loneliness that characterizes Lilly throughout.

Similarly, Will Eisner's *New York: The Big City* (1986) assembles various vignettes from the (now defunct) *Will Eisner Quarterly*, imposing shape on them with thematic chapter headings—and through the overall packaging of the book as a collection of linked episodes set in a specific place. By traditional literary standards, *The Big City* is not a "novel" at all but something like a series of sketches; yet the organizing of those sketches into book form gives the project, again, a cumulative effect greater than the sum of its parts. Significantly, both *Daddy's Girl* and *The Big City* are composed of short pieces culled from larger anthologies, in contrast to those graphic novels that compile whole issues of comic books in the traditional format.

Some graphic novels use episodic structure to build longer narratives that ultimately become more focused and cohesive than expected. For example, Dan Clowes's *Ghost World* (1997), originally serialized in his series *Eightball*, quietly builds toward a moment of crisis in the tense relationship between two friends, Enid and Becky. Each successive episode depicts the anomie and cynicism of these two young women in a different situation; taken together, the episodes push toward that moment when Enid will have to choose either to go away to college or to remain in her ambiguous, unresolved relationship with Becky. Thus, though Clowes seems at first to surrender to the enervation of the two women, he also suggests the limitations imposed by their persistently ironic and hopeless outlook. Deceptively low-affect, *Ghost World* finally builds to a powerful conclusion that suggests betrayal, self-defeat, and irrecoverable loss.

In contrast, more prosaic and less interesting examples of this kind of repetitive and episodic structure may be found in most of the so-called graphic novels culled from the continuities of periodic superhero comics. To read a single volume that collates several months' worth of superhero "continuity" between two covers is to be reminded of just how *dis*continuous the experience of reading a monthly serial really is, for, typically, each successive chapter includes much redundant exposition as well as brief, teasing glimpses of subplots still gestating. These subplots may linger, fecklessly, for chapter after chapter, without gaining momentum, then abruptly, arbitrarily, leap to the fore. Thus even a very good adventure serial of this type may read poorly in collected form.

(2) On the other hand, the serial packaging of a long-form comic lends certain structural and design elements that can be used to reinforce the shape and continuity of an overarching story. For example, in the aforementioned *Watchmen*, as originally serialized in twelve issues, packaging underscores the prevailing mood of paranoia and expectancy. On each successive back cover, the slowly advancing minute hand of a clock, or watch, counts down toward midnight, and the series' apocalyptic finale. Also, the front covers depict not characters but extreme close-ups of significant objects, anticipating the reappearance of the object in the first panel of each chapter, so that, for instance, a bloodied "smiley face" button appears both on the front of the first issue and in the first panel of the story proper. These objects are associated with key characters and help to focus each successive chapter around one such character.

Also, Moore and Gibbons cannily exploit the "wait time" between the penultimate and final chapters by ending issue No. 11 with a terrible disclosure: that the megalomaniacal plot just described by the story's villain (antihero, if you prefer) has already been carried out, resulting in a catastrophic explosion in the heart of New York City. As the final page of No. 11 wipes out various supporting players in a blinding white flash, we realize that the villain has already succeeded; the dialogue shown in the preceding pages does not anticipate his success but crowns it. While the story has been cross-cutting between the villain's lair and the streets of New York, time has not been unfolding linearly, for the New Yorkers we have been watching are already dead; it is too late for the "heroes" to do anything about it.

Figure 58. A highly-charged interchapter break: the last page of *Watchmen* No. 11, and the first page of No. 12. By Alan Moore and Dave Gibbons. © 1987 DC Comics. Used with permission. All rights reserved.

And then we are forced to wait a month (or more) for the succeeding installment. When No. 12 begins, the opening pages—wordless, full-page panoramas of mass death—break away from the prevailing gridlike, nine-panel layout of the rest of the story, at last revealing the carnage wrought by the villain's plot (fig. 58). The synapse between issues No. 11 and No. 12 is a cliffhanger in the classic sense, except that it is built around a fait accompli, not a thing to be prevented. What happens just before the synapse is the very thing that the superheroes were supposed to stop, so that the cliffhanger consists of wondering how the world will respond, not whether this horror can be avoided. (This is just one of many subversions of genre that *Watchmen* performs.)

A similar moment occurs between the sixth and seventh chapters of Peter Milligan and Duncan Fegredo's *Enigma*, originally serialized in eight issues by DC's Vertigo line in 1993. In this aggressive dismantling of the superhero genre—like *Watchmen*, *Enigma* is a superhero tale indebted to alternative comics—the protagonist, Michael Smith, witnesses a series of bizarre and horrific events precipitated by the coming of the Enigma: his favorite 1960s comic book superhero, now come to life. These events conspire to force Michael into confronting his own homosexuality. The series' crowning moment occurs when Michael consummates his relationship with the Enigma in a sexual sense—that is, when he makes love to the icon of his childhood. Milligan's script

Figure 59. Another heavily fraught break: the last page of *Enigma* No. 6, and the first of No. 7. By Peter Milligan and Duncan Fegredo. © 1993 Peter Milligan and Duncan Fegredo. Used with permission.

moves the reader to this emotion-fraught moment at the end of the sixth chapter, or issue, then picks up the story at the beginning of the seventh *after* the event, in a post-coital reverie that deliberately teases the reader with the thought of what he has missed: "Actually you should have seen it. You really missed something" (fig. 59).

Again, the packaging of the story as eight issues reinforces its dramatic argument. Fegredo's cover illustrations embed panels of line drawing within fully painted images of the titular Enigma, commenting on the collision of two frames of reference—which I'm tempted to call "reality" and "fantasy"—within the story itself. The cover to the last issue, however, inverts this design motif, and instead embeds a small painted panel of the Enigma within a larger line

drawing of the protagonist, Michael Smith (fig. 60). This reversal is in keeping with the story's shifting emphasis, from the surreal and hyperviolent encounters of the early chapters to Michael's quiet self-realization in the latter half. Like *Watchmen*'s consistent cover scheme, the shifting designs of *Enigma* provide an opportunity to influence the reader's take on the story in specific ways before the reader has even opened the package.

In short, packaging and seriality can underscore plot and theme, though the breakneck scheduling of periodicals usually discourages the exploitation of this potential. Creators must be both very fast and possessed of a strong a priori grasp of structure to make scheduling and packaging work to the advantage of narrative. At the same time—and here lies a

Figure 60. Symbolic packaging: Duncan Fegredo's covers to *Enigma* No. 7 and No. 8. © 1993 Peter Milligan and Duncan Fegredo. Used with permission.

paradox—packaging and seriality are most effective artistically in books that *do* adhere to a strict periodic schedule, because the consistent intervals between chapters can become an anticipated part of the reading experience itself. Thus I have drawn the above two examples from series published by DC Comics in traditional comic book form, series that adhered to a more or less monthly schedule.

Yet the serial relationship between chapters can be manipulated in other, less strictly periodic comics as well: witness the ironic triumph of Spiegelman's *Maus* volume 2, whose second chapter, "Auschwitz (Time Flies)," records the author's own struggle with guilt, depression, and inertia over a period of some three years (see chapter 5). "Time Flies" exploits the interchapter "break," or pause, to recontextualize the entire story so far: *now* we are suddenly told that Vladek, whose recollections are the book's foundation, has died long since. Thus we are forcibly reminded that what Spiegelman has depicted as "the present" is already past, no less so than the memories of the Holocaust that his father shares. This disclosure forces the reader to reorient him or herself with respect to time, and with respect to Vladek, whose pending death will now haunt the rest of the book. By repositioning the reader at the beginning of this chapter—that is, by using this structural break to introduce an entirely new vantage, one from which Vladek's death is known and unavoidable—Spiegelman at once undercuts and ratifies the strong sense of realism that characterizes all of Art's scenes with his father. As in *Watchmen* and *Enigma*, Spiegelman uses the chapter as a discrete structural element to enable a crucial change in perspective. This change serves Spiegelman's all-important strategy of ironic authentication (as discussed previously).

The example of *Maus* leads to point (3), which ought to be an obvious one but is hidden by the very use of the term "graphic novel." Authors whose work is serialized while still in progress can and do reply to the public reception of their work, by commenting (in direct or coded fashion) on readers' reactions, or by altering the substance of their work in response to reader feedback (as did Dickens on occasion). The point would seem obvious in the case of an ongoing comic book series, in which the readers' advice and feedback may be solicited quite openly, but also applies to personal, self-directed work that would seem entirely aloof from reader response, such as *Maus*. As noted in chapter 5, "Time Flies" represents, among other things, an elaborate, even tortuous, response to the fame Spiegelman garnered from the first volume of *Maus*, published five years before. The critical reaction to his work gets drawn into the work itself, in the form of a blackly comic scene in which reporters and merchandisers vie for Spiegelman's attention, oblivious to the bodies of Nazi victims piled up around him. Despite the fact that *Maus* was always intended to be read as a single work, coherent in form and expression, we stand to lose something important if we obscure the circumstances of its original publication in parts (see Kannenberg, "Form" 151–54).

Serialization, then, can allow graphic novels to comment on the terms of their own reception, or otherwise to change in mid-stream in response to that reception—and, again, serialization can undercut or reinforce a graphic novel's structural cohesion. Serial units (chapters or installments) can be used to impose structure on a novel, or, alternately, they can compromise structure through digression, redundancy, and the attenuation of suspense. More broadly, I would argue that, though some novelists can turn serialization to their advantage, what makes a good serial may not make a good novel, and, vice versa, what makes a good novel may make a poor serial.

Many popular "mainstream" comic books, for instance, sustain plotlines for months or even years at a time and offer something like novelistic development of character and theme. Yet most of these series do not yield cohesive "novels" when collected in book form. Though it is now common to break down ongoing series into successive, self-contained "arcs," often by different authors or teams, mainstream comic books still tend to be cumulative rather than organic in structure. Such series tend either to capitalize on the legendary status of some familiar property (for example, Batman), or to nurse long-term subplots in an open-ended continuity, subplots that remain unresolved at the end of each arc and are manifestly designed to lure the reader back for another soap-opera-like installment. While such comics may exploit the creative and marketing advantages of self-contained arcs, they still accrete story material without the long-term structural aims of a *Watchmen* or *Enigma*. Seldom will a long-running monthly serial achieve the kind of closure aimed at in, for instance, Neil Gaiman's fantasy series *Sandman* (1989–96), in which a series of short tales provided a deliberate, drawn-out denouement after the title's climactic arc.

By the same token, stories that are planned to work as collected volumes may frustrate the expectations of serial readers, leading to a loss of readership, and of economic support—which are the most powerful incentives for persisting in serialization in the first place. As noted in chapter 3, Gilbert and Jaime Hernandez alienated many of their readers in the latter half of the original *Love & Rockets* series by serializing several graphic novels at once, including Gilbert's dauntingly complex *Poison River*. Though begun with distinct and well-structured chapters, *Poison River* eventually devolved into a series of unstructured chunks, or allotments of pages, with no concessions to the periodical readership in terms of exposition or notes—even as the gap between successive issues of *Love & Rockets* stretched wider and wider. Readers balked at the difficulty of *River*'s narrative arc, with its nonlinear structure and uncued flashbacks, and the story became notorious for its byzantine complexity.

Throughout this difficult period, Gilbert Hernandez himself continued to pour considerable energy into *River*, which he has described as a very demanding, even consuming, "stream-of-conscious" effort (Hernandez to the author, 22 Mar. 2000). Also, as noted in chapter 3, he took on additional book-length projects, very different in character, as a relief from the pressures that *River* had created (hard as this may be to fathom). Along the way, *Poison River's* coherence was compromised by this grueling process, compelling Hernandez to do additional work: again, the novel's single-volume edition boasted some fifty new pages of chapter headings and story material to smooth out its knotty complexities. According to Hernandez, this part was easy; it was fitting the story into so few pages in the first place that was hard. In the aftermath of *River*, Gilbert and Jaime struggled to keep pace with each other, so as to put *Love & Rockets* out on a more reliable schedule; this proved difficult enough that the brothers, for a time, chose to discontinue the series in favor of individual publishing projects.

Acclaimed Canadian cartoonist Chester Brown faced a similar problem with his surreal, slow-moving, and now-suspended comic book series *Underwater* (1994–97), an atmospheric treatment of the growth and development of a young girl's mind from birth onwards. With dialogue that mixed snippets of English with a weird invented language, evoking the child's gradual acculturation into speech, *Underwater* offered what many readers saw as a frustrating experience, glacial in its rhythms and ungenerous to its periodic readership (accustomed to the more tightly paced stories in Brown's previous series, *Yummy Fur*). Reviewer Robert Boyd summed up the dilemma posed by the series: "The whole narrative concept of *Underwater* seems to depend on reading it all in one go, but we get it in little, unsatisfying bits. I understand acutely the need to amortize the costs of production, which serialization accomplishes, but if you're going to serialize something, each chapter should at least acknowledge the form—each chapter should be a semi-autonomous story unit. . . . But *Underwater's* chapters read like they were cut randomly from a larger narrative" (42). As if in response to reader's complaints, Brown stepped up the rate of his work, trying to get *Underwater* out on a more regular schedule. He also moved away from his habit of irregular layouts, back to a standard, rectilinear, six-panel grid, a move that, as Boyd suggests,

would seem to threaten the integrity of the work as a whole. Finally, he suspended the project in mid-story—something Gilbert Hernandez was apparently urged to do with *Poison River* as well, according to correspondence with this author—and launched into a conventionally paced serial of more definite duration, the historical *Louis Riel* (1999–2003).

Projects like *Poison River* and *Underwater* suggest the difficulties that face serialized graphic novels that aspire toward unconventional structure (as in *River*) or pacing (as in *Underwater*). In such cases, the standard comic book or magazine-length installment may not be an adequate unit for serialization, and as a result the serial reading experience is fragmented and unsatisfactory, unlike those graphic novels whose rhythms are keyed to the traditional comic book installment, such as *Watchmen*. In short, projects like *Poison River* and *Underwater* anticipate the finished novel without providing whole, satisfying chapters along the way. Their ambitions make for frustrating serials, though they are serialized nonetheless, mainly for economic reasons.

Such is arguably the case with Dave Sim's bizarrely autobiographical epic *Cerebus* (as described in chapter 1). In *Cerebus*, tightly structured chapters (for example, the discrete chapters in the novel *High Society*, originally serialized in issues 26 through 50) eventually gave way to roughly twenty-page allotments divided without regard to the monthly series as such. These allotments would sometimes end, for instance, in mid-scene. Perhaps because of this change in approach, sales of the monthly *Cerebus* comic book dropped even as sales of the collected *Cerebus* volumes rose—a phenomenon also at work in other long-term comic book serials, and christened "the *Cerebus* effect" by *Comics Journal* columnist Bart Beaty ("*Pickle*" 1). Yet Sim's work presents an especially difficult case because its larger ambitions, as a series of graphic novels totaling three hundred issues' worth of story, would seem to be compromised by the author's frequent topical jabs at the comic book industry and other targets. Though these satiric forays remain interesting artifacts of the series qua series—revealing as they do Sim's awareness of his monthly readership—they often serve to waylay or reroute the main storyline. As argued in chapter 1, the resulting collections at times seem dated and unfocused. Yet, economically if not creatively, these collected volumes constituted as important a vehicle for Sim as the comic book itself.

A good serial, then, may not make a good novel, despite its ambitions. Conversely, a good novel may make a poor serial: take *Poison River*, say, or, for a more recent example, *The Sands* by Tom Hart, which was partially serialized, then abruptly halted when the author (and his publisher, the now-defunct Black Eye Books) came to the conclusion that the story could not be effectively parceled out in periodic installments because of its pacing. *The Sands* as a series disappeared, to be completed later as a single volume (Beaty, *"Pickle"* 2). One result of this has been some debate within the small press about the viability of simultaneously publishing comic book series and planning for their eventual compilation (a debate sparked by Beaty and played out in the pages of *The Comics Journal* in 1998–99).[3]

But what of the possibilities for graphic novels that, like most contemporary novels, are not serialized but simply published in toto? A number of examples come to mind from the book trade: for instance, Joyce Brabner, Harvey Pekar, and Frank Stack's *Our Cancer Year*, published by Four Walls, Eight Windows (1994); Paul Karasik and David Mazzucchelli's adaptation of Paul Auster's *City of Glass*, published by Avon as the first in an abortive series (1994, reprinted by Picador in 2004); Howard Cruse's *Stuck Rubber Baby*, published by DC's Paradox Press (1995); or Raymond Briggs's *Ethel & Ernest*, first published by Britain's Jonathan Cape (1998). In addition to these, there are recent examples from the direct market that have crossed over into the book trade—all-new bookshelf volumes from comics specialty publishers such as Fantagraphics Books (for example, Jason's *The Iron Wagon*, 2003), Drawn and Quarterly (for example, Joe Sacco's *The Fixer*, 2003), and Top Shelf Productions (for example, Craig Thompson's *Blankets*, 2003).

Despite recent gains, the prospects for such books are discouraging, due to the financial constraints that weigh on both authors and publishers. On the author's side, the amount of time required to produce a novel-length comic may be prohibitive, unless she/he enjoys some means of support during that time. Notwithstanding the above exceptions, serialization seems essential to underwriting the production of works in the long form, because it pays authors as they go, and offers publishers the added advantage of promoting the eventual novel through tantalizing installments (see Groth, "Partisan Response" 3). Barring serialization, a comics author with his or her eye on the graphic novel typically needs some other kind of work to keep body and soul together, or some sort of substantial advance—something hard to come by in the undercapitalized world of alternative comics.

Even an author who *does* receive an advance for a graphic novel, as in the case of Howard Cruse for his 210-page *Stuck Rubber Baby* (1995), may find that the sheer craftwork required to complete the project cannot be financed by that advance. Cruse faced a terrible dilemma when, by his own admission, the two-year project he had envisioned ended up requiring *four* years to bring to press. *Stuck Rubber Baby* was, and is, a dense and demanding project: a semi-autobiographical fiction about growing up gay in the midst of the Civil Rights movement, populated by dozens of distinct characters and covering many years. Cruse's advance (bear in mind that he was being published by Paradox, a division of DC Comics, and not by an undercapitalized small publisher) was not enough to cover that extra time. This, according to Cruse, engendered "a personal budgetary crisis of unnerving proportions," as the author was forced to divert much-needed attention to fund-raising in the midst of his "full-time drawing" (*Stuck* acknowledgments, n. pag.). Cruse attacked this problem in ingenious ways: he sought foundation grants with the help of testimonials from fellow artists and, finally, ended up selling original artwork for the book *in advance of its being drawn*, to individual sponsors whose support enabled him to finish. *Stuck Rubber Baby*, a rich, complex story—a novel in the traditional sense—required heroic effort both on and off the drawing board to bring to press (and this from one of the largest publishers to specialize in comics and graphic novels).

Cruse's novel, inevitably compared to Spiegelman's *Maus*, was published in a climate of expectation created by *Maus*'s success (note that Spiegelman too relied on a grant, in his case a Guggenheim Foundation fellowship, to underwrite the completion of his project). Yet it took years for *Stuck Rubber Baby* to reach retail shelves, years in which Cruse had to divide his attention between actually crafting the work and seeking funds to keep the process going. The climate of expectation, post-*Maus*, was not enough to sustain a project of *Stuck Rubber Baby*'s scope. Obviously, these observations should not be taken as proof positive that comics are unsuited for the long form. Nor should we fall into the trap of regarding every successful book-length comic, whether serial in origin or not, as simply an unaccountable freak exception to some immutable, oppressive rule. To do so would be to confuse logistical hurdles with inherent formal limitations. Yet to forecast the future prospects of long-form comics, we need to be aware of the real economic and structural difficulties that obstruct the creation of cohesive graphic novels. Even now, despite the blooming interest in graphic novels among mainstream publishers, serialization remains the one economically proven means of getting book-length comics into print. Serialization, however, brings with it an entirely new set of challenges—indeed, a different aesthetic—which constrains, even as it enables, the creation of longer works.

In sum, to make a fetish of the "graphic novel," without reckoning on the serial nature of most comics, is to neglect the crucial economic and generic contexts of this struggling literary form. Privileging the graphic novel package also means ignoring the strengths of other long-form comics genres, such as the comic book and the short story (to say nothing of short-form comics such as strips, which we have knowingly neglected here). Granted, the graphic novel has at last been embraced by the book market, and the term, though misleading from a literary standpoint, is now commonplace enough that it needs no air quotes around it. What's more, it represents a byroad to critical acceptance and a new maturity. Yet a too-exclusive embrace of the term *graphic novel* risks eliding much of what is interesting in comics history, mystifying the economic relations on which the art form depends, and cheating us of an appreciation for those great comics that do *not* look at all like novels. Future criticism needs to contextualize the graphic novel thoroughly, so as to understand more clearly the achievements of a Gilbert Hernandez or an Art Spiegelman. Critics should also be wary of importing aesthetic standards that cannot appreciate the varied forms that comics have explored, and will continue to explore.

CONCLUSION

The hopeful yet at times misleading reception of the graphic novel offers an unusually clear example of what may happen when a popular form, in all its repleteness and variety, is repositioned vis-à-vis literary study. Indeed, as the foregoing discussion suggests, importing comics into prevailing canons of literary value, without regard to their special formal characteristics and the specialized circumstances of their making, may mystify their origins and impoverish our appreciation of the medium. After all, every satisfyingly self-contained graphic novel represents a triumph over logistics and circumstance; every serialized graphic novel represents a negotiation between short- and long-term aims. Not knowing this—that is, not knowing about the serial publishing and marketing of comics—places one at a disadvantage when evaluating graphic novels in terms of their novelistic structure and formal ambitions. In a nutshell, we need to know where these works come from, and what conditions enable and constrain their production. We also need to know what readerly habits and expectations shape their reception.

Such considerations threaten to throw a wrench into the critical recognition of alternative comics as literature; yet that recognition is nonetheless deserved, indeed overdue. The richness of contemporary alternative comics warrants an expansive and searching criticism, one that not only acknowledges the artistic potentialities of comics but also turns an eye, reflexively, on the very criteria by which we ascribe value to literary works in general. Despite—or perhaps because of—the constraints of serial publication, alternative cartoonists like Gilbert Hernandez have explored long-form storytelling and dazzling variations on narrative structure. Despite the cloistral limitations of comic book fandom, alternative cartoonists have overstepped the limits of formula fiction, plunging into piercingly frank self-examination and powerful sociopolitical argument. Increasingly, cartoonists are staking claim to comics, especially long-form comics, as a literary art, one capable of supporting ambitious, disarmingly original and questioning work. In defiance of decades of stultifying convention, alternative comics have expanded the possibilities of the form, reminding us of what a challenging, unpredictable, and tension-filled experience reading comics can be.

NOTES

1. COMIX, COMIC SHOPS, AND THE RISE OF ALTERNATIVE COMICS, POST 1968

1. Notable precursors to *Zap* emerged from college humor magazines. Frank Stack's *The Adventures of Jesus*, published in 1964 in a photocopied edition of about fifty copies, stemmed from Stack's work with Gilbert Shelton on the *Texas Ranger*, the magazine for the University of Texas at Austin. Jack Jackson, a friend of Shelton and the *Ranger* crowd, credited Stack's cartoons with inspiring his own comics booklet, *God Nose*, also produced in 1964 (Rosenkranz 16–25; Harvey, *Comic Book* 211). Yet these formative publications were seen by few at the time; claims for Stack and Jackson as the "firsts" reflect their later stature as much as their historical priority. Ditto for Shelton, whose mock-superhero "Wonder Wart-Hog" bowed during the same period and eventually earned a short-lived newsstand (not underground) magazine in 1967, pre-*Zap* (Rosenkranz 90). (Shelton went on to create the "Fabulous Furry Freak Brothers," comix hippies par excellence, who became staples of the underground press.) Another precursor was the late Joel Beck, a cartoonist for the UC Berkeley *Pelican*, whose booklets of the early sixties were later reissued by comix publisher The Print Mint (Estren 49, 316; Rosenkranz 20, 58–59). These proto-comix, however, were obscure, and did not exploit the comic book format the way *Zap* did; hence claims for their primacy are always couched in terms of "predating" *Zap*, a testament to Crumb's greater impact.

2. Regarding the mid-1950s shakeup in magazine (and therefore comic book) distribution, discussion has been scarce, though Nyberg's *Seal of Approval* does address the problem (125–26). The withdrawal of the once preeminent American News Company from distribution in May 1957 appears to have had a great impact; so too did the damage done to smaller distributors, e.g., Leader News, by the public backlash against comic books. See Vadeboncoeur 4–8, Irving 24–26, and contemporary news coverage of American's cave-in (e.g., Freeman, "Selling Problem"; "American News to Sell Assets"; "Newsstand Giant"). Regarding the encroachment of television, see, e.g., Witty et al. (1963) for an essay that links the decline in comics reading to the rise of television viewing.

3. The semi-autonomous Comics Code Authority, whose seal of approval emblazoned the covers of most comic books from 1955 onwards, worked to insure publishers' compliance with the rigid Code adopted by the majority of comic book publishers in late 1954. As originally adopted, the Code—a strategic concession to public criticism and congressional pressure—not only curbed the depiction of violence and sexual behavior but also forbade

explicit criticism of public figures and, in general, demanded adherence to an authoritarian ideal (in which the law is never wrong and lawbreakers are never right). Targeted at such comics as the infamous horror, suspense, and satire titles from trend-setting publisher E.C., the Code effectively snuffed the kind of antiauthoritarian comics later celebrated by the underground. For the history and significance of the Code, see Nyberg's *Seal of Approval*. For a general treatment of comics censorship, including the global influence of the late-1950s American crisis, see Lent, ed., *Pulp Demons*, and Leonard Rifas's review of same.

4. *Mad* (in both comic book and magazine format) has been cited repeatedly as a major influence, both on underground comix and on American satire in general. *Mad* founder/editor Harvey Kurtzman was the single figure from mainstream media most cited by the comix and a direct inspiration for such cartoonists as Crumb, Lynch, and Spiegelman. Regarding the *Mad*/comix connection, see Groth and Fiore 24–38; Estren 37–38; Rosenkranz 275; *Bijou Funnies* No. 8 (1973), an underground pastiche of *Mad* with a cover by Kurtzman himself; and Spiegelman's comic-strip eulogy for Kurtzman ("Genius").

5. The Cartoonists Co-Op Press, a short-lived publishing collective formed in 1973 by Bill Griffith and other Bay Area artists, circulated an advertisement in comics form (drawn by Willy Murphy) that satirized the comix publishing business for making undergrounds "almost as stupid and disgusting as . . . *overground* comics." This ad depicts underground publishing as an impersonal, corporate process presided over by a "Mr. Bigg," whose comix factory spews out tons of sub-par publications yet cannot boast sales to match. The ad implicitly links questions of quality, creative ownership, and, of course, sales (Estren 252–53). In 1973 Griffith had already inveighed against a rising tide of retrograde comix in an editorial in the San Francisco *Phoenix* ("A Sour Look"). See also Rosenkranz 217–18.

6. For historical background on fandom and direct sales, consult Sabin, *Adult*, chapter 5, and Schelly, *The Golden Age of Comic Fandom*. See Schelly in particular for accounts of key moments in fan history, circa 1964–65 (71–97). (Schelly's history is an invaluable fund of detail and anecdote.) For a study of fandom today, see Pustz.

7. The greatest fund of detail on the history of the market can be found in the scattered writings of veteran dealer/collector Robert Beerbohm, e.g., "Unstable Equilibria" (1997) and "Secret Origins" (2000). The most trenchant analyses of the relationship between the market and comic book content are McAllister's "Cultural Argument and Organizational Constraint" (1990) and "Ownership Concentration" (2001).

8. Though many of the celebrated novels of the eighteenth and nineteenth centuries were three-deckers aimed at the circulating libraries, still the libraries' impact on literary form seems to have been neglected. I have here relied on Jacobs, "Anonymous Signatures," and Erickson, *The Economy of Literary Form*.

Additional historical background on circulating libraries and novel-publishing can be found in Blakey, *The Minerva Press, 1790–1820*; Curwen, *A History of Booksellers* (1873, rpt. 1968), pages 421–432; and Griest, *Mudie's Circulating Library and the Victorian Novel*—the latter two concerned especially with Mudie's, the most popular and powerful of the Victorian libraries. See also Watt 1999, Cross 1985, and, for a fascinating cross-media comparison, Roehl and Varian, "Circulating Libraries and Video Rental Stores."

9. Lane's success was notorious, and his impact on popular literacy and leisure inspired severe social criticism. In Victorian England, the phrase "Minerva Press" had a pejorative potential rather like the phrase "Harlequin Romance" in our own time (Blakey 1). Like Harlequins, Minerva novels were routinely condemned as sensationalistic trash, yet faithfully read by many middle-class readers (Cross 174). Watt, in *Contesting the Gothic*, links the nineteenth-century condemnation of Minerva novels to pandemic cultural anxiety over the growth of "an undisciplined reading public," whose promiscuous consumption (and production) of genre literature was implicitly linked with "a destabilizing form of modernity"—and explicitly gendered as female (80–82). (The concern about popular literacy revealed here anticipates the concern raised in the 1940s and fifties by American comic books, only here it is feminine propriety, not childhood innocence, that is under threat.)

10. Fan historian Richard Kyle has been credited with coining, circa 1964–65, both "graphic story" and "graphic novel." In 1967, Bill Spicer's fanzine *Fantasy Illustrated*, to which Kyle contributed, became *Graphic Story Magazine*, and helped legitimize these terms (see Schelly 130; Harvey, "Novel" 104–5). George Metzger's *Beyond Time and Again* (1976), which Kyle helped publish, may have been the first book-length comic billed as a graphic novel (Rosenkranz 75; Harvey, "Novel" 106). However, Eisner's *A Contract with God*, which bore the term "graphic novel" on its cover, was the first widely recognized example of the genre and became the catalyst for general use of the term. Eisner apparently believed that he had coined a new term, out of desperation to market his book.

2. AN ART OF TENSIONS: THE OTHERNESS OF COMICS READING

1. The cinema/comics analogy, intuitive and long-lived, can be found in many of the seminal popular studies of the art form, often as part of a brief précis of formal characteristics meant to accompany an otherwise historically oriented treatment (see, e.g., Steranko 1:3; Perry 14; Horn 56–57). Ironically, Eisner himself has often been cited as the master of "cinematic" technique in comics (see, e.g., Steranko 2:116). Eisner himself told Steranko that he came to regard comics as "film on paper" but in later interviews and writings would claim theater and print as

his prime influences. In 1973 Eisner told John Benson that print "has always been the most attractive [medium] to me. . . . There's an intimacy in reading that to me transcends motion pictures" ("Art and Commerce" 7). For a recent theoretical comparison of comics and film, see Christiansen.

2. One notable exception to this, Phyllis Hallenbeck's 1976 article for the *Journal of Learning Disabilities* (reprinted in Thomas 136–41), focuses on the use of comics to teach left-to-right sequencing and visual discrimination to students with learning disabilities. Tellingly, this article focuses on a population for whom traditional remediation strategies have proved ineffective and to whom standard expectations are assumed not to apply. Another noteworthy exception, *not* to be found in Thomas, is James W. Brown's "Comics in the Foreign Language Classroom: Pedagogical Perspectives," published in *Foreign Language Annals* in 1977. Brown defines comics as "a *forme mixte*, a polysemiotic genre consisting of many codes," and pays attention to such formal elements as layout, pictorial characterization, and ballooning of text. Brown is invoked as a helpful precedent in later articles by teachers (including some reprinted in Thomas). Significantly, Brown's work comes from an international perspective, with a substantial debt to francophone semiotics; in fact the conceptual foundation of the piece is French research from 1967 to 1976. Though Brown does emphasize the "transparency" and ease of the form, his essay exhibits little of the anxiety over comics that has so disfigured the American critical tradition.

3. Circa 1993–98, Cartier participated in a European collective known as Stakhano, dedicated to producing wordless comics albums for an international audience (see Beaty, "Stakhano"). Regarding the international reach of mute comics, see what is almost certainly the world's largest anthology of such comics, *Comix 2000*, a millennial project assembled in 1999 by the French comics collective L'Association (J.-C. Menu, ed.) This two-thousand-page anthology of pantomime comics, wildly inconsistent, includes contributions from twenty-nine countries and more than three hundred creators.

4. "Torn Together" originally appeared as the inside front cover of issue No. 7 of Spiegelman and Mouly's *Raw* (1985). This issue, subtitled "The Torn-Again Graphix Magazine," had deliberately hand-torn covers (taped inside each copy was a corner torn from the cover, though not necessarily from the cover of that particular copy). Subsequent reprintings of the strip have restored the torn-off upper left corner, which Swarte has drawn to *appear* torn.

3. A BROADER CANVAS: GILBERT HERNANDEZ'S *HEARTBREAK SOUP*

1. Mario's involvement with the original series was minimal after issue No. 3 (1983), but it was his initial prodding that

made *Love & Rockets* a reality. The resultant comic book, the self-published *Love & Rockets* No. 1, captured the attention of Fantagraphics Books, who offered to publish the series professionally. The Fantagraphics *L&R* began in 1982, and Gilbert and Jaime Hernandez have continued their association with Fantagraphics to the present. See Fiore, Groth, and Powers 72–74; Cooke 37–40.

2. Los Bros have acknowledged both the diversity and the zeal of their fan following. In a collaborative Gilbert/Jaime strip from 1994, hyping *Love & Rockets* in a distributor's catalog (reprinted in *Hernandez Satyricon*), Luba boasts of the series' "strong-willed independent women," while a character drawn by Jaime speaks of "minorities shown in a respectful and even inspiring light." In a more self-deprecating vein, the commemorative booklet *Ten Years of Love & Rockets* (1992) includes a strip by Jaime (also reprinted in *Satyricon*) that gently pokes fun at the readers' strong responses to the book. Here Jaime's principal characters, Maggie and Hopey, mouth dialogue taken from fan letters—e.g., "I think I have a crush on Maggie" and "I never thought I'd ever fall in love with a comic book character." Such responses testify, not only to a faithful readership, but to authors who engaged that readership openly and intimately, aware that their joint creation had become a part of readers' lives.

3. For convenience, page citations throughout this chapter generally refer not to the *Love & Rockets* magazine but to the collected, single-volume edition of *Palomar* (2003). The novel *Poison River* is an exception: since it is not included in the collected *Palomar*, I cite its definitive separate edition (1994). In all cases I have identified the original (magazine) publication dates of the stories. On occasion I have also named smaller *Love & Rockets* compilations in which certain stories can be found. Fantagraphics has published a shelf's worth of such compilations, some twenty to date (1985–2003), which are known collectively as *The Complete Love & Rockets* or (sometimes) simply "Love & Rockets Collections." In many cases, Los Bros substantially revised and expanded their stories for these compilations, and it is such revised, definitive versions that are gathered in the single-volume *Palomar*. (No additional changes appear to have been made for the one-volume edition.)

4. During this so-called respite, Hernandez's exploration of high art traditions peaked in "Frida" (*L&R* No. 28, 1988, reprinted in *Flies on the Ceiling*), a short, surreal and intensely suggestive pictorial biography of Mexican painter Frida Kahlo drawing on Hayden Herrera's *Frida* (1991). With the editorial guidance of Fantagraphics editor Kim Thompson (see Gaiman, Interview 95), Hernandez here achieves a stunning visual/verbal repartee, and reveals a contextual awareness of art and politics that portends the complexities of *Poison River*.

5. Nericcio points out that Hernandez "captures and deftly comments upon the dynamics of cinema," and shows that these cinematic touches inform a larger critique of U.S. cultural imperialism (95). Thus, Hernandez's movie references reveal

an overarching interest in the way "image technologies" impact the culture of Palomar and of Latin America in general (94–95). Movies become part of, not only the technique, but also the content of Hernandez's stories: note, for instance, that Palomar's movie theater (run by Luba) displays posters for various bygone American and European films, posters that playfully suggest both the range of Hernandez's cinematic inspirations and the cultural relationship between Palomar and the "outside world." For more on *Heartbreak Soup*'s debt to film, see, e.g., Fiore et al. 87–88.

6. The tables of contents for *L&R* No. 34 (December 1990) and No. 37 (February 1992) include short blurbs designed to bring readers up to speed with *Poison River*, but, predictably, they are so brief and elliptical as to be useless to the uninitiated. The story chapters themselves contain no expository captions, title pages, or other cues to catch readers up. As Hernandez says on the title page of the last chapter of *Human Diastrophism* (*L&R* No. 26, June 1988): "For any new reader of this story; forget it, it's hopeless. . . ." Even more so with *Poison River!*

4. "I MADE THAT WHOLE THING UP!": THE PROBLEM OF AUTHENTICITY IN AUTOBIOGRAPHICAL COMICS

1. The interaction between Pekar's life and his art has been made only more complex by the notoriety of Shari Springer Berman and Robert Pulcini's film adaptation of *American Splendor* (released to acclaim in 2003). The film blends fictionalized versions of Harvey Pekar and Joyce Brabner (played by Paul Giamatti and Hope Davis respectively) with appearances and commentary by their real-life counterparts; moreover, it combines dramatic recreation, archival footage (of Pekar's famed appearances on the *David Letterman Show*) and sequences of animation inspired by the *American Splendor* comics. See Pulcini & Berman 2003.

2. Interestingly, Seth's own work has undermined Pekar's ethic of authenticity by blurring fact and fiction. His ostensibly autobiographical novel *It's a Good Life, If You Don't Weaken* (1996), about Seth's obsessive inquiry into the life of a bygone magazine cartoonist from the 1940s, has been "outed" as a fiction, despite the presence of such real-life supporting characters as Seth's family and fellow cartoonist Chester Brown.

3. Of course, not all autobiographical comics show their protagonists; some merely imply them through dialogue and/or captioned prose. For instance, Harvey Pekar's "Bat" (*American Splendor* No. 16, 1991), drawn by Joe Zabel and Gary Dumm, is seen through the protagonist's eyes and does not reveal his complete likeness until the very end—in a disturbing change of viewpoint. But my comments here pertain to the majority of autobiographical comics, which are concerned if not obsessed with depicting the self.

4. This discussion of selfhood assumes the unified, inner self as a guiding concept or goal, notwithstanding poststructuralism's realization that the "self" may be no more than the successive guises we choose to adopt. I speak of the "inner self" not as an objective presence but as a thing desired or article of faith. Indeed, it may be the very absence, or unlocatable quality, of the self that makes us desire it so. For discussion of recent theories of self and self-imaging, see Dowd.

5. Hernandez would later reject this suicidal ending in a short, mock-heroic strip titled "Destroy All Fanboys" (*Comics Journal* No. 200, Dec. 1997). Though this later strip's posturing borders on self-parody, its blustery rejection of "self-pity" does suggest that Hernandez was attempting to resolve the professional crisis that had marked his late-period work on the original *Love & Rockets* (see chapter 3).

6. Of course, Gusdorf's "original sin" metaphor implies a fallen state, as if by setting our lives forth in autobiography we are lapsing from a state of Edenic innocence. It might be argued—indeed, *has* been argued, by such critics as Gunn— that composing one's autobiography is not a matter of falling from innocence but rather one of (re)creating oneself through performance. Gusdorf's metaphor assumes a prior, prelapsarian self, internal and inviolate, while Gunn assumes no such thing, preferring instead to emphasize the self's dependence on social expression for its very existence. (Note Gunn's insistence on the "worldliness" of autobiography, as opposed to the Edenic purity assumed by Gusdorf's phrase.) For Gusdorf, autobiography remains insufficient, a never-ending "struggle" for an "absolute" knowledge of self (48), whereas Gunn sees autobiography as performance, not only sufficient in itself but necessary for our social being.

5. IRONY AND SELF-REFLEXIVITY IN AUTOBIOGRAPHICAL COMICS: TWO CASE STUDIES

1. For examples of Spiegelman's formalist experimentation, see *Breakdowns* (1977, now sadly out of print) and *Read Yourself Raw* (1987). For comprehensive analysis of this work and its relationship to *Maus*, see Kannenberg, "Form, Function, Fiction," chapter 3.

2. A footnote about the birth of Spiegelman's daughter Nadja (b. 13 May 1987) reveals just how long it took Spiegelman to create the first few pages of "Auschwitz (Time Flies)" (2:43). Whereas Spiegelman was typically able to complete a page of *Maus* in "less than two weeks" (Juno 12), this passage evidently took much, much longer. Indeed, as Kannenberg has pointed out, this chapter apparently encapsulates some three years of work.

3. Belief in the strictly denotative, or referential, power of photographic images persists despite widespread recognition of

their constructed and deeply coded nature. For more on this, see Rugg's discussion of such commentators as Roland Barthes and Alan Sekula in *Picturing Ourselves* (12–13). Barthes discriminates between "denotative" and "connotative" aspects of photography; Sekula, likewise, separates the photograph's "informative" from its "affective" powers. Such faith in the photograph's referentiality, as W. J. T. Mitchell has observed, lends photography a "mystique of automatism and natural necessity" that makes it all the more difficult to approach photos critically (*Iconology* 60–61). Decades of criticism notwithstanding, the technology of photography encourages the common view of photographic images as neutral and slavishly referential (though one suspects that the growth in digital imaging technology will eventually make skeptics of us all).

6. WHITHER THE GRAPHIC NOVEL?

1. Since the first mainstream success for graphic novels circa 1986, several American publishers (Penguin, Avon, Marlowe & Co., Doubleday) have launched but then abandoned graphic novel lines.

2. As this book was entering final edits, I discovered, bemusedly, that another book has laid claim to the title *The Rise of the Graphic Novel*—a cursory guidebook published by NBM in 2003 (Weiner).

3. In *Comics Journal* 207 (Sept. 1998), Beaty's "*Pickle, Poot*, and the *Cerebus* Effect" (1–2), which questions the publishing practices of small publishers, is followed by Gary Groth's angry rejoinder, "A Publisher's Partisan Response" (3–4). Groth, co-publisher of *The Comics Journal* as well as Fantagraphics Books, emphasizes the economic necessity of serializing prior to book publication, even when republication brings substantial alterations to the finished work (a practice decried by Beaty). In *Comics Journal* 212 (May 1999), Rich Kreiner follows up with "*Pay-as-You-Go-Pleasures*: In Defense of Serialized Comics," an essay extolling the aesthetic "attractions" of the serial form as such (1–3).

WORKS CITED

Note: Small-press comic books are often kept in print via successive reprintings, and the collectors' market treats such publications as books rather than periodicals. When listing them here, therefore, I have followed the conventions for books rather than serials (though where applicable I have supplied the specific month of publication). Also, I have listed comics trade magazines by issue number, not only date, because of their sometimes unpredictable scheduling. I trust readers will understand that these unusual objects require an unusual approach.

Abbott, Lawrence L. "Comic Art: Characteristics and Potentialities of a Narrative Medium." *Journal of Popular Culture* 19 (Spring 1986): 155–76.

Adams, Sam. "Return Flight: The Second Coming of *Love and Rockets*." *Philadelphia City Paper*, 15–22 Mar. 2001: 25–26.

Adams, Timothy Dow. *Light Writing & Life Writing: Photography in Autobiography*. Chapel Hill: University of North Carolina Press, 2000.

———. *Telling Lies in Modern American Autobiography*. Chapel Hill: University of North Carolina Press, 1990.

Alagbé, Yvan. "Etoile d'Orient." *Le Cheval sans Tête* Vol. 5: *Nous sommes les Maures*. Ed. Yvan Alagbé and Olivier Marboeuf. Wissous, France: AMOK, May 1998. 35–41.

"American News to Sell Assets." *New York Times*, 18 June 1957: 53.

Arnold, Andrew D. "Graphic Sketches of Latino Life." *Time*, 19 Feb. 2001: 64.

Asbury, Dana. "Photographing the Interior: The Self-Portrait as Introspection." *Self = Portrayal*. Ed. James Alinder. Carmel, Calif.: The Friends of Photography, 1978. n. pag.

Avril, François, and Philipe Petit-Roulet. *Soirs de Paris*. Paris: Les Humanoïdes Associés, 1989.

B., David. *L'Ascension du Haut Mal*. 6 vols. Paris: L'Association, 1996–2003. Translated by Kim Thompson as *Epileptic*. New York: Pantheon, 2005.

Baetens, Jan, ed. *The Graphic Novel*. Proceedings of the Second International Conference on the Graphic Novel, KU Leuven, Belgium, 12–13 May 2000. Leuven: Leuven University Press, 2001.

Barker, Martin. *Comics: Ideology, Power, and the Critics*. Manchester and New York: Manchester University Press, 1989.

———. *A Haunt of Fears: The Strange History of the British Horror Comics Campaign*. London: Pluto, 1984. Rpt., Jackson and London: University Press of Mississippi, 1992.

Beaty, Bart. "AMOK's Culture of Excellence." *The Comics Journal* 209 (Dec. 1998): 19–23.

———. "The Compelling Experimentation of Marc-Antoine Mathieu." *The Comics Journal* 196 (June 1997): 29–34.

———, ed. "Critical Focus: *Understanding Comics.*" *The Comics Journal* 211 (Apr. 1999): 57–103.

———. "Fire Up the Micro-Press: Stakhano." *The Comics Journal* 198 (Aug. 1997): 35–38.

———. "*Pickle, Poot,* and the *Cerebus* Effect." *The Comics Journal* 207 (Sept. 1998): 1–2.

———. "The Search for Comics Exceptionalism." In Beaty, ed., "Critical Focus: *Understanding Comics.*" 67–72.

Beerbohm, Robert. "Secret Origins of the Direct Market, Part Two: Phil Seuling and the Undergrounds Emerge." *Comic Book Artist* 7 (Mar. 2000): 116–125.

———. "The Unstable Equilibria of Unlimited Growth Systems." In "The Comic Book Crisis." 28–32.

Bell, John, ed. *Canuck Comics: A Guide to Comic Books Published in Canada.* Montreal: Matrix Books, 1986.

Benstock, Shari. *The Private Self: Theory and Practice of Women's Autobiographical Writings.* Chapel Hill: University of North Carolina Press, 1988.

Beronä, David A. "Pictures Speak in Comics without Words: Pictorial Principles in the Work of Milt Gross, Hendrik Dorgathen, Eric Drooker, and Peter Kuper." In Varnum and Gibbons, eds., *The Language of Comics: Word and Image.* 19–39.

Blakey, Dorothy. *The Minerva Press, 1790–1820.* London: Oxford University Press, 1939.

Boyd, Robert. "Seasonal Disorder: Spring With Drawn & Quarterly." *The Comics Journal* 198 (August 1997): 41–44.

Brabner, Joyce, Harvey Pekar, and Frank Stack. *Our Cancer Year.* New York and London: Four Walls, Eight Windows, 1994.

Brown, Chester. *Louis Riel.* 10 issues. Montreal: Drawn & Quarterly Publications, 1999–2003. Rpt. in *Louis Riel* [book]. Montreal: Drawn & Quarterly, 2003.

———. *Underwater.* 11 issues. Montreal: Drawn & Quarterly, 1994–97.

Brown, James W. "Comics in the Foreign Language Classroom: Pedagogical Perspectives." *Foreign Language Annals* 10 (Feb. 1977): 18–25.

Brown, Joshua. "Of Mice and Memory." Review essay on *Maus* I by Art Spiegelman. *Oral History Review* 16:1 (Spring 1988): 91–109.

Brown, Merle E. "The Idea of Fiction as Fictive or Fictitious." *Stand* 15.1 (1974): 38–46.

Brubaker, Ed. *A Complete Lowlife.* Marietta, Ga.: Top Shelf Productions, 2001.

Bruss, Elizabeth W. "Eye for I: Making and Unmaking Autobiography in Film." In Olney, ed., *Autobiography: Essays Theoretical and Critical.* 296–320.

Buhle, Paul. "The New Scholarship of Comics." *Chronicle of Higher Education,* 16 May 2003: B7–B9.

Callahan, Bob, ed. *The New Comics Anthology.* New York: Collier Books, 1991.

Carrier, David. *The Aesthetics of Comics.* University Park: Pennsylvania State University Press, 2000.

Cartier, Eric. *Flip in Paradise.* Paris: Rackham, 1990.

Chabon, Michael. *The Amazing Adventures of Kavalier & Clay.* New York: Random House, 2000.

Christiansen, Hans-Christian. "Comics and Film: A Narrative Perspective." In Magnussen and Christiansen, eds., *Comics & Culture* 107–21.

Clell, Madison. *Cuckoo.* Portland, Ore.: Green Door Studios, 2002.

Clowes, Daniel. *Ghost World.* Seattle: Fantagraphics Books, 1997.

———. *Twentieth Century Eightball.* Seattle: Fantagraphics Books, 2004.

"The Comic Book Crisis." Special insert in *The Comics Journal* 199 (Oct. 1997). [32 pp.]

Cooke, Jon B. "A Love of Comics." Interview with Mario Hernandez. *Comic Book Artist* 15 (Nov. 2001): 34–42.

"Creators' Rights." Special section in *The Comics Journal* 137 (Sept. 1990): 65–106.

Cross, Nigel. *The Common Writer: Life in Nineteenth-Century Grub Street.* Cambridge: Cambridge University Press, 1985.

Crumb, Robert. *The Complete Crumb Comics,* Vol. 9. Seattle: Fantagraphics Books, 1992.

———. "The Many Faces of R. Crumb." *XYZ Comics.* Milwaukee: Kitchen Sink Enterprises, June 1972. [n.pag.] Rpt. in *Complete Crumb,* Vol. 9. 21–22.

———. *Zap Comix* No. 0. San Francisco: Apex Novelties, 1968.

———. *Zap Comix* No. 1. San Francisco: Apex Novelties, 1968.

Cruse, Howard. *Stuck Rubber Baby.* New York: Paradox Press/DC Comics, 1995.

Curwen, Henry. *A History of Booksellers.* 1873. Rpt., Detroit: Gale Research Company, 1968.

Daniels, Les. *Comix: A History of Comic Books in America.* New York: Outerbridge & Dienstfrey/E. P. Dutton, 1971.

De Haven, Tom. "Comics." *New York Times Book Review,* 31 May 1998: 9+.

Delany, Samuel R. "The Politics of Paraliterary Criticism." *Shorter Views: Queer Thoughts & The Politics of the Paraliterary.* Hanover and London: Wesleyan University Press/ University Press of New England, 1999. 218–70.

Diereck, Charles, and Pascal Lefèvre, eds. *Forging a New Medium: The Comic Strip in the Nineteenth Century.* Leuven, Belgium: VUB University Press, 1998.

Doherty, Thomas. "Art Spiegelman's *Maus*: Graphic Art and the Holocaust." *American Literature* 68:1 (Mar. 1996): 69–84.

Dorfman, Ariel. *The Empire's Old Clothes: What the Lone Ranger, Babar, and Other Innocent Heroes Do to Our Minds*. New York: Pantheon, 1983.

Dorfman, Ariel, and Armand Mattelart. *How to Read Donald Duck: Imperialist Ideology in the Disney Comic*. 1975. Trans. and with an updated introduction by David Kunzle. New York: International General, 1991.

Doucet, Julie. *Lève Ta Jambe Mon Poisson Est Mort!* Montreal: Drawn & Quarterly Publications, 1993.

———. *My Most Secret Desire*. Montreal: Drawn & Quarterly Publications, 1995.

Dowd, James J. "Aporias of the Self." *Alternative Identities: The Self in Literature, History, Theory*. Ed. Linda Marie Brooks. New York and London: Garland, 1995.

Drechsler, Debbie. *Daddy's Girl*. Seattle: Fantagraphics Books, 1996.

Eakin, Paul John. *Fictions in Autobiography: Studies in the Art of Self-Invention*. Princeton, N.J.: Princeton University Press, 1985.

Eisner, Will. "Art and Commerce: An Oral Reminiscence." Interview with John Benson. *Panels* 1 (Summer 1979): 4–21. [Recorded Dec. 1973.]

———. *Comics & Sequential Art*. Tamarac, Fla.: Poorhouse Press, 1985.

———. *Graphic Storytelling*. Tamarac, Fla.: Poorhouse Press, 1995.

———. *New York: The Big City*. Princeton, Wis.: Kitchen Sink Press, 1986.

Elder, Robert K. "A Drawn-out 'Love' Affair: Brothers Hernandez Revive Stellar Comic 'Love & Rockets'." *Chicago Tribune*, 4 Feb. 2004: 4.

Erickson, Lee. *The Economy of Literary Form: English Literature and the Industrialization of Publishing, 1800–1850*. Baltimore and London: Johns Hopkins, 1996.

Estren, Mark James. *A History of Underground Comics*. 1974. Rev. ed. Berkeley, Calif.: Ronin Publishing, 1987.

Fiedler, Leslie. "The Middle Against Both Ends." *Encounter* 5.2 (Aug. 1955): 16–23. Rpt. in *The Collected Essays of Leslie Fiedler*, Volume II. New York: Stein and Day, 1971. 415–28.

Fiore, Robert, Gary Groth, and Thom Powers. "Pleased to Meet Them. . . ." Interview with Gilbert, Jaime and Mario Hernandez. *The Comics Journal* 126 (Jan. 1989): 60–113.

Fischer, Hervé. "Ecriture phonétique et pictogrammes dans les bandes dessinées." *Communications* 9:2–3 (1984): 191–200.

Fleener, Mary. *Life of the Party*. Introduction by Ray Zone. Seattle: Fantagraphics Books, 1996.

Fletcher, Robert P. "Visual Thinking and the Picture Story in *The History of Henry Esmond*." *PMLA* 113:3 (May 1998): 379–94.

Frank, Thomas. *The Conquest of Cool: Business Culture, Counterculture, and the Rise of Hip Consumerism*. Chicago: University of Chicago Press, 1997.

Freeman, William M. "Selling Problem Faces Magazines." *New York Times,* 26 May 1957: 95.

Fresnault-Deruelle, Pierre. "Du linéare au tabulaire." *Communications* 24: *La bande dessinée et son discours*. Paris: Ed. du Seuil, 1976. 17–23.

Frome, Jonathan. "Identification in Comics." In Beaty, ed., "Critical Focus: *Understanding Comics*." 82–86.

Gaiman, Neil. Interview with Gilbert and Jaime Hernandez. *The Comics Journal* 178 (July 1993): 91–123.

Genette, Gerard. *Paratexts: Thresholds of Interpretation*. Trans. Jane E. Lewin. Cambridge and New York: Cambridge University Press, 1997.

Gilbert, James. *A Cycle of Outrage: America's Reaction to the Juvenile Delinquent in the 1950s*. New York: Oxford University Press, 1986.

Gombrich, E. H. "The Mask and the Face: The Perception of Physiognomic Likeness in Life and in Art." *Art, Perception, and Reality*. Ed. Maurice Mandelbaum. Baltimore and London: Johns Hopkins, 1972. 1–46.

Goodrick, Susan, and Don Donahue, eds. *The Apex Treasury of Underground Comics*. New York: Links Books, 1974.

Gopnik, Adam. "Comics and Catastrophe: Art Spiegelman's *Maus* and the History of the Cartoon." *New Republic*, 22 June 1987: 29–34.

Gordon, Ian. "Beyond the Funnies: Comic Books, History, and Hegemony." *American Quarterly* 52.1 (Mar. 2000): 145–50.

———. "'But Seriously, Folks . . .': Comic Art and History." *American Quarterly* 43.2 (June 1991): 341–46.

———. *Comic Strips and Consumer Culture, 1890–1945*. Washington, D.C.: Smithsonian Institution Press, 1998.

Goulart, Ron. "Golden Age Sweatshops." *The Comics Journal* 249 (Dec. 2002): 70–81.

———. *Great American Comic Books*. Lincolnwood, Ill.: Publications International, 2001.

Gravett, Paul. "Euro-Comics: A Dazzling Respectability." *Print* 42:6 (Nov.-Dec. 1988): 74–87, 204–6.

———. "Hergé and the Clear Line: Part Two." *Comic Art* 3 (Summer 2003): 70–79.

Green, Justin. *Binky Brown Meets the Holy Virgin Mary*. 1972. Rpt. in *Justin Green's Binky Brown Sampler*. San Francisco: Last Gasp, 1995. 9–52.

Griest, Guinevere L. *Mudie's Circulating Library and the Victorian Novel*. Bloomington and London: Indiana University Press, 1970.

Griffith, Bill. "A Sour Look at the Comix Scene." *San Francisco Phoenix*, 13 Apr. 1973. Rpt. in *Panels* 1 (Summer 1979): 28–29.

Groensteen, Thierry. "Histoire de la bande dessinée muette." Part 1. *9e Art* [The Ninth Art] 2 (1997): 60–75.

———. "Histoire de la bande dessinée muette." Part 2. *9e Art* [The Ninth Art] 3 (1998): 92–105.

———. "Les petites cases du Moi: L'autobiographie en bande dessinée." *9ᵉ Art* [The Ninth Art] 1 (1996): 58–69.

Groth, Gary. "A Publisher's Partisan Response." *The Comics Journal* 207 (Sept. 1998): 3–4.

Groth, Gary, and Robert Fiore, eds. *The New Comics.* New York: Berkley, 1988.

Gunn, Janet Varner. *Autobiography: Towards a Poetics of Experience.* Philadelphia: University of Pennsylvania, 1982.

Gusdorf, George. "Conditions and Limits of Autobiography." Trans. James Olney. In Olney, ed., *Autobiography: Essays Theoretical and Critical.* 28–48.

Halkin, Hillel. "Inhuman Comedy." Review of *Maus* II by Art Spiegelman. *Commentary*, Feb. 1992: 55–56.

Hallenbeck, Phyllis N. "Remediating with Comic Strips." *Journal of Learning Disabilities* 9:1 (Jan. 1976): 22–26. Rpt. in Thomas, *Cartoons and Comics in the Classroom.* 136–41.

Harvey, Robert C. *The Art of the Comic Book: An Aesthetic History.* Jackson: University Press of Mississippi, 1996.

———. *The Art of the Funnies: An Aesthetic History.* Jackson: University Press of Mississippi, 1994.

———. "The Graphic Novel, Will Eisner, and Other Pioneers." *The Comics Journal* 233 (May 2001): 103–6.

———. "Shop System: Interview with Will Eisner." *The Comics Journal* 249 (Dec. 2002): 62–69.

Haspiel, Dean, and Josh Neufeld, eds. *Keyhole* 1. Kingston, R.I.: Millenium Publications, June 1996.

———, eds. *Keyhole* 3. Narragansett, R.I.: Millenium Publications, Jan. 1997.

Hatfield, Charles. "*Heartbreak Soup:* The Interdependence of Theme and Form." *Inks: Cartoon and Comic Art Studies* 4:2 (May 1997): 2–17.

Heller, Steven. "A Clear Line to Many Layers." *Print* 41 (Sept.-Oct. 1987): 78–86.

Hernandez, Gilbert. *Birdland.* 4th ed. Seattle: Eros Comix, 1996.

———. "Destroy All Fanboys." *The Comics Journal* 200 (Dec. 1997): 108.

———. *Fear of Comics.* Seattle: Fantagraphics, 2000.

———. *Girl Crazy.* Milwaukie, Ore.: Dark Horse Comics, 1997.

———. *Luba in America.* Seattle: Fantagraphics, 2001.

———. *New Love.* 6 issues. Seattle: Fantagraphics, 1996–97.

———. *Palomar: The Heartbreak Soup Stories.* Seattle: Fantagraphics, 2003.

———. *Poison River. Love and Rockets* Book 12. Seattle: Fantagraphics, 1994.

———. Private correspondence to the author [electronic mailing]. 22 Mar. 2000.

Hernandez, Gilbert, and Jaime Hernandez. *Flies on the Ceiling.* Vol. 9 of *The Complete Love & Rockets.* Seattle: Fantagraphics, 1991.

———. *Las Mujeres Perdidas.* Vol. 3 of *The Complete Love & Rockets.* 2nd ed. Seattle: Fantagraphics, 1990.

———. *Love & Rockets Sketchbook* Vol. 2. Seattle: Fantagraphics, 1992.

———. *Ten Years of* Love & Rockets. Seattle: Fantagraphics, 1992.

Hernandez, Gilbert, Jaime Hernandez, and Mario Hernandez. *Chelo's Burden.* Vol. 2 of *The Complete Love & Rockets.* Preface by Gary Groth. 2nd ed. Seattle: Fantagraphics, 1989.

———. *Hernandez Satyricon. Love and Rockets* Book 15. Seattle: Fantagraphics, 1997.

———. *Love & Rockets.* 50 issues. Seattle: Fantagraphics, 1982–96.

Hill, George E. "Word Distortions in Comic Strips." *The Elementary School Journal* 43 (1942–43): 520–25.

Hogarth, Burne. Interview with Gary Groth. Part 2. *The Comics Journal* 167 (Apr. 1994): 84–104.

Horn, Maurice. "The World of Comics: An Analytical Summary." *The World Encyclopedia of Comics.* Ed. Maurice Horn. New York: Chelsea House, 1976. 47–62.

Horowitz, Sara R. *Voicing the Void: Muteness and Memory in Holocaust Fiction.* Albany: State University of New York, 1997.

Huestis, Peter. "*Love and Rockets* is Dead/Long Live *Love & Rockets!*" *Your Flesh* 34 (Fall 1996): 66–71.

Iadonisi, Rick. "Bleeding History and Owning His [Father's] Story: *Maus* and Collaborative Autobiography." *The College English Association Critic* 57:1 (1994): 41–56.

Irving, Christopher. "Unlocking the Mystery of Gold Key Comics." *Comic Book Artist* 22 (Oct. 2002): 16–31.

Iser, Wolfgang. *The Act of Reading: A Theory of Aesthetic Response.* Baltimore: Johns Hopkins, 1978.

Jacobs, Edward. "Anonymous Signatures: Circulating Libraries, Conventionality, and the Production of Gothic Romances." *ELH* 62 (Fall 1995): 603–29.

Jay, Paul. *Being in the Text: Self-Representation from Wordsworth to Roland Barthes.* Ithaca and London: Cornell, 1984.

———. "Posing: Autobiography and the Subject of Photography." *Autobiography & Postmodernism.* Eds. Kathleen Ashley, Leigh Gilmore, and Gerald Peters. Amherst: University of Massachusetts Press, 1994. 191–211.

Juno, Andrea, ed. *Dangerous Drawings: Interviews with Comix and Graphix Artists.* New York: Juno Books, 1997.

Kannenberg, Gene, Jr. "The Comics of Chris Ware: Text, Image, and Visual Narrative Strategies." In Varnum and Gibbons, eds., *The Language of Comics: Word and Image.* 174–97.

———. "Form, Function, Fiction: Text and Image in the Comics Narratives of Winsor McCay, Art Spiegelman, and Chris Ware." Diss., University of Connecticut, 2002.

———. "Graphic Text, Graphic Context: Interpreting Custom Fonts and Hands in Contemporary Comics." *Illuminating Letters: Typography and Literary Interpretation.* Ed. Paul C. Gutjahr and Megan L. Benton. Amherst: University of Massachusetts Press, 2001. 165–92.

Kinneir, Joan, ed. *The Artist by Himself: Self-Portrait Drawings from Youth to Old Age*. New York: St. Martin's, 1980.

Kirby, Jack. Interview with Ben Schwartz. *The Jack Kirby Collector* 23 (Feb. 1999): 19–23.

———. *Jack Kirby's New Gods*. New York: DC Comics, 1998.

Knowles, Chris. "Down Palomar Way." Interview with Gilbert Hernandez. *Comic Book Artist* 15 (Nov. 2001): 44–55.

Kominsky-Crumb, Aline. *Love That Bunch!* Seattle: Fantagraphics Books, 1990.

Kreiner, Rich. "*Pay-as-You-Go-Pleasures*: In Defense of Serialized Comics." *The Comics Journal* 212 (May 1999): 1–3.

Kunzle, David. *The History of the Comic Strip*. Vol. 1: *The Early Comic Strip: Narrative Strips and Picture Stories in the European Broadsheet from c. 1450 to 1825*. Berkeley and Los Angeles: University of California Press, 1973.

———. *The History of the Comic Strip*. Vol. 2: *The Nineteenth Century*. Berkeley and Los Angeles: University of California Press, 1990.

Kurtzman, Harvey, et al. *Frontline Combat*. Vol. 1. West Plains, Mo.: Russ Cochran, 1982.

———. *Two-Fisted Tales*. Vols. 1–3. West Plains, Mo.: Russ Cochran, 1980.

Lasch, Christopher. *The Culture of Narcissism: American Life in an Age of Diminishing Expectations*. New York: Norton, 1978.

Lefèvre, Pascal. "The Importance of Being 'Published': A Comparative Study of Different Comics Formats." In Magnussen and Christiansen, eds., *Comics & Culture*. 91–105.

———. "Recovering Sensuality in Comic Theory." *International Journal of Comic Art* 1:1 (Spring/Summer 1999): 140–49.

Lejeune, Philippe. *On Autobiography*. Ed. and with a foreword by Paul John Eakin; trans. Katherine M. Leary. Minneapolis: University of Minnesota Press, 1988.

Lent, John A. *Comic Strips and Comic Books in the United States: An International Bibliography*. Vol. 4 of Bibliographies and Indexes in Popular Culture. Westport, Conn.: Greenwood Press, 1994.

———, ed. *Pulp Demons: International Dimensions of the Postwar Anti-Comics Campaign*. London: Associated University Presses, 1999.

Levin, Bob. "Rice, Beans and Justin Greens." *The Comics Journal* 203 (Apr. 1998): 101–7.

Lutes, Jason. *Jar of Fools*. Montreal: Black Eye Books, 1997.

Lynch, Jay, and Skip Williamson, eds. *Bijou Funnies* 8. Chicago: Bijou Publishing Empire, 1973. [An underground homage to *Mad* magazine.]

Magnussen, Anne, and Hans-Christian Christiansen, eds. *Comics & Culture: Analytical and Theoretical Approaches to Comics*. Copenhagen: Museum Tusculanum Press, University of Copenhagen, 2000.

Markee, Patrick. "American Passages." Review of *Love & Rockets*, Vols. 1–15, by Los Bros Hernandez. *The Nation*, 18 May 1998: 25–27.

Mathieu, Marc-Antoine. *Julius Corentin Acquefacques, prisonnier des rêves*. 4 vols. Paris: Delcourt, 1990–95.

Matt, Joe. *Peepshow*. Montreal: Drawn & Quarterly Publications, 1992– . [13 issues to date.]

———. *The Poor Bastard*. Montreal: Drawn & Quarterly Publications, 1997.

McAllister, Matthew P. "Comic Book Research: A Bibliography and Brief History." Paper presented at the Mass Communication Division of the 1989 Annual Meeting of the Southern States Speech Association.

———. "Cultural Argument and Organizational Constraint in the Comic Book Industry." *Journal of Communication* 40 (Winter 1990): 55–71.

———. "Ownership Concentration in the U.S. Comic Book Industry." *Comics & Ideology*. Ed. Matthew P. McAllister, Edward H. Sewell, Jr., and Ian Gordon. New York: Peter Lang, 2001. 15–38.

McCloud, Scott. *Understanding Comics*. Northampton, Mass.: Tundra Publishing, 1993.

McKenna, Kristine. "What He Saw: Gary Panter's Apocalypse Now." *L.A. Weekly*, 4–10 Jan. 2002.

Menu, Jean-Christophe, ed. *Comix 2000*. Paris: L'Association, 1999.

Milligan, Peter, and Duncan Fegredo et al. *Enigma*. 8 issues. New York: Vertigo/DC Comics, 1993. Rpt. in *Enigma* [book]. New York: Vertigo/DC, 1995.

Mitchell, W. J. T. *Iconology: Image, Text, Ideology*. Chicago: University of Chicago Press, 1986.

———. *Picture Theory: Essays on Verbal and Visual Representation*. Chicago: University of Chicago, 1994.

Moodian, Patricia, ed. *Wimmen's Comix* 1. Berkeley, Calif.: Last Gasp Eco-Funnies, 1972.

Moore, Alan, and Dave Gibbons. *Watchmen*. 12 issues. New York: DC Comics, 1986–87. Rpt. in *Watchmen* [book]. New York: Warner Books, 1987.

National Association of Comics Art Educators [Website]. 2002. 28 February 2005. <http://www.teachingcomics.org>.

Nericcio, William Anthony. "Artif[r]acture: Virulent Pictures, Graphic Narrative and the Ideology of the Visual." *Mosaic* 28:4 (Dec. 1995): 79–109.

"Newsstand Giant Shrinks Away." *Business Week*, 25 May 1957: 59+.

Nodelman, Perry. *Words About Pictures: The Narrative Art of Children's Picture Books*. Athens: University of Georgia Press, 1988.

Nyberg, Amy Kiste. *Seal of Approval: The History of the Comics Code*. Jackson: University Press of Mississippi, 1998.

Olney, James, ed. *Autobiography: Essays Theoretical and Critical*. Princeton, N.J.: Princeton University Press, 1980.

Panter, Gary. Interview with Dale Luciano. In Groth and Fiore, eds., *The New* Comics. 224–36.

———. Interview with John Kelly. *The Comics Journal* 250 (Feb. 2003): 206–44.

———. "Jimbo Is 'Running Sore.'" In Spiegelman and Mouly, eds., *Read Yourself Raw*. 51–55.

Peeters, Benoit. *Case, Planche, Récit: lire la bande dessinée*. Rev. ed. Paris: Casterman, 1998.

Pekar, Harvey. Interview with Gary Groth. In Groth and Fiore, eds., *The New Comics*. 212–23.

———. "The Potential of Comics." *The Comics Journal* 123 (July 1988): 81–88.

Pekar, Harvey, et al. *American Splendor*. Garden City, N.Y.: Dolphin/Doubleday, 1986.

———. *More American Splendor*. Garden City, N.Y.: Dolphin/Doubleday, 1987.

———. *The New American Splendor Anthology*. New York: Four Walls Eight Windows, 1991.

Pekar, Harvey, and David Collier. *American Splendor: Unsung Hero*. Milwaukie, Ore.: Dark Horse Comics, 2003.

Pekar, Harvey, and R. Crumb. *Bob and Harv's Comics*. New York: Four Walls, Eight Windows, 1996.

Pekar, Harvey, Colin Warneford et al. *American Splendour: Transatlantic Comics*. Milwaukie, Ore.: Dark Horse Comics, July 1998.

Pekar, Harvey, Joe Zabel, and Gary Dumm. "Bat." *American Splendor* No. 16 (Nov. 1991): n. pag.

Perry, George, with Alan Aldridge. *The Penguin Book of Comics*. Rev. ed. London: Penguin, 1971.

Pollman, Joost. "An Art of the Real: About the Adulthood of Contemporary Comics." *International Journal of Comic Art* 1:2 (Fall 1999): 107–26.

Pulcini, Robert, and Shari Springer Berman. *American Splendor: The Official Shooting Script*. New York: Welcome Rain, 2003.

Pustz, Matthew J. *Comic Book Culture*. Jackson: University Press of Mississippi, 1999.

Randall, William Lowell. *The Stories We Are: An Essay on Self-Creation*. Toronto: University of Toronto, 1995.

Renza, Louis. Review of *Educated Lives: The Rise of Modern Autobiography in America* by Thomas Cooley. *American Literary Realism* 10 (1977): 317–20.

Rifas, Leonard. "Addressing Lent's Demons"/"International Aspects of the American Anti-Comic Book Crusade." Review of Lent, ed., *Pulp Demons*. *The Comics Journal* 221 (Mar. 2000): 93–98.

Roehl, Richard, and Hal R. Varian. "Circulating Libraries and Video Rental Stores." *First Monday*, Vol. 6, No. 5 (May 2001). 28 February 2005. <http://firstmonday.org/issues/issue6_5/roehl/ index.html>.

Rosenkranz, Patrick. *Rebel Visions: The Underground Comix Revolution, 1963–1975*. Seattle: Fantagraphics, 2002.

Rothberg, Michael. "'We Were Talking Jewish': Art Spiegelman's *Maus* as 'Holocaust' Production." *Contemporary Literature* 35:4 (Winter 1994): 661–87.

Rugg, Linda Haverty. *Picturing Ourselves: Photography and Autobiography*. Chicago: University of Chicago Press, 1997.

Sabin, Roger. *Adult Comics: An Introduction*. London: Routledge, 1993.

———. *Comics, Comix & Graphic Novels*. London: Phaidon, 1996.

Schelly, Bill. *The Golden Age of Comic Fandom*. Rev. ed. Seattle: Hamster Press, 1999.

Seth [pseud.], Chester Brown, and Joe Matt. Interview with Mark Daly and Rich Kreiner. *The Comics Journal* 162 (Oct. 1993): 51–56.

Seth [pseud.]. *It's a Good Life, If You Don't Weaken*. 1996. Rev. ed. Montreal: Drawn & Quarterly Publications, 2001.

Shapiro, Stephen A. "The Dark Continent of Literature: Autobiography." *Comparative Literature Studies* 5 (1968): 421–54.

Sim, Dave. *High Society*. Kitchener, Ont.: Aardvark-Vanaheim, 1986.

———. Interview with Tom Spurgeon. *The Comics Journal* 184 (Feb. 1996): 68–106.

Sommer, Anna. *Remue-Ménage/Damen Dramen*. Paris: L'Association, 1996.

Sontag, Susan. *On Photography*. New York: Farrar, Straus and Giroux, 1977.

Spiegelman, Art. *Breakdowns*. New York: Nostalgia Press, 1977.

———. *Comix, Essays, Graphics and Scraps (From Maus to Now to* Maus *to Now)/Comics, Essays, Grafiken und Fragmente*. Italy: Sellerio Editore—La Centrale dell'Arte, 1999.

———. "Commix: An Idiosyncratic Historical and Aesthetic Overview." *Print* 42 (Nov.-Dec. 1988): 61–73, 195–96.

———. *The Complete Maus*. [CD-ROM.] New York: Voyager Publishing, 1996.

———. "Drawing Pens and Politics: Mightier Than the Sorehead." *The Nation*, 17 Jan. 1994: 45–46. Rpt. as "Little Orphan Annie's Eyeballs" in *Comix, Essays, Graphics and Scraps*. 17–18.

———. "H. K. (R. I. P.)."/"A Furshlugginer Genius!" *New Yorker*, 29 Mar. 1993: 75–77. [A eulogy and appreciation, in comics form, for the late Harvey Kurtzman.]

———. Interview with Andrea Juno. In Juno, ed., *Dangerous Drawings*. 6–31.

———. "Introduction." *Breakdowns*. Rpt. in *Comix, Essays, Graphics and Scraps*. 26.

———. *Maus: A Survivor's Tale*. 2 vols. New York: Pantheon, 1986 and 1991.

———. "Symptoms of Disorder/Signs of Genius." Introduction. *Justin Green's Binky Brown Sampler*. By Justin Green. San Francisco: Last Gasp, 1995. 4–6. Rpt. in *Comix, Essays, Graphics and Scraps*. 94.

Spiegelman, Art, and Chip Kidd. *Jack Cole and Plastic Man: Forms Stretched to Their Limits.* San Francisco: Chronicle Books, 2001.

Spiegelman, Art, and Françoise Mouly. Interview with Joey Cavalieri, Gary Groth, and Kim Thompson. In Groth and Fiore, eds., *The New Comics.* 185–203.

———. Interview. *Comics Feature* 4 (July–Aug. 1980): 49–56.

———, eds. *Read Yourself Raw.* New York: Pantheon, 1987.

"State of the Industry/State of the Art Form." Special issue. *The Comics Journal* 188 (July 1996).

Staub, Michael E. "The Shoah Goes On and On: Remembrance and Representation in Art Spiegelman's *Maus.*" *MELUS* 20:3 (Fall 1995): 33–46.

Steranko, Jim. *The Steranko History of Comics.* Vol. 1. Reading, Penn.: Supergraphics, 1970.

———. *The Steranko History of Comics.* Vol. 2. Reading, Penn.: Supergraphics, 1972.

Sturm, James. "Comics in the Classroom." *Chronicle of Higher Education,* 5 Apr. 2002: B14–B15.

Sullivan, Darcy. "Marvel Comics and the Kiddie Hustle." *The Comics Journal* 152 (Aug. 1992): 30–37.

Swarte, Joost. "Torn Together." *Raw* No. 7. Ed. Art Spiegelman and Françoise Mouly. New York: Raw Books & Graphics, 1985. 2 [inside front cover].

Thomas, James L., ed. *Cartoons and Comics in the Classroom: A Reference for Teachers and Librarians.* Littleton, Colo.: Libraries Unlimited, Inc., 1983.

Töpffer, Rodolphe. "Essay on Physiognomy." 1845. Rpt. in *Enter: The Comics.* Translated and edited, with an introduction, by E. Wiese. Lincoln: University of Nebraska Press, 1965. 1–36.

Vadeboncoeur, Jim. "The Great Atlas Explosion." *The Jack Kirby Collector* 18 (Jan. 1998): 4–8.

Varnedoe, Kirk, and Adam Gopnik. *High and Low: Modern Art, Popular Culture.* New York: Museum of Modern Art/Abrams, 1990.

Varnum, Robin, and Christina T. Gibbons, eds. *The Language of Comics: Word and Image.* Jackson: University Press of Mississippi, 2001.

Ware, Chris. "I Guess." *Raw,* Vol. 2, No. 3. Ed. Art Spiegelman and Françoise Mouly. New York: Penguin, 1991. 76–81.

———. Interview with Andrea Juno. In Juno, ed., *Dangerous Drawings.* 32–53.

———. *Quimby the Mouse.* Seattle: Fantagraphics, 2003.

Watt, James. *Contesting the Gothic: Fiction, Genre and Cultural Conflict, 1764–1832.* Cambridge: Cambridge University Press, 1999.

Watterson, Bill. *Weirdos from Another Planet!: A Calvin and Hobbes Collection.* Kansas City, Mo.: Andrews and McMeel, 1990.

Waugh, Coulton. *The Comics.* 1947. Rpt., Jackson: University Press of Mississippi, 1991.

Weiner, Stephen. *The Rise of the Graphic Novel.* New York: NBM Publishing, 2003.

Wertham, Fredric. "Comics in Education: A Reply." *High Points* 39:7 (Oct. 1957), 18–22.

———. *Seduction of the Innocent.* New York: Rinehart, 1954.

Wiater, Stanley, and Stephen R. Bissette, eds. *Comic Book Rebels: Conversations with the Creators of the New Comics.* New York: Donald I. Fine, 1993.

Witek, Joseph. *Comic Books as History: The Narrative Art of Jack Jackson, Art Spiegelman, and Harvey Pekar.* Jackson: University Press of Mississippi, 1989.

———. "Comics Criticism in the United States: A Brief Historical Survey." *International Journal of Comic Art* 1:1 (Spring/Summer 1999): 4–16.

———. Review of *Understanding Comics* by Scott McCloud. *Inks: Cartoon and Comic Art Studies* 1:1 (Feb. 1994): 42–47.

———. "Uncued Closure in *Love & Rockets.*" Paper presented at the "Comic Art and Comics" section of the Popular Culture Association Conference, Las Vegas, 28 Mar. 1996.

Wright, Bradford. *Comic Book Nation: The Transformation of Youth Culture in America.* Baltimore: Johns Hopkins University Press, 2001.

Young, Frank, ed. "Comic Art in the '90s: *Misfit Lit* Discussion Panel." With Burne Hogarth, Gilbert and Jaime Hernandez et al. *The Comics Journal* 149 (Mar. 1992): 48–64.

Young, Frank. "Peeping Joe." Review of *Peepshow* by Joe Matt. *The Comics Journal* 149 (Mar. 1992): 37–40.

Young, James E. "The Holocaust as Vicarious Past: Art Spiegelman's *Maus* and the Afterimages of History." *Critical Inquiry* 24 (Spring 1998): 666–99.

Zinsser, William. *Inventing the Truth: The Art and Craft of Memoir.* Boston: Houghton-Mifflin, 1987.

Zorbaugh, Harvey, ed. *Journal of Educational Sociology* 18:4 (Dec. 1944). A special issue devoted to the comics controversy.

INDEX